Farhad Malekian

Utipolitianist International Criminal Court

nova
science publishers
www.novapublishers.com

DOI: https://doi.org/10.52305/UXTD1207

NOTICE TO THE READER

Additional color graphics may be available in the e-book version of this book.

Library of Congress Cataloging-in-Publication Data

Names: Malekian, Farhad author
Title: Utipolitianist International Criminal Court / Farhad Malekian.
Description: Hauppauge : Nova Science Publishers, 2025. | Series: Laws and legislation | Includes bibliographical references and index. |
Identifiers: LCCN 2025005388 (print) | LCCN 2025005389 (ebook) | ISBN 9798895303870 hardcover | ISBN 9798895304501 adobe pdf
Subjects: LCSH: International Criminal Court | International Criminal Court--Philosophy | Criminal justice, Administration of | International criminal courts
Classification: LCC KZ7312 .M35 2025 (print) | LCC KZ7312 (ebook) | DDC 345./01--dc23/eng/20250211
LC record available at https://lccn.loc.gov/2025005388
LC ebook record available at https://lccn.loc.gov/2025005389

Published by Nova Science Publishers, Inc. † New York

To the Mother of Justice,
Naledi Pandor

Contents

Abstract

The term 'vassal' highlights the inextricably intertwined system of corruption at the International Criminal Court that was founded on *utipolitianist theory*. This is a theory of the exploitation of the entire body of the Court, which indicates a new clandestine hegemony of colonialism. It is a theory adopted by the masters of the modern norms of international criminal law, including guns, wars, self-defence, decision-making power, sanctions, justice, and judgments. The existence of such platforms is itself one of the primary barriers to the proper application of international criminal justice and the promotion of the rights of victims. Utipolitianists veto victims' rights, which in turn become negotiable cargo in the Security Council. Norms are modified to promote the exploitation of the provisions of the Statute of the ICC. The philosophy of morality is no longer present and is instead used as a weapon of mass destruction by utipolitianists, thereby ceasing to exist as an unbiased subject of human rights law. Consequently, our moral faculties are unable to achieve their objectives. Jurisprudential philosophies become the tools of utipolitianist governments, which in turn results in a failure to ban the commission of international crimes. The rules of international criminal procedures cannot function if utipolitianist hegemony consumes the rights of victims. As long as the power of the Security Council is maintained, the ICC will remain the vassal court of certain governments.

Introduction

Our discussions in this book are very brief as it would require several volumes to cover this subject comprehensively. The notion of morality put forward in this book may disappoint some readers and fail to meet their expectations. This becomes particularly significant when viewed through the lens of the International Criminal Court, which is often seen as subservient to the superpower states. Many readers may naturally anticipate the book to take a stance on the actual definition of morality and the relevance of contemporary issues. While this may occur in specific instances when discussing morality within the book, the approach to these discussions will differ from those taken in my previous works. In this book, we will address the violations of the regulations of the International Criminal Court in terms of their moral, legal, and political implications. Additionally, I may also pose certain questions about the concept of morality in the context of political and legal actions—which are currently the most contentious aspects of theories concerning justice, morality, peace, and equality.

We will examine the question of what parameters need to be met in relation to the metaphor of morality and what its given particular substance in connection to the matter of legal norms or rules of law in the content of international human rights law should really be. However, the most significant question about the notion of morality is whether a trustworthy system of human rights that is based on the practical principles of morality exists that does not contradict the rights of its subjects and their personal values, i.e., the principle of *somebodiness*.[1] These are the factors that make it an imperative phenomenon for the body of human rights, which in turn has to be consistent and based on the notion of morality and the equal rights of men. This is

[1] Read Farhad Malekian, International Criminal Law, the Law of Somebodiness, the Law of Nobodiness (New York: Nova Science Publishers, 2021); Farhad Malekian, International Criminal Law: The Legal and Critical Analysis of International Crimes (2 vols. 1991); Farhad Malekian, The Monopolization of International Criminal Law in the United Nations, A Jurisprudential Approach (Stockholm: Almqvist Wiksell International, 1st ed., 1993).

particularly essential as it concerns the jurisdiction of international criminal courts.

The notion of morality should therefore be free to influence the opinions of individuals belonging to all different categories. With the expression category, we are obviously not speaking about the categorisation of men and their level of rights. That is not my purpose, and I do not attempt here to disregard the equality of our rights and express opinions without considering what I am supposed to present in connection with the definition of morality in the international criminal court, where the court is obliged to respect certain principles. With the use of the expression "category," the intention is to emphasise that our different occupations and positions within different state apparatuses do not have any value in the evaluation of the notion of morality, which is supposed to be the basic reason for the formulation of a considerable number of international conventions on human rights. Although I do not reject the fact that the notion of international human rights is unfortunately linked with the image of political association in practice, a state can, but should not, connect its definition to its own acts in order to interpret the law differently.

There are hardly any definitions of the provisions of international human rights laws that have not been taken under the control of political associations in order to redefine them based on their own conclusions and interpretations. Ultimately, while one may define the system of international human rights without the notion of morality, doing so is meaningless in practice and harms the system of international criminal courts. This is because if the notion of morality does not exist, the notion of human rights becomes a game between the political authorities and the legal authorities of criminal jurisdictions—as we have already seen. A clear example of this is the position of international criminal courts, both permanent and *ad hoc*, under the full control of the politically strong governments of the world. This is why the system of morality in the inner structure of our international human rights law does not function as it should, and is also why we are currently facing the collapse of morality within the substance of international criminal justice, i.e., its vassal position, as well as the increase in the number of victims in the global community of nations.

The vassal position of international criminal justice concerns violations of the basic principles of morality during times of occupation, war, and colonisation in the name of the imposition of sanctions and the implementation of international human rights principles. This indicates that the notion of morality, which should be an integral part of our legal systems, lacks real strength and is controlled by political institutions. Of course, anarchy and the use of force persist, and the violence we continue to see is especially intimate. This is, however, not the creation of the modern history of civilisation. The fact is that the social civilisation of humanity has always been strongly connected to the political behaviour of the authorities in power. As a result, the notion of morality has varied overtime and differed from nation-to-nation. Additionally, its form has been based on the extent to which immorality is situated in the mind of the relevant power in force.

We should also add that the old morality of the authorities has been revived with more gunpower, and, as a result, conventions of human rights have been used as the tools of the modern system of power, morality, and law. We have to say that governments are receiving more power and authority than ever before, based on the advanced development of weapons. Therefore, as we will see in the coming chapters, the system of morality represents a monopoly on the legitimate use of physical force against those who do not accept the conditions of a strong nation that puts forth its will and interests with the power of a gun. In the current international arena, politicians have been transformed into laws, and laws have been transformed into the moral vision of certain authorities. Consequently, the right to use physical force is directly connected to who-knows-who, who-works-for-whom, and finally, who-fails-to-obey-whom. This in turn paves the way for the final decisions of the vassal international criminal court.[2]

Farhad Malekian
Uppsala, Sweden,
3rd March; 4th June
23rd June; 12th September 2023
f.malekian.in.crim.l@telia.com
f.malekian.in.crim.l@gmail.com.

[2] Id.

Chapter 1

Organised Utipolitianism in International Criminal Justice

1. Permanent Virtue of Morality

I will begin with a description of the differences between traditional and contemporary moral thinking about the philosophy of law and its very deep interconnectedness with the development and promotion of justice. Of course, if there is a genuine philosophy, it would not depend on utipolitianist powers. When it comes to traditional moral philosophy, I am referring to the evolution of law in ancient civilisations, such as those of the Persians, Egyptians, Romans, and Greeks. All of these theories of morality are directly linked to philosophers such as Socrates, Plato, and Aristotle. From the sixth century onwards, the development of international law has been greatly influenced by modern moral philosophy. Moreover, modern moral philosophy also has its roots in the traditional or ancient theories of morality, and the subject of morality has therefore been treated with broad reference to the philosophies of Socrates, Aristotle, Zarathustra, Avicenna, and Plato. Their ideas on the philosophy of law and morality have had a significant influence on imperative argumentation for many reasons.[3] The term 'reason' is commonly used to make decisions, and is often accompanied by arguments between subjects or parties to the law.

One could argue that moral philosophy is not only an imperative aspect of traditional philosophy, but that is has also influenced our ideas about drafting and adopting international human rights conventions—regardless of whether or not they are enforced. Our point is that the moral system that is displayed within the body or surface of human rights instruments is essentially purely decorative and not productive. This point has been consistently

---

[3] Study Farhad Malekian, Imperative Philosophy of International Criminal Justice: Visible Power – Invisible Essence (New York: Nova Science Publishers, 2022); Farhad Malekian, Powertionism in International Criminal Justice (New York: Nova Science Publishers, 2022); Farhad Malekian, Tour de force of Moral Virtue in International Criminal Justice (New York: Nova Science Publishers, 2022).

demonstrated through the United Nations Security Council's negotiations and meetings— particularly concerning its most powerful members. Most members of the United Nations lack the virtue of decision, or righteous action that they should innately possess.[4]

It is difficult for an ordinary individual to understand the immoral philosophy of the Council while having in mind that the "quasi-jural" of morality has to exist, even if the members of the Council are essentially against its existence. The reason for this is that all members have a particular duty that is essential when it comes to certain members and certain important decisions. All this means that the concept of morality must not only be visually represented, but must also be observed within all actions taken by the Council members. We not only accept good decisions, but also strive for the highest good if the Council has any legal purpose for its immoral existence. The structure of an international organisation should thus contain morality.

Our common understanding is that the concept of morality in the law must endure and not privilege any one party over the others. The objective is not to maximize pleasure for some while minimising opportunities for others. It is a sign of either rightness or lawfulness that must be equal. The distinction between morality and immorality becomes evident through this method of evaluation. Despite sharing the same philosophy, they can still contradict each other. Morality would not be a topic of discussion if that were not the case. In the absence of the law, our personal interests and understandings would suffice. This is also the case within the system of international human rights and the provisions of the Charter of the United Nations, particularly the provisions of Chapter VII, which were allegedly drafted and codified to prevent war, injustice, inequality, and immorality.

The presence of Chapter VII reflects the existence of both inequality and immorality in general. In other words, the UN Charter was created in order to find the most rational way to achieve true happiness among all nations, not the opposite. *The mission of the Charter should have been to attain the best results and promote courage, temperance, and wisdom among all members of the organisation. The Charter mandates that all members be decent individuals, seek good, and refrain from any kind of immorality in their decisions and actions. Despite this, Chapter VII operates to the contrary.*

There are very few Security Council decisions that can be attributed to just, present objectives and that coincide with the philosophy of morality as a

[4] Farhad Malekian, Concreting Righteousness in International Criminal Justice (New York, Nova Sciences Publishers, 2024).

whole. The United States government is the most prominent decision-making power, and all other decisions are made based on the interests and ambitions of every permanent member. Furthermore, the Security Council's decisions lack a sufficient understanding of morality, which is not only weak, but practically non-existent. One might question what was to be expected from the provisions of the Charter of the United Nations. The answer may be that in the case of morality's efficiency within the fundamental principles of Chapter VII, we take a serious political position. Additionally, there may be different speculations regarding the most important principles of morality. Unfortunately, I believe that there is no moral principle in the relevant chapter. Despite this, governments are still influenced by the will and attitudes of the relevant Council members. The acceptance or rejection of violations is dictated by the wants and desires of the powerful members. Thus, morality and the law are only tools used to control the law and other members. As a result, there is a strong interdependency between the permanent members and other members, which forms a method of legal slavery. The subjects of UN laws are referred to as vassal *states parties*.

This indicates that the situation has generally depended on the reasons on which we have based the foundation of morality since the dawn of the philosophy of morality. What does the legacy of our arguments consist of? Even after more than 2,000 years, the same discussions persist. This implies that philosophers of morality, whether they are part of the Charter of the United Nations or in school, have not been able to establish a platform for themselves unless they validate the political opinions of the authorities currently in power. The reason for this is simply based on the use of utipolitianism by certain powers against the established morality of the natural law and its equal treatment of all its subjects, regardless of their position. It also implies that authorities also oppose the fundamental philosophy of utilitarianism. Accordingly, it is true that they promote misunderstandings, mistreatments, and confusion within the scope of the moral virtue and uncertainty of laws with the goal of promoting their utipolitianist theories by impairing the trustworthiness of the conclusions of the philosophy of law, which should be based on morality.

The Security Council appears to be an anomaly within the system of international law and within the realm of law in general. This anomaly makes it challenging to achieve a clear understanding of the system of international criminal justice because the doctrines of the science of morality may not be conveyed effectively.[5] The primary reason for this challenge lies in the hidden, precarious interests held by those who wield power over the law, regardless of the content of that law. The foundational truths that should serve as the guiding principles of legal science are often disregarded due to the erosion of moral virtue and its relevance. It is crucial to acknowledge that the science of morality does not manifest as a visible practical art; rather, morality's essence defines our existence, emphasising the essential need for moral principles. Our existence is perpetually intertwined with the interpretation of needs, the genuine virtue of humanity, and the profound necessity to uphold a profound respect for individuality.

If such respect is not achieved, then the natural existence of man will remain at the mercy of the daily decisions made by Security Council members, thereby making the position of respect of the principle of morality unstable. This implies that all actions are potentially aimed at some end, and if these goals are not met, doubts arise about their initial reasons for existence. This is also true as it concerns legal philosophy, which aims to establish regulations for all. If these intentions are disregarded, then the entire essence and purpose of these regulations become absurd and fall prey to a one-sided traditional theory of *utilitarianist justice*. The same theory applies to moral philosophy, which relies on its structure being respected. This structure can easily deteriorate due to the authorities' disobedience and their attempts to monopolise the law and its enforcement.

---

[5] Consult Robert Cryer, 'The Doctrinal Foundations of International Criminalisation,' in M. Cherif Bassiouni, ed., International Criminal Law, Vol. 1, (2008), pp. 107-128. See also Robert Cryer, Prosecuting International Crimes, Selectivity and the International Criminal Law Regime (Cambridge University Press, Cambridge, 2005); Farhad Malekian, Powertionism in International Criminal Justice (New York: Nova Science Publishers, 2022); Georg Schwarzenberger, 'The Problem of an International Criminal Law,' 5 Current Legal Problems (1950) 265; Edward M. Wise, 'Prolegomenon to the Principles of International Criminal Law,' 16 New York University Law Review (1970) 562; Farhad Malekian, International Criminal Law: The Legal and Critical Analysis of International Crimes (2 vols. 1991); Farhad Malekian, Principles of Islamic International Criminal Law: A Comparative Search (2011); Farhad Malekian, The Monopolization of International Criminal Law in the United Nations: A Jurisprudential Approach (2nd ed., 1995); M. Cherif Bassiouni (ed.), International Criminal Law (5 vols., 1999); Farhad Malekian, 'International Criminal Responsibility,' in M. Cherif Bassiouni (ed.), International Criminal Law, (1999).

2. Tracking the Quest of Justice

When we engage in a pursuit, particularly within the realm of moral philosophy, a strong and pure foundation of what we are seeking appears to be the primary requirement for the validity of our arguments. This implies that moral philosophy cannot be equated with morality and the promotion of equality if it is influenced by the whims of those in power. No positive outcomes can be attained through a passive adherence to norms. This is because all legal norms should be rooted in the fundamental principles of morality, which in turn should be our guiding light. Evaluating what is right or wrong within the interpretation of legal rules must be based on a prior understanding of practical morality. The pursuit of applying moral substance cannot be avoided by resorting to the conventional theory of utilitarianism, which itself relies on the utilitarian theory. The presence of such a moral instinct poses a significant challenge to the concept of morality.

This leads us to further subject utilitarianism to utipolitianism, suggesting the complete political exploitation of the United Nations Charter to achieve our own political gains that align with our interests. Consequently, disputes within the Security Council transform into institutions, norms adapt their essence, and the idea of absolute control over the legal framework, including the entire United Nations Charter, gains credence. Those who advocate for moral philosophy and believe in its essence within international human rights instruments are misguided and become pawns of utipolitianism rather than objective proponents of human rights instruments. As a result, our moral compasses fail to fulfil their purpose, and those who interpret politics in the name of moral philosophy end up serving utipolitianism instead of the core tenets of moral judgment theory.

Since the philosophy of moral justice primarily has been, or at least initially was, in the hands of a certain few states of the Security Council within the system of international law, the authoritative prescription of the right reason for the prescription of the rule of law and its benefits in the Charter becomes impossible to achieve. This concerns the rights, obligations, and duties to which these prescriptions of moral philosophy of reasoning give rise. Indeed, the difference between morality, ethics, and law may not be very deep at all, and may rather be a question of the vocabulary used to define the terms. Thus, whether we call law morality, ethics, or just law, it should not modify the substance of the law and should just be the moral domain of the philosophy of trust to the essence of the equal existence of all nations under the provisions of the Charter. In other words, the notion of utipolitianism should not be the master of peace, justice, morality, or war. The fact is that the Charter was established to bid farewell to all wars and the use of force.[6]

If we suppose that we were writing the theory of justice and morality, the theory of righteousness should have been present as well.[7] It would have been better to present it in terms of a morality that treated all men both within and outside an international organisation with the same principles of justice or with the same eyes of equality. The main goal of justice as fairness is achieved once it is pure and can omit all principles of personal or institutional utility outside the vocabulary of human rights, which are wrong and immoral. In such cases, we have adopted the principle of morality rather than the principle of utility.

Of course, there could be other significant principles concerning the distribution of justice, however justice without the concept of morality within the basic structure of the United Nations is meaningless, and therefore can never establish equality and only serves the interests of those in power. I hesitate to explain the principle of difference with urgency and would still brand my argument with the recognition of the principle of morality as the necessary substance for the proper existence of the law. This is particularly significant if the UN Charter is going to be powerful and effective in the long term.

We must actually decide whether we are going to evaluate the existence of the law in the Charter of the United Nations or strengthen its existence within the statutes of its different bodies. The only proof that the utipolitianism put in the Charter of the United Nations by the Security Council, and particularly the occupation of the power of the ICC and the controls placed upon it, is to realize that the ICC is not based on the principle of morality and has instead been monopolized. This means that the ICC is unable to address to certain very significant questions of international criminal justice, accountability, and the attribution of international criminal responsibility for the purpose of punishment. In other words, punishment is invisible and has largely only applied to African leaders. This reflects selectivity within the court. This is why the philosophy of moral justice has a significant role in the ultimate strength of the decisions of the United Nations and the prevention of international crimes committed by the powertionist governments. Applying

---

[6] Clara Nieto, Masters of War: Latin America and U.S. Aggression from the Cuban Revolution through the Clinton Years (foreword by Howard Zinn; translated by Chris Brandt, 2003); Farhad Malekian, Powertionism in International Criminal Justice (New York: Nova Science Publishers, 2022).

[7] Examine Farhad Malekian, Concreting Righteousness in International Criminal Justice (New York, Nova Sciences Publishers, 2024).

such a policy would be very difficult within the system of morality, law, and jurisprudence of a vassal international criminal court.[8]

The only proof that a constitution functions properly is that victims can see it and feel it, and the population of the world sees that it prevents the commission of international crimes. *How can we trust the sources of our experiences in the system of criminal justice when it does not react to the utipolitianism of the law in the Charter of the United Nations and its practical use in the Security Council? Similarly, we cannot identify the sole evidence of justice, which includes the essence of morality. The statute of the law cannot function if the utipolitianist doctrine proposes the destruction and monopolisation of the entire philosophy of the law.[9] Nothing can ever convince the rights of any victim when the knife and gavel of justice remove happiness to promote utipolitianism in the interest of certain members. We have not merely given all the proof of the law to most powerful states in the UN, we have also violated the principles of criminal justice under the framework of the ICC.*

We have forgotten the fact that the happiness of every victim is a necessary condition for the implementation of justice and a successful, permanent international peace. The general happiness of humanity is therefore not promoted within the provisions of our international legal organisation, i.e., the UN. It seems that, by the same rule of monopolisation of the law, utipolitianist governments do desire things that are decidedly different from the philosophy of morality of the law and its equal treatment of its subjects.[10] They desire, for example, the virtue of morality, which is much greater than the presentation of lies and the full absence of rights. *The utipolitianist doctrine denies that people desire to see the virtue of morality and also maintains that the virtue of morality of the law is abstract. However, people have the right to say when the virtue of the law needs to be heard. Regardless of utipolitianists' judgments, moralists should have privilege in recognising the ingenious conditions that demonstrate the virtue of moral philosophy in the interpretation and application of the law. Simply put, utipolitianists use the powerlessness of the victims to their benefit.*

---

[8] Study Farhad Malekian, Tour de force of Moral Virtue in International Criminal Justice (New York: Nova Science Publishers, 2022); Farhad Malekian, Powertionism in International Criminal Justice (New York: Nova Science Publishers, 2022); Farhad Malekian, Imperative Philosophy of International Criminal Justice: Visible Power – Invisible Essence (New York: Nova Science Publishers, 2022).

[9] Farhad Malekian, The Monopolization of International Criminal Law in the United Nations, A Jurisprudential Approach (Stockholm: Almqvist Wiksell International, 1st ed., 1993).

[10] *Id.*

Judgments thus must not violate the rights of victims. It is an imperative binding principle of justice to produce moral justice for the common will of natural rights for all men.[11] This is the primary principle of justice. This should be the truth when we talk about the existence of the law and its benefits for the common interests of human happiness and the protection of the natural environment from destruction. Therefore, it is not permitted to depart from the notion of morality to any degree. Otherwise, we would restrict the principle of morality and consequently, the notion of happiness. Although we realize that the ingredients of happiness are potentially varied, as a norm, happiness is the respect of rights and not the monopolisation of rights by a weapon— the UN Security Council. This means that every norm of the law is inherently desirable—not only when a utipolitianist government decides what the criteria of moral happiness should be. Desirability means being free of control.

3. Moral Character of Utipolitianism

The code of utipolitianism does not indicate that the interests of powertionist governments can be restricted. Rather, it states that their interests are broad and can increase with the passage of time. For instance, the development of states and the significant expansion of international communication with different views have increased the power of the powertionist governments under the code of utipolitianism. Such strong governments seek out the destruction of the collective interests of all states in the name of promoting the collective happiness of all humanity.

This can be seen in their desires, meaning that the norms of the law, the provisions of adopted resolutions, and the relevant interpretations of the law only serve them and do not work for the common interests of all governments. In addition, the norms of the law cannot be interpreted by the moral principles of equality, only by the immoral principle of selectivity. Quality, along with dogma, mean nothing except respect for the political interests of strong governments. They are not trying to create equality, peace, justice, love, and happiness for all men, but rather only for themselves.

---

[11] Farhad Malekian, Powertionism in International Criminal Justice (New York: Nova Science Publishers, 2022); also Farhad Malekian, Conundrums of Paternalism in International Criminal Justice (New York: Nova Science Publishers, 2024); Farhad Malekian, Exploitation of Christian Islamic International Criminal Justice (New York: Nova Science Publishers, 2024); Farhad Malekian, Concreting Righteousness in International Criminal Justice (New York: Nova publishers, 2024).

The previous explanation indicates the existence of the monopolisation of the system of justice, whether in the Security Council, the United Nations, or in the spheres of vassal international criminal courts—both *ad hoc* and permanent. Therefore, it may not be superfluous to mention that the common misapprehensions of the *utipolitianist* policies of the big governments create very serious international conflicts, which causes us to always be at war as a result. These wars are so obvious and uncivilised that it is impossible for any government to not acknowledge them, particularly when the Western governments and NATO promote the wars of *utipolitianist* governments. Here, we refer to the utipolitianist governments use of UN and ICC power against governments that do not affirm the political views of the powertionist governments. Therefore, no morality remains in law and we are instead left with the concerto of barbarity and its savagery.

Even if substantial change in the rules of humanitarian law of armed conflict are adopted, it would be difficult to implement them in their true forms due to the political influence of the big governments on the interpretation of the rules of the law and, as a whole, what constitutes justice. Therefore, any opinion against which governments are biased is rejected immediately and considered invalid. In general, there is so little consciousness of the rights of other governments on the part of the powertionist governments, and every matter comes generally under the estimation of utipolitianism as a tool of possession of power and dictating your own interests. We normally think it is not necessary to say anything against the evil power of governments concerning the essence of morality. We may say that the situation depends upon which political theory we have concerning moral character or the philosophy of utipolitianist, influential power.

This is because the existence of the veto power implies the notion of monopolisation, and monopolisation is the idea of utipolitianist control, and utipolitianism is the theory of the utipolitianist doctrines of the Security Council, which empower the idea of powertionism within international criminal justice.[12] *This indicates that the theory of utipolitianism promoted the power of powertionist governments in the final stage of its applicability under the nature of the vassal court. That is why there is no justice for the victims of international crimes in the corridors of international criminal courts, and the courts are solutions for reducing the legitimated power of victims. In other words, if you see real justice, then justice is law, but all laws under the system*

[12] Farhad Malekian, The Monopolization of International Criminal Law in the United Nations, A Jurisprudential Approach (Stockholm: Almqvist Wiksell International, 1st ed., 1993, 1995).

of international human rights and the power of international criminal courts are not justice. In other words, laws are not justice, but authentic justice is law.

Thus, if there is a true law that justice desires, that will be seen in its application. The systems of international human rights and international criminal justice are not laws at all, as long as their moral virtue is not present in the practical application of the case law. There are a number of cases that demonstrate that even speaking about morality is equated with being mad.

4. Utipolitianism Ignoring Massacres

The unfortunate fact is that there is no moral virtue in the system of international criminal justice. If there were, we would have seen it, and the ICC would not continue to let the most serious international criminals escape prosecution and punishment. The ICC does not respect its own norms of justice and instead upholds the policy of utipolitianist international criminal justice. That is why the ICC is largely a vassal court and selectively chooses cases based on the principle of who-knows-who. With this simple picture of ethical justice, the ICC prosecutor admits to the commission of crimes that are committed by powerful governments in the name of the implementation of the principles of international human rights law.

Above all else, the ICC prosecutor is a dependent subject of international utilitarianism and actually works for it. This has been seen since the court was established in its subordinate vassal position because of the influence of the utipolitianism of great power, as well as the hidden theory of monopolisation under the Charter of the United Nations. This reveals that the only principle that does not exist under the Statute of the ICC is law itself. This has been affirmed through the genocide of the population of Gaza. Over 45,000 people have been killed, the majority of whom are children, and many more bodies still lie under the rubble.[13] Despite this, the ICC Prosecutor is blind to this suffering, not only in their mind, but also in their eyes.

---

[13] On genocide see Majd Mohammad Gholi, *The Great Famine & Genocide in Iran: 1917-1919* (2nd ed., University Press of America, 2013); Majd Mohammad Gholi, Victorian Holocaust Iran in the Great Famine of 1869-1873 (Hamilton Books, 2018); Machteld Boot, Genocide, Crimes Against Humanity, War Crimes: Nullum Crimen Sine Lege and the Subject Matter Jurisdiction of the International Criminal Court (Nomos Verlagsgesellschaft, 2002); Farhad Malekian, 'Armenian Genocide and the Questions of Responsibility of the Turkish Government,' House of Commons Conference on the Armenian Genocide, Armenian Solidarity, British-Armenian All-Party Parliamentary Group, No Security Publication

Even dogs, cats, snakes, lizards, skunks, cockroaches, donkeys, and camels can see and escape from being harmed by carpet bombing massacres, but Karim Khan unfortunately cannot.[14] *This is how the morality of the system of international criminal justice along with its laws and regulations work, and it includes the orders of utipolitianism.* This indicates that the purpose of the system of human rights and international criminal courts is not, in reality, to hold the real terrorists accountable, but rather to punish those who do not follow the terrorist criminal orders of powertionist governments under the theory of *utipolitianist* vassal designs. If utipolitianism is the same as "*utisecurity*" then it also reflects the power of the Security Council permanent members. With the new term "utisecurity," I refer to the extreme use of security for itself. As a result, the Security Council is used to controlling the internal and international authority of all states. That is why the ICC acted too late— long after the massacre of thousands of Palestinians. The fact is that the prosecutor is a vassal of his masters and is afraid of Israeli authorities.

In this case we are confronted with international criminal justice that lacks eyewitnesses or has eyewitnesses that are accused of corruption and conspiracy. The concept of utipolitianism grows in importance because the focus of the interests of the powertionist governments is to control any notion of international democratic law, even though it does not exist. This is the challenge facing both utipolitianist theory and international criminal justice theory, both of which have the same qualified norms of legacy stemming from traditional colonial power. The system of international criminal justice and its court are nothing more than the development of the rules promoted by the politicians of colonial powers who guide the world in the direction of their own goals and interests. Consequently, the belief in the democratic values of the system of international criminal justice and its monopolised court is nothing more than a *fata morgana* dream.

Therefore, there has been very little improvement, if any, concerning the notion of correct and authentic equality as it concerns violations of international criminal obligations. Utipolitianists have thus always been the tailor of justice and decides how criminal justice norms should be seen and

---

(2007); W. Michael Reisman, 'Legal Responses to Genocide and Other Massive Violations of Human Rights,' 59 Law and Contemporary Problems (1996). See also John A. Berry & Carol Pott Berry, (eds.), Genocide in Rwanda: A Collective Memory (Howard Univ Pr, 1999); Howard Adelman, & Astri Suhrke (eds.), The Path of a Genocide: The Rwanda Crisis, from Uganda to Zaire (Transaction Publ,1999); David William Pear, 'The US-Led Genocide and Destruction of Yemen,' https://www.unz.com/article/the-us-led-genocide-and-destruction-of-yemen/ (October 12, 2019).

[14] He acted very tardily.

evaluated. As a result, the guilty have always been viewed as the victims along with the offenders of brutal international crimes. This situation is likely to have little impact on the promotion of the equal imposition of international criminal rules and the enhancement of equal criminal justice. There has always been a growing belief in the establishment of authoritarianism in international criminal courts as having a vassal character for the populations of so-called Third World countries.

5. Imposing Utipolitianist Heavy Weapons

Naturally, the most obvious alternative to authoritarianism in international criminal justice would be to establish a pure international criminal court independent from utipolitianist power. However, such a court has always been a dream, not a reality. Therefore, the classification of those who have committed international crimes is as old as criminal science itself, and there is an embarrassment of selectivity among different criminals, which also seems to overlap with the idea of utipolitianism and their interest in the accusation of others and granting themselves impunity. Like the advocates of utipolitianist powers, international criminal court provisions, decisions, and conduct have become the central dilemma concerning the creation of various pressures on the victims without achieving any greater equality of arms within the jurisprudence of international criminal jurisdiction.

The question then arises concerning the extent to which utipolitianist governments are accountable for their actions and how much they control the vocabulary of the law. Inhuman conduct is continuously being carried out in the shadow of the guns of authoritarian powers, as we are currently seeing in Gaza. What, then, are the opportunities available for, and obstacles in the way of, achieving banished rights—except to resort to self-defence against occupation forces through the establishment of resistance movements? In accusing an occupied nation of terrorist conduct, we are affirming our own savage opinions about the annihilation of the Palestinians.[15] This is one

[15] Minister of International Relations and Cooperation of the Parliament of the Republic of South Africa Naledi Pandor cleary declares that "It is an honour to address you here today at the inaugural Global Anti-Apartheid Conference on Palestine. This is a watershed moment as it is the start of the global anti-apartheid movements on Palestine from around the globe coming together and joining forces in the struggle for justice for the Palestinian people. We would like to express our deep appreciation to Reverend Frank Chikane for spearheading the efforts to make this conference a reality at a pivotal moment for Palestinians who are fighting for their survival amidst mass starvation, military onslaught, and unspeakable war

obvious problem created by the utipolitianist theory, which not only sounds immoral, but also barbaric. In rejecting the crude equality and rights of a nation, the international criminal court faces Western utipolitianist theory being used against its own foundation.

Therefore, there is a broad distinction between utipolitianist/authoritarian criminal provisions and right-wing equality based on the moral effects and substance of decisions. Through the examination of the entire system of international criminal provisions, one can see that the politics of barbaric

---

crimes and atrocities. It has never been so urgent for the progressive forces around the globe to come together in a collective effort to exert maximum pressure to end the genocidal campaign underway in Gaza, and to end the apartheid system in Israel and the Occupied Territories which is worse than what we experienced in our own country. The ongoing genocidal atrocities being committed by Israel in the Occupied Territories has put renewed focus on the urgent need for the wider international community to demand decolonisation and an end to Israel's settler colonialism. Progressive forces need to push for the fulfilment of the inalienable right of the Palestinian people to self-determination, which has been systematically denied since the British mandate, as well as the right of refugees in the diaspora to return. South Africa is of the view that the international community has an obligation to find a comprehensive and just resolution to the Palestinian issue. So far, the traditional approach to conflict resolution has failed to achieve peace in the Israel–Palestine conflict. It is possible that a different approach, one that uses a human rights perspective on conflict resolution, could produce what the old approach could not. A human rights approach asserts that the principles and practices enshrined in the Universal Declaration of Human Rights, including equality and non-discrimination, participation, inclusion, and accountability, and the importance of the rule of law should guide all the stages of the peace process. South Africa calls for international solidarity and increased pressure to support the just cause of the Palestinian people to achieve their legitimate demand for a viable independent state alongside the state of Israel. South Africa stands ready to work more closely with Palestine and believes that the only way to bring about a lasting peace in the Middle East is to have a comprehensive and negotiated settlement, without preconditions, to end the Israeli occupation of the Palestinian territories and Israel's continued blockade and siege of Gaza. South Africa recognises the connection between the Palestinian struggle for self-determination and the wider global movement for liberation from both colonialism and other associated forms of structural and institutionalised racism. South Africa has consistently shown its commitment to the Palestinian cause over the past 30 years of democracy, and we are also intent on supporting efforts to bring the Palestinian factions closer together so that they speak with one voice and have a common vision on the way forward. The people of South Africa and Palestine share an indivisible bond of solidarity, forged by the crucible of the two nations' respective liberation struggles. South Africa has, since the dawn of democracy in 1994, always been an ally of Palestine and has constantly highlighted the struggles of the Palestinian people, supported them in international bodies, and offered material assistance within its means. The Palestinian experience evokes memories of South Africa's own history of racial segregation and oppression. As oppressed South Africans, we experienced first-hand the effects of racial inequality and discrimination, and we identify fully with the struggle for freedom and self-determination in Palestine." *South Africa FM: 'We will not rest until Palestine's freedom is realized.'* Visit https://mondoweiss.net/2024/05/south-africa-fm-we-will-not-rest-until-palestines-freedom-is-realized/.

decisions against the victims has shifted into the idea of powertionist governments of the United Nations Security Council. This means that there is no idea of establishing rights for the victims of genocide in Gaza.[16] It also reflects the monolithic power of force and rejection of the rights of the weak by the utipolitianist governments and their Western allies. In searching for clues, we do not need to create groups of investigators, lawyers, judges, or prosecutors to prove that international crimes have been committed. This is because we only need to look at Gaza and the deaths of thousands of civilians to see clear evidence of the criminality and disability of the system of International Criminal Court, which is currently functioning under the influence of utipolitianist powers, particularly the American and British governments.

However, the problem is that we have to find the first independent Court in the world that is not a vassal court. The supreme law of morals does not exist in the ICC as it is supposed to. It is wishful thinking to believe that the law of the ICC intends to bring criminals under its policy of prosecution. All it has done up until today has been to punish the leaders of African nations. The fact is that the prosecutor of the ICC seems to be swinging between the nails of power for survival. This is not an exaggeration.

Over the past nine months, the crimes of the Israeli government continued with the permission of utipolitianist powertionist governments like the United Kingdom, the United States, and other Western governments. This is not solely the fault of Karim Khan, but rather the fault of all prosecutors of the ICC. Thus, Karim Khan is actually committing and aiding in the commission of international crimes because he did not resign from his position when he did not act. This is the first act to observe and register in the name of morality of the immorality of the International Criminal Court in The Hague. Of course, such actions represent an abuse of moral justice and the exploitation of the system of international criminal justice being promoted by the office of the prosecutor.

The remaining arguments against the prosecutor of the ICC actually come from his employers, who are all the greatest criminals of all time. The general implications that embarrass conscientious lawyers, if they exist, are that Karim

---

[16] W. Michael Reisman, 'Legal Responses to Genocide and Other Massive Violations of Human Rights,' 59 Law and Contemporary Problems (1996). See also John A. Berry & Carol Pott Berry, (eds.), Genocide in Rwanda: A Collective Memory (Howard Univ Pr, 1999); Howard Adelman, & Astri Suhrke (eds.), The Path of a Genocide: The Rwanda Crisis, from Uganda to Zaire (Transaction Publ,1999); David William Pear, 'The US-Led Genocide and Destruction of Yemen,' https://www.unz.com/article/the-us-led-genocide-and-destruction-of-yemen/ (October 12, 2019).

Khan is actually a utilitarian who agrees with the policies of criminal governments.[17] The very simple question is: if he cannot understand that he has long been violating the basic principles of international human rights law and international criminal justice, is he of sound mind? Nonetheless, he is professionally capable of covering for himself and saying that he is waiting for the right time to make the right decision. Therefore, he gives himself the opportunity to omit moral rules. In this way, he succumbs to the temptation posed by his position even if it means breaking the rules of international criminal justice. This generates greater opportunities for him and protects his salary through the sale of justice. This is why we argue that moral virtue does not exist in the system of international criminal justice as it is supposed to.

6. Prosecutor as a Utipolitianist Tool

The problem is that the philosophy of law and its power are under the control of certain governments, and consequently, the self-indulgence of certain members contributes to what happens in the Security Council and the entire United Nations. *The intention here is not to suggest that the excuses made for the crimes committed by certain members of the organisation are damaging the reputation of the system of international human rights law. The fact is that human rights have no power when it comes to the criminality of Western powers. Our system of international human rights actually cheats our own conscience of humanity, which is drafted and ratified as norms of morality. Even though human rights treaties speak about the rights and equality of all nations, they are just presenting the immorality of Western authorities at a time when they need to be respected.*

Politicians have no souls, no limits, and no consciences. Human rights instruments can show how certain Western countries can speak about human rights and codify them in the form of conventions, albeit with several different faces and ambitions. The complicated nature of utipolitianism proves that rules of conduct within international conventions cannot be framed in a way that there are no exceptions made for certain individuals. The fact is that barely

[17] Examine Farhad Malekian, Conscience of Lawyers in International Criminal Law, the Burden of Doppelgängers (New York: Nova Science Publishers, 2021); Farhad Malekian, Conscience of Prosecutors in International Criminal Law, the Heart of the Matter (New York: Nova Science Publishers, 2021); Farhad Malekian, Conscience of Judges in International Criminal Law, the Heart of Judgements (New York: Nova Science Publishers, 2021).

any kind of action under the power of the powertionist governments can be securely identified as presenting the principle of equality between nations. This means that the decisions made through the utipolitianist policies of governments are always imposed by force, which is not acceptable.

There is no ethical rule in the principles of inequality of the Charter, and this in turn prompts the violation of moral virtue and principles of international human rights law. We do not have bad feelings concerning the rigidity of the laws of the system of international criminal justice or human rights and the reason for our feelings is based on the fact that the United Nations Charter has a considerable number of faces, i.e., evil political policies, and it uses such malevolent power whenever it deems fit. There exists no moral system of justice under the policy of utipolitianism, which can unequivocally refer to equality and the positive contribution of certain members to the interests of the rules of law that are formulated in the Charter. These are the real difficulties that the system of morality faces under the arguments presented both under the philosophy of ethics as well as in the nonexistence of the conscientious guidance of evil powertionist governments. In fact, the term morality now means providing weapons, approving of the conduct of terrorist governments, and sanctioning governments that do not obey the given orders of the utipolitianist governments and instead struggle for political and economic independence.[18]

We must remember that the system of international criminal justice and the body of the United Nations are not private institutions, and that they actually function as the private possessions of the big, powerful states. It is no secret that the big, powerful nations receive impunity for the most serious international crimes that they have committed. Barack Obama, Hillary Clinton, Tony Blair, and Rishi Sunak, to name but a few, have committed international crimes but walk with full impunity. That is the same concerning crimes committed by H.W. Bush, George W. Bush, Joe Biden, Antony Blinken, John F. Kirby, Lloyd Austin, Boris Johnson, Rishi Sunak, and a number of others, to name but a few examples, but they are on vacation.

The aforementioned individuals have killed millions of individuals and yet are supported and protected not only by their governments, but also by the very established ideology of utipolitianist governments. Such cases create conflict between various significant principles of international criminal justice

[18] Berlin Taken to Court over Arms Deliveries to Israel Is Germany Complicit in War Against Gaza? (Asia Haidar und Juliane von Mittelstaedt, 19.04.2024). Visit https://www.spiegel.de/international/world/is-germany-complicit-in-war-against-gaza-a-eec8c88f-0b8b-45e4-ab31-24c29d1df1e2.

and human rights that are supposed to promote the principles of morality among all nations. This implies equality and justice. The fact is that there is no trace of moral obligation under the legal power of the ICC or the United Nations that can guarantee the security of arms among all nations. *Positive action in the interest of the victims of big, powerful governments is rarely taken. Consequently, the principle of morality is powerless in practice and any semblance of morality in the Security Council or the Office of the Prosecutor of the ICC works against the victims.*

Many European governments, with the assistance of the United States, have killed millions since the ICC was established, however these crimes have never been acknowledged by the ICC. The powertionist government has controlled all superiority with the existence of the ICC and many international human rights organisations. If morality were the ultimate source of moral obligations under the system of international criminal justice and international human rights then we would see it, however the deaths of millions of children at the hands of the European weapons' industry proves the opposite. The application of the standards of the rules of international criminal courts and human rights may be difficult in practice. All human rights laws claim to have independent authority and a serious presentation of the human rights of all civilisations, but the fact is that interference in their rules of application is sanctioned by the governments that decide which other governments receive sanctions. Prejudice and bigotry grow rapidly due to the unacknowledged encouragement of utilitarianism and its control, which do not reflect the desires of the victims.

This is precisely what is happening in Gaza, where the racist, fascist, and dictatorial Zionist regime is using the practical philosophy of utility in order to occupy the remaining lands of the Palestinian nation. As American philosopher John Rawls stated, those who support the utility principle reject the existence of fairness for others and cannot see any reason to respect the rights of other individuals, groups, or nations. The principle of utility means maximising pleasures in an illogical way. The principle of morality presumably necessitates and calls for a form of respect that was once common and that should not be violated by any means. It is essential for all nations to follow the principle of morality, which ultimately requires the rejection of the principle of utipolitianism in the Charter of the United Nations and the practice of the ICC. It does follow from the *utipolitianist* doctrine that is formulated in the Charter or the ICC that the rights of other nations and their existence are trivial or insignificant within the statutes of the relevant bodies. This is a dangerous international policy that was created by governments and which will result in more suffering for victims if it remains a tool of injustice used by international bodies.

7. Games of Utipolitianist Governments

It is unfortunate that we experience and witness the loss of the lives of millions of individuals and still do not react properly. It is necessary to express certain rules of equality and the implementation of the principles of international human rights instead of the principle of utipolitianism. Under the sphere of the Charter, international utipolitianism has taken advantage of the immoral rights of offenders and rescinded the rights of weaker nations. Utipolitianists may say that maximising the ordinary efficacy of rules and principles in the Charter is meant to assist poor nations. While this is not true, the face of utipolitianism is based on the fact that the practice shows the contrary. We should not put aside the fact that the equal respect of the territorial integrity of all nations is not only essential, but that it is also a fundamental principle for the existence of peace, justice, and self-determination globally.

When we talk about the philosophy of morality under the system of the United Nations or international criminal justice, we also set certain boundaries that must be respected as they are an integral part of self-respect. When the average utility of powertionist governments is much higher than any notion of violation, then we are violating civilian legislation. *That is why it is believed that law is not morality, but morality must be a common law of human civilisation. Additionally, this also means that certain principles of social existence should never be violated. This indicates that no law should violate the general moral standard of civilisation.*[19] *For instance, we cannot prohibit the delivery of food to the victims of international crimes by asserting that we are fighting against our enemies when, in reality, there is no enemy but only people struggling against the barbaric occupation of their lands. Such people cannot be called enemies, but rather resistance groups. Despite this, brutal occupying forces label their actions as acts of self-defence against enemies or a war of civilisation against barbarism.*

Brutality can demonstrate the level of morality of the gross violations of the system of international criminal justice and human rights law as a whole.

---

[19] Consult Farhad Malekian, Classical Morality in International Peremptory Criminal Law (Newcastle: Cambridge Scholars Publishing, 2018); also Farhad Malekian, Allegations by Political Laundering (Cambridge Scholars Publishing, 2019).

This implies the control of an international criminal court through the use of force and placing it in the position of a vassal court. The point is that we must not lose sight of the whole truth and avoid utipolitianism, instead supporting the principle of moral equivalence, which demands that we uphold the rights of victims. We should not subject ourselves to the utipolitianist principles of authoritarian governments. A clear example of this is the Israeli Zionist government's crimes and aid given by certain Western countries, such as the United States, the United Kingdom, Germany, France, Australia, Sweden and many other countries.[20] The Swedish government has even prohibited journalists from investigating documents relating to the sale of weapons to the criminal Israeli Zionist regime. It is not possible to increase the average application rate of international criminal justice and human rights law, since both are tools of utipolitianist standards. However, in the aforementioned case, we refer to the brutal violation of the principles of morality and the history of human civilisation.[21]

We may therefore conclude that utipolitianism generally aims at encouraging its alliances to adopt and apply a policy of aggression against states that have been colonised by colonial powers. There is no limit to the brutality of actions of powertionist governments and violations of the principles of justice. If, for whatever reason, the rights of victims are presented by the old colonial states, they are eventually rejected by the powertionist governments because of the original policy of utilitarianism which wants equality and human rights for all. Sometimes there may be some loss of self-esteem among the old colonial states. However, these attitudes have changed because international human rights laws are constantly developing. This is one

---

[20] All these identify the concept of democracy of Western utipolitianist governments. "For instance, the brutal invasion of Iraq was called *Operation Iraqi Freedom* and given a saintly title. *Operation Unified Protector* was the name given to the destruction that took place in Libya. In 2011, it was carried out by a NATO aggressive attack concerning the Libyan Civil War, which was in reality planned by the United States to destroy the Ghazafi's plans for the Arabs' oil. The aggressive attacks were seen as the enforcement of the United Nations Security Council resolutions of 1970 and 1973. *Operation Enduring Freedom* was the decorative name given to the unjust, aggressive invasion of Afghanistan. The decoration name was orchestrated by the U.S. government for both the first stage of the war in Afghanistan and its widespread scale of armed attacks in the name of the *Global War on Terrorism*. All these were carried out in the name of democracy, human rights, and justice. That is what the paternalism international human rights and international criminal justice looks like. This is precisely the way in which the big, powertionist government is contributing economically and militarily to the genocide of Palestinians by the Zionist government in Israel." Farhad Malekian, Conundrums of Paternalism in International Criminal Justice (New York: Nova Science Publishers, 2024), pp.15-6.

[21] Id.

of the reasons why utipolitianism increases and fosters its alliances by permitting new NATO members. Eventually, there is no way around this drawback of the policy of the powertionist governments under the theory of utipolitianism. It is consequently an inevitable price that is paid by the victims of urban policy.

I am largely referring to the provisions of Chapter VII of the United Nations Charter, which ultimately brought the atomic gift upon Nagasaki and Hiroshima and has also permitted the most inhuman annihilation, obliteration, and holocaust of the Palestinian population ever seen. As a result, moral judgments do not exist as they should, and consequently, the values of humanity are not balanced with the moral substance of the law. Instead, they are balanced with undifferentiated mixed conduct that falsifies the notion of injustice as morality of the law and immorality as justice of the law. All this speaks to supremacy and the close relations between violators and principles of morality as its own property for monopolisation of whatever deduction or interpretation seems necessary for the intentions of utipolitianist future designs. This is why utipolitianist governments have preferred to fight large-scale conventional wars and proxy wars. This is an integral moral policy of utipolitianist governments. One clear example of this is the war between Ukraine and Russia, which is, in reality, the war waged by the United States (and NATO) against Russia. Moreover, NATO is not a defensive alliance. It is important to remember what they did in Libya, Afghanistan, Iraq, Lebanon, and Syria. Their illegal bombing of Yugoslavia was another direct violation of the UN Charter.

8. Tailors of Moral Justice

The difference between the holocaust of the innocent Jews and the holocaust of the Palestinians is that the former was mainly committed by the German Nazi government, while the Palestinian holocaust is being carried out by the Israeli fascist Zionist government, which has been supported by many Western governments and the utipolitianist theories of the United Nations Charter.[22] Hence, presuming that utipolitianism is essentially superior to the idea of Nazism is not wrong. If we were to compare the two holocausts, the former holocaust would pale in comparison to the latter. This is because the holocaust

[22] Study John J Mearsheimer and Stephen Walt, The Israel Lobby and U.S. Foreign Policy (New York: Farrar, Straus and Giroux. 2007).

against Palestinians has been committed over the course of over seventy years and has been carried out with advance military technology. Furthermore, many Western governments are compliant accomplices and collaborators in the execution of this holocaust. Therefore, the Palestinian holocaust may conceivably represent the largest case of international crimes ever committed in the modern history of civilisation.[23]

Therefore, no notion of morality can be seen under the aggressive pressures carried out by the utipolitianist theories of powertionist governments, and, eventually, the concept of morality within international human rights law and international criminal justice dies. When this occurs, it means that we have killed the most powerful and attractive prospect of the system of law in general and the systems of international law in particular. The lines of reasoning about international human rights then lose their strength of purity, and their real face and fake promotion of justice for all men with different phrases such as freedom, equality of race, language, or so forth are proven to just be propaganda.

The powertionist governments cannot argue that this interpretation is wrong if they have any person within their governments who can understand the definition of moral wisdom, but since it is rare to find such a wise man in their organisation, any idea of maximising the average level of morality is lost to the theory of maximising the average level of utilitarianist plans through wrongful interpretations. In fact, powertionist governments have chosen to uphold three principles of injustice: utilitarianism, the monopolisation of weaker nations, and sanctioning states that do not accept their conditions. I

---

[23] Consult also Anatomy of a Genocide: Report of the Special Rapporteur on the situation of human rights in the Palestinian territories occupied since 1967. The summery of the report of 25 March 2024 clarifies that "After five months of military operations, Israel has destroyed Gaza. Over 30,000 Palestinians have been killed, including more than 13,000 children. Over 12,000 are presumed dead and 71,000 injured, many with life-changing mutilations. Seventy percent of residential areas have been destroyed. Eighty percent of the whole population has been forcibly displaced. Thousands of families have lost loved ones or have been wiped out. Many could not bury and mourn their relatives, forced instead to leave their bodies decomposing in homes, in the street or under the rubble. Thousands have been detained and systematically subjected to inhuman and degrading treatment. The incalculable collective trauma will be experienced for generations to come. By analysing the patterns of violence and Israel's policies in its onslaught on Gaza, this report concludes that there are reasonable grounds to believe that the threshold indicating Israel's commission of genocide is met. One of the key findings is that Israel's executive and military leadership and soldiers have intentionally distorted jus in bello principles, subverting their protective functions, in an attempt to legitimize genocidal violence against the Palestinian people." https://www.ohchr.org/sites/default/files/documents/hrbodies/hrcouncil/sessions-regular/session55/advance-versions/a-hrc-55-73-auv.pdf (visited 03/11/2024).

have detailed the two new terms "powertionist" and "powertionism" in a separate work. The very immoral principles of utipolitianist governments modify the notion of moral justice and present it as the implementation of international human rights law. In other words, powertionist governments use the theory of utipolitianism to serve their economic, military, and political interests. For the utipolitianist governments, there is no distinction between international human rights law (HRL) and international humanitarian law (IHL) since they use both concepts to explain their own situations and interests.

Powertionism is an innovative legal term coined by the author used to emphasize the greed of our governments. This greed is demonstrated through how such governments interpret international legal rules based on their agendas and their desire to pursue and strengthen their political, military, and economic interests. As a result, certain governments have adopted hypocritical, autocratic, egregious, and *reductio ad absurdum* standards, while other governments continue to suffer under the hegemonic policies of the former. Powertionism sings a song of superiority instead of one of multilateralism. The epidemic of powertionism first arose within the systems of international human rights law and international criminal justice when governments nominated themselves to be permanent members of the United Nations, Security Council, and NATO, and subsequently began imposing hypocritical sanctions upon other states. This book illuminates the truth relating to the objectives of governments working to conceal the true nature and impact of their deadly weapons as a result of the punitive or deluded decisions made by NATO or others. We can no longer ethically consent to the domination of power, the waging of proxy wars, and the ambiguous incitement of the commission of international crimes by permitting the chauvinistic policies of powertionist governments.[24]

The immoral governmental conception of justice is therefore the very criterion used in the interpretation of international human rights law and international criminal justice. Consequently, the original position of the basic elements of human rights conventions is not only violated, but also openly insulted under the provisions of Chapter VII of the United Nations. A different variation of the initial conditions for the adoption of the principles of international human rights law with the motivation of promoting equality between all nations has been mocked by states and governments that are

---

[24] Farhad Malekian, Powertionism in International Criminal Justice (New York: Nova Science Publishers, 2022).

supposed to promote and create international stability, peace, equality, and respect for the principle of morality. The governments adopted these principles at the time of creation of the Charter in order to maximise the average of morality, humanity, and justice. However, instead they have maximised the advantages of the immoral principle of utipolitianism with evil utility. *The preceding remarks indicate that the three immoral principles of justice may still be upheld even after the Gazan genocide, the Gazan holocaust, or the commission of the international crime of blackboard-barbarism end.*[25]

It is unethical to state that the immoral principles that are the consequence of creating and formulating the Security Council principles promote human rights norms. They have virtually the same character as the evil notions of humanity that are carried out by satanic governments. The motivational assumption of satanic governments does not itself determine the character of the whole evil nature of those governments. Still, it presents the power of injustice in the sphere of global legislation and rules of law. The vassal states follow the order of their masters, and those satanic governments were chosen due to different motivations of the system of international criminal justice and its procedural reasonings. Any such expression such as such as charlatan or satanic titles against those governments is certainly short of expressing the evil nature of many evil individuals who such governments serve. This emphasises the flexibility of the theory of justice and the tailors of its clothes in the hands of big political parties or the office of the prosecutor of the ICC in international criminal courts. This means we have unfortunately oversimplified the notion

---

[25] Consult Farhad Malekian, *International Crime of Blackboard-Barbarism* (New York: Nova Science Publishers, 2025); Examine also See On genocide see Majd Mohammad Gholi, *The Great Famine & Genocide in Iran: 1917-1919* (2nd ed., University Press of America, 2013); Majd Mohammad Gholi, Victorian Holocaust Iran in the Great Famine of 1869-1873 (Hamilton Books, 2018); Machteld Boot, Genocide, Crimes Against Humanity, War Crimes: Nullum Crimen Sine Lege and the Subject Matter Jurisdiction of the International Criminal Court (Nomos Verlagsgesellschaft, 2002); Farhad Malekian, 'Armenian Genocide and the Questions of Responsibility of the Turkish Government,' House of Commons Conference on the Armenian Genocide, Armenian Solidarity, British-Armenian All-Party Parliamentary Group, No Security Publication (2007); W. Michael Reisman, 'Legal Responses to Genocide and Other Massive Violations of Human Rights,' 59 Law and Contemporary Problems (1996). See also John A. Berry & Carol Pott Berry, (eds.), Genocide in Rwanda: A Collective Memory (Howard Univ Pr, 1999); Howard Adelman, & Astri Suhrke (eds.), The Path of a Genocide: The Rwanda Crisis, from Uganda to Zaire (Transaction Publ,1999); David William Pear, 'The US-Led Genocide and Destruction of Yemen,' https://www.unz.com/article/the-us-led-genocide-and-destruction-of-yemen/ (October 12, 2019).

of morality in the tailor's house, which creates its strategic models using law, morality, and the rights of victims.

Chapter 2

The Dilemma of Utipolitianist Vassal International Criminal Justice

1. Judgments in Contemplative Equilibrium

What we want to understand from the principles of international human rights law and international criminal justice is how they treat their various subjects. Although all subjects of international human rights law and even the systems of international criminal justice and the United Nations should be the same concerning their rights and principles, this is not the case in practice. The practices of these systems of law demonstrate that the only matter that is not essential, but should be, in the context of the system is the object of equality. This is not at all a secret. The entire structure of the United Nations speaks about equality, and yet the interpretations of its principles and their practical implementations differ without any respect for the principle of morality. *Therefore, the conception of human rights and its justice, which should symbolise or embody our final judgments in contemplative equilibrium, present another picture of justice. As a result, human rights justice becomes a decorative principle within our arguments, reasoning, and, naturally, the final judgments. We should remember that the moral basis of international human rights law is the most fundamental principle of the rightfulness of the system of international criminal justice, which should be respected if the notion of authentic justice is valued.*

Unless we have not realised this fact and have attempted to accept falsehoods as the truth and the truth as falsehoods, the conception of utipolitianism is growing steadily. The strains of commitment to justice and human rights and protection of the rights of victims under the procedures of vassal international criminal courts have become just a utopian dream. This arises from the fact that we tend to reject the goodness of the moral reality and legal equality between the subjects of law, concluding that the division of power politics and their utipolitianist interests are correct and therefore just. Consequently, the categorisation of governments and the value of their international legal personalities become norms of international justice, including within the Security Council and the ICC. This obviously threatens the promotion of justice and the reestablishment of the rights of various oppressed nations in the world. Additionally, we have not acted rationally for the sake of the principles of justice. The judgments of the ICC and the resolutions of the Security Council have become metaphors for violations. In other words, our decisions must promote happiness and contain only the objective truth.

Our decisions are not objective and contain different policies of utipolitianism, which in turn destroy the rights of victims of international criminal violations. This is also true when we are referring to the policy and views of the ICC, which generally protects the views of the big criminal governments of the world. The fact is that the ICC is the product of the Western states, even though we call it an international criminal court. It is absolutely essential to know how a vassal international criminal court can have international standards of accountability and react to crimes that are committed by the founders of the Court. Two said founders are the American and British governments, both of which have directly engaged in the commission of international crimes, including in Syria, Afghanistan, Iraq, Libya, Lebanon, and Palestine. They even fuelled the war between Iran and Iraq. All these wars were fought to serve their utipolitianism. These governments have actively killed massive numbers of people in the aforementioned countries, thereby causing significant harm to the balance of justice that the Court claims to uphold.

However, despite the killing of millions, utipolitianist governments operate with full impunity, and the vassal international criminal court's prosecutor or judges do nothing about their crimes since they are all owners of its norms and statutes. Prosecutors and judges do not even try to excuse them for the massive killings of innocent civilians of other nations while their own civilisation is safe under the principle of utipolitianism, which is governed by Chapter VII of the Security Council. They do not even try to help the victims and their civilisations. Criminal governments have even been nominated for Nobel Prizes for their criminal conduct and the commission of genocides that were carried out to seize the natural resources of other countries. However, as an established principle of treaty laws, when governments enter into an agreement, they have to accept the consequences. Although we understand that the United States government is not a party to the ICC, it is still obligated to respect the Court's rules. This is based on the principle of *jus cogens*, which strictly prohibits governments from committing international crimes for any reason. This principle also encourages us to follow the rules of international criminal law in good faith and to respect and avoid the imposed notion of vassalisation upon states and international criminal justice, which promotes subjugation.

The reality is that governments should not only honour the legacy of the framework of justice law, they should also avoid making arbitrary decisions that may harm the body of international human rights and the Charter of the United Nations. However, all these matters are controlled by the legal and political policy of the theory of utipolitianism, which indicates the monopolisation of the law, the rejection of any form of morality, and the objection to any interpretation of the policies of the powertionist governments that conflict with their economic, political, and military interests.[26] One cannot agree with the unjust principle that the provisions of Chapter VII of the Charter are correct and should be enforced while there is a real possibility that such immoral and terrorist provisions of the relevant chapter of the Charter could be abolished if the majority of states were to vote for it. At the same time, we are aware that such suggestions can be prevented by governments that enjoy the immoral principle of utipolitianism, i.e., vassal states that are subordinate to their masters.[27]

---

[26] Examine Farhad Malekian, Allegations by Political Laundering (Cambridge Scholars Publishing, 2019); Farhad Malekian, 'Emasculating the Philosophy of International Criminal Justice in the Iraqi Special Tribunal,' Cornell International Law Journal, 58/5 (2005), pp.675-725; Farhad Malekian, 'Comparative Substantive International Criminal Justice,' in Ronald C. Slye (ed.), The Nuremberg Principles in Non-western Societies: A Reflection on their Universality, Legitimacy and Application (2017), pp. 10-44.

[27] "For instance, the apartheid cases in the General Assembly and the Security Council, document that two of the permanent members and their allies had no interest in ending the apartheid system, and therefore the result and motive quality was wrong, since it ended in the same circuitous result. This is the same in the case of Palestine, despite whatever positive decision is taken in the General Assembly; the Security Council still has not established the rights of the Palestinians in the occupied territories. In other words, the positive aspects of the General Assembly resolutions are barred by the Security Council decisions. According to Kant, slowly and gradually brings the relevant Palestinian territories under complete occupation or possession of the occupying power is a not morally worthy result. The decisions of the Security Council on the occupation were taken for a wrongful intention. Consequently, the moral worth of the Security Council resolutions depends on its motives and the result. An action should be carried out for the right purpose and the right reason and not to the advantage of some and ignorance of the rights of others.16 This is what I discuss in my article Judging International Criminal Justice in the Occupied Territories. The original title of the article was, in fact, Crucifying International Criminal Justice in the Occupied Territories. Imminently before publication, I was officially informed in an e-mail that the entire article would be rejected if the term 'crucifying' would not be replaced with the term 'judging.' Farhad Malekian, The Mirage of International Criminal Law: Kant Metaphysics of Mens Rea (Cambridge: Cambridge Scholars Publishing, 2018), pp.42-43; Pietro Stefanini, 'Palestine and the Mirage of International Criminal Justice – Can the ICC

I shall not comment further on the persuasive condition of international human rights law, which demands justice, humanity, and morality at all times. The balance of human rights requires that all nations engage with their rights and not become subjects of international crimes at the hands of different utipolitianist powers. Such reasoning about human rights is based on the outcome of the negotiations carried out between different groupings of states. Therefore, it constitutes proof that human morality that has to be respected. However, as previously stated, once all the details about human rights and international criminal justice roles are analysed, it may become clear where the final balance of reasons is being presented. Consequently, the reasons make up the structure of the development of the law and promoting the philosophy of reasonable and valuable justice for all nations. If this happened, we could find better solutions to allow our arguments to develop and reject utipolitianist policy. It is therefore very important and essential to search for the elimination of injustice and determination of morality in the inner Statute of the International Criminal Court. If this is not possible or important to us, then we are presenting a fake law for the international community as a whole.

2. Maximising Average Utipolitianism

The system of the United Nations and its relevant branches must support justice, humanity, and morality, all of which should be integral parts of international peace. If this duty is not fulfilled, the bodies of the organization will not be able to represent justice in the international spheres of law. This means that the theory of good faith disappears from the surface of the international rule of law and is endangered by violations and utility by the powertionist governments of the world. It may be useful to maintain the grounds of justice in all matters in favour of all nations of the world and to restrict their private utility to a few governments. *The moral codes of international human rights law and international criminal justice must be recognised and respected in the international policies of all states and therefore, the philosophical standpoint of justice that is based on the principle of morality and equality of the rights of nations should not be replaced with the utipolitianism of the Security Council. This is why the theory of maximising the average utility of the rules of law, and particularly international criminal*

---

improve the Security of the Palestinians,' available at http://platform.almanhal.com/Files/2/90090 (Visited on 1 November 2017).

justice, must not be used as by the UN to impose the values of justice with full injustice.

In fact, any denial of international morality that violates the relevant provisions of international criminal law can lead to the commission of international crimes and lead to criminal accountability. As a general rule of justice, governments that adopt a limited legal definition of the notion of morality violate the rules or the basic elements of the UN, IHR, and ICC most frequently. The governments in question prioritise monopolising law and wealth rather than promoting moral potential for all nations. The issue of justice arises when governments' political interests determine the path to justice, even if their natures harm other nations. They do not strive to create fair conditions for other nations or for those whose resources are exploited by their military actions. The hierarchy of interests in the minds of these utipolitianist governments implies the unjust implementation of international justice in vassal courts, amounting to the violation of others' rights and loss of millions of lives.

In addition, the veil of ignorance in the office of the utipolitianist International Criminal Court is rapidly developing and the killing of children *en masse* has become the norm in the implementation of international human rights law and the morality of the law. Even more surprisingly, the Israeli authorities kill children with the irrational logic that they would one day be terrorists.[28] A Zionist politician stated the following, quoting Hitler:

> We are not guests in our land, this whole land is ours. And now, the one who we had to get with him somehow because he also lived here, and we have to be humane and, all of course. He shows that he represents the deepest Islamo-Nazim. As it is clear for us, that we cannot live with .... As Hitler may his name be erased, once said: "I cannot live with this world if there is one Jew left in it." We could not live in this land if even one such Islamo-Nazi remains in Gaza. And not before we return to Gaza, and turn it into Hebrew Gaza. Do you want to turn Gaza into Hebrew

---

[28] See Farhad Malekian and Kerstin Nordlöf, Confessing the International Rights of Children: The Basic documents with Analysis (Cambridge: Cambridge Scholars Publishing, 2012); Farhad Malekian and Kerstin Nordlöf,'International Legal Status of Children' in Jay S. Albanese (ed.), The Encyclopaedia of Criminology & Criminal Justice (United States: Wiley-Blackwell (5 volumes, 2013), vol. III, pp. 1173-1178; Farhad Malekian, Kerstin Nordlöf, Prohibition of Sexual Exploitation of Children Constituting Obligation Erga Omnes (Cambridge: Cambridge Scholars Publishing, 2013); Farhad Malekian, Kerstin Nordlöf, The Sovereignty of Children in Law (Cambridge: Cambridge Scholars Publishing, 2012).

> Gaza? Unequivocally, yes. Because if not, if Gaza will not turn into Jaffa, then Jaffa will turn into Gaza. Friends, this is the whole story.

The motivations of the criminal Zionist government are evident in various records. More surprisingly, the UN itself has practically no power to prevent crimes against "terrorist children." The international political circumstances in which we may try to convince the powerful nations about their crimes are also veiled by the legacy of hiding the truth and the presentation of lies. The nature of the selection of crimes and violations has become a norm within the international criminal courts, the consequence of which determines the theory of impunity for criminals. The utipolitianist governments therefore do not object to the practices of the criminal jurisprudence of the ICC, since there is no real difference between the offices of those governments and the office of the vassal prosecutor.[29] This is the theory of faith, morality, conscience, and judgments in the Court. A clear example of this is the office of Karim Khan in the ICC, as previously mentioned.

3. Worthless Utipolitianist Monopolisation

There are no objective grounds for relying on the distribution of international human rights provisions among nations of the world only to then tolerate systematic injustices under the authority of the UN Security Council. Again, any ethical, moral, or complementarity arguments that are presented by many governments around the world for the monopolisation of the Charter are considered insufficient and therefore cannot be invoked as a basic proof for injustices. These arguments prove that we are working with frozen systems of international human rights, international humanitarian law, and international criminal justice that have lost their explanatory power on account of proper enforceability.[30] This means that the arguments are derived from the very principles of morality regarding the essence of human unity, which serves no purpose and is cancelled out by the evil interests of governments.

---

[29] The Statute of the ICC clearly states that "3. The Prosecutor and the Deputy Prosecutors shall be persons of high moral character, be highly competent in and have extensive practical experience in the prosecution or trial of criminal cases. They shall have an excellent knowledge of and be fluent in at least one of the working languages of the Court." Article 42. Emphasis mine.

[30] Farhad Malekian, The Monopolization of International Criminal Law in the United Nations, A Jurisprudential Approach (Stockholm: Almqvist Wiksell International, 1st ed., 1993).

The expectations put forward by the principles of moralist theories are constructed by the argument for the utility principle of injustice under the umbrella of justice. We have generally considered the principle of morality and the meaning of the priority of rights in the shadow of our own interests. This is particularly evident concerning political, legal, and moral thoughts when they are evaluated by the United Nations Security Council—which is a dictatorial political organ. It seems appropriate at this point to say that there is a different conception of justice from which we derive our principles. Thus, we may argue with different theories in order to prove that our arguments and interpretations are authentic. This is particularly done by our governments without referring to any notion of basic morality existing for the sake of the law.

In other words, we may offer a different definition of autonomy in our arguments from that which is generally identified and recognised. While the theory of autonomy seems significant, it is also used as a power to strengthen the scope of utipolitianism in the interest of the big powers of the Council. It is therefore a mistake to highlight the theories of big powers with the theory of autonomy. This is because what the Security Council is doing is essentially a violation of universal moral ethics. Such moral principles should not be evaluated and restructured by the utipolitianist leaders of governments. We have seen that these principles of the universal moral law or the principles of equality of all human beings are not upheld, even in their most basic forms.

It is impossible to hypothesize about a moral theory that only exists to impose the policies of utipolitianist powers given the monopolised plans of utipolitianist governments. These governments actually impose the rules of monopolisation and a hollow idea of equality. At the same time, the real force of the idea that moral principles are essential for the concept of equality arises from the structure of our international conventions on human rights. They define the moral law in its invisible essence. Thus, when we say man is equal, we are referring to the notion of morality. This means that men should be, and are, capable of acting ethically. However, there are a considerable number of problems that hinder us from reaching an ideal conception of justice. Moreover, as we have seen, since it will never be clear what is ideal and what is not, such conflicts help the wrongful utilitarian idea of domination of power to develop in the Security Council of the United Nations.

The notion of morality and the goal of not prioritising or privileging any one individual over another is unachievable. That is why speaking about the notion of morality is not only a joke given the provisions of the Security Council, it also represents an abuse of the theory of morality. Thus, even if we suppose that moral legislation is to be approved and decided for the implementation of proper justice, the entire force of the application of such morality remains in the hands of the big powers' governments. *The notion of morality cannot be proper and acceptable in the Security Council with such monopolised provisions as long as it does not characterise men as free, equal, and rational beings. This is also significant and imperative concerning equality among governments.*

4. Utipolitianist Autonomous Monopolisation

The description of the original position of morality is based on the description of the basic foundations of the arguments for the protection of the concept of equality between nations and governments. It is an attempt to interpret these concepts of equality in the semantic structure. I am not arguing here about different interpretations of morality and our personal or governmental understandings, which cause significant damage to the structure of international human rights and international criminal justice. Rather, I am referencing the basis of the texts of the Security Council of the United Nations and their invisible evil nature. The fact is that the notion of morality has been reduced to the point of non-existence.

Certainly, we would like to see and read texts differently and evaluate them with full respect, however they are just decorative words that do not promote any related notions of justice or fairness.[31] This is also why the concept of morality has been criticised by Rousseau and Kant on various occasions.[32] Moreover, the notion of autonomy is preferred as it concerns the

---

[31] Note below.

[32] Israel's escalating use of torture against Palestinians in custody a preventable crime against humanity: UN experts (05 August 2024). Available at https://www.ohchr.org/en/press-releases/2024/08/israels-escalating-use-torture-against-palestinians-custody-preventable. Farhad Malekian, 'Mutilating the Philosophy of Justice in the Time of Armed Conflicts,' Contemporary Journal of International Criminal Law (2007); Farhad Malekian, The Concept of Islamic International Criminal Law, A Comparative Study (1994); Farhad Malekian, 'The Miserable Wedding of Naturalism into Positivism,' 2 ID EST Journal (2009). Immanuel Kant, Religion within the Limits of Bare Reason (1795), p. 87. Launched by Jonathan Bennett, Available online at http://www.earlymoderntexts.com/pdfs/kant1795part4.pdf; Alf Ross, On Law and Justice (London: Stevens & Sons Limited, 1958); Vagn Greve, 'Sheep or Wolves' 4 European Journal of Crime, Criminal Law and Criminal Justice (2005), 515-552; Hans Kelsen, 'What is Justice?' Justice, Law and Politics in the Mirror of Science (1957); Farhad Malekian, 'The Functions of International Criminal Law and the Problem of Positivism and Neutralism Philosophy,' Contemporary Journal of International Criminal Law (2007).

provisions of the Security Council and certain members. This is why the position of the American, British, and French governments in the Security Council can be described as taking advantage of the autonomous monopolisation of the discipline of morality and self-control of the rules of the organisation, as opposed of the application of united morality to all nations of the United Nations.[33]

Consequently, the most plausible explanation of this monopolized situation of the Security Council of the United Nations with certain matters of interest in the mind of a government is to say that the members of the UN have fallen into a trap. As a result, nearly all members continue to find themselves in very difficult situations due to the policies stemming from to the Big Powers legislation of 1944 or the UN. States have therefore walked into an organisation that, in reality, belongs to certain members and controls their nations and resources. States that reject this reality face difficulties and have sanctions imposed on them by the big powers. The principles upon which the organisation acts are not adopted based on an understanding of human rights and the protection of morality, but the contrary. Therefore, the position of most members of the organisation is that they are financed by the powertionist governments, which also means they have to follow their rules and morality.

The specific rules of the organisation governing human rights are therefore tentative, even if a government follows the organisation's orders, i.e., acts on the unjustified rules of the Security Council and follows the orders of certain members, it indicates how that member is different. This indicates that states act based on a standard external to the visible provisions of the organisation's charter. In this way, states or their governments act in accordance with certain members' desires rather than their sense of moral duty. There are two ways of explaining it: either their actions are based on the veil of ignorance of the governments, or they deprive themselves of their natural rights, legal rights, or human rights. Thus, countries act in accordance with the morality expressed by the powerful governments and against the basic morality of their own or the universal morality for all men. In the end, we choose the quality of the controlled principles of powertionist governments instead of our own—we are sold.[34]

---

[33] Farhad Malekian, The Monopolization of International Criminal Law in the United Nations, A Jurisprudential Approach (Stockholm: Almqvist Wiksell International, 1st ed., 1993).

[34] "On the same wavelength, Kant believes that the principle of the categorical imperative is an objective phenomenon and is therefore a rationally necessary and unavoidable principle that we are obliged to fulfil, even though we may have some natural desires or inclinations opposite from the rationality principle. This is why, according to Kant, the Security Council does not follow the rationality principle, and this has nothing to do with its permanent

The core of our argument is that the vast majority of governments make collective decisions based on what is dictated to them instead of making their own choices. Equally, rational governments should not permit circumstances such as those that have given rise to the fruitless search for the principles of justice. Surely, the arguments for those principles of human rights and morality are fixed. We should check the documents of human rights and evaluate them in the context of the brutal and aggressive position of the contemporary politics of utipolitianist governments. We must remember that the principles chosen in the Charter of the United Nations apply to the basic structure of our international relations and the premises characterising these stemming principles of justice. Assuming that the reasoning in the Charter and its principles of justice are correct and not monopolised, then governments can observe that the powerful governments act in accordance with their personal political principles that they have adopted and believe to be rational and perfect descriptions of humanity and morality.

5. Utipolitianist Drama in the Security Council

Militarily powerful governments which want to be powertionists change the original positions of equality, humanity, and morality. By acting from such privatized perspectives, the general conditions of justice naturally change, and the determining elements of justice and morality inevitably become paralysed.[35] Consequently, when we knowingly act against the principles of justice within the United Nations or through the adoption of a resolution, we assume that we have the right to limit any suggestions that do not align with our desires. Thus, we extend the rights of interpretation and promotion or rejection of any theory that does not meet and satisfy the will of certain powerful members. One reason for governments to do this is to have the principles of legality under their control. In the end, this results in the notion of morality continually being infringed upon.

members; instead, this irrationality comes from the basic elements of the Charter. According to his metaphysics, all specific moral requirements are justified by the principle of rationality. When we do wrong, our wrongful action is surely irrational and therefore immoral. Alternatively, let us put it the other way around, all immoral actions carried out by the Security Council are indeed immoral. They seriously breach the principle of the categorical imperative." Farhad Malekian, The Mirage of International Criminal Law: Kant Metaphysics of Mens Rea (Cambridge: Cambridge Scholars Publishing, 2018), p.145.

[35] Farhad Malekian, Paralysing International Criminal Justice (New York: Nova Science Publishers, 2021).

Of course, it will not be so easy to decide what constitutes the most favorable interpretation and expression of the principle of legality in the system of international law. I believe that the principles of justice should be chosen and decided under certain international conditions that are workable and suitable to the administration of justice. This is much more significant in the case of administration of international criminal justice, which has a very important role to play in the maintenance of international legal order and peace. One of the important aspects of the principle of *de lege lata* is to see whether it incorporates those commonly shared presumptions of justice as presented by the principle of legality. The shared principles of equality may simply be entered into the principle of legality but they may practically be interpreted in a very narrow way. The aim of the commonly shared principles of international criminal law is to establish acceptable principles of justice. This is why states enter into international criminal conventions. The philosophical idea is to create a unique set of criminal principles acceptable to all nations. The conventions of international criminal law are supposed to apply to all injustices and inequalities based on the principle of legality or *de lege lata*. International criminal justice has to satisfy the row between the mind and reality. Without doubt, the idea of international criminal justice should not be restricted and limited to specific groups, states, or individuals in the international legal community. But, of course, reality is different. A permanent member of the Security Council can give effect to many unsolved questions of international law. The Council can especially take decisions concerning the questions of international criminal law-the character of which denote a breach of peace, threat to peace, or acts of aggression. Thus, a powerful nation under its political independence can interpret the original purpose of the system of international criminal law. This interpretation gives a temporary definition to the principle of *de lege lata* and justice. The interpretation basically consists of political, economic, and military interests of the state claiming to express the words of justice or the concept of rightness and fairness. The expression scarcely has a negative effect on the interests of the state itself. [36]

The principle of justice in the system of the Security Council and the United Nations Charter may be analogous to colonialism and contradicts the principles of categorical imperatives. This means that we may violate the imperative function of the system of international criminal justice by taking

[36] Farhad Malekian, 'Emasculating the Philosophy of International Criminal Justice in the Iraqi Special Tribunal,' Cornell International Law Journal, 58/5 (2005), pp. 717-718.

control of the hypocrisy of the United Nations with military force.[37] The language of the Security Council is very clear and does not require any further elaboration. It says, "Accept my order, or we will remove you from your position or even make your nation disappear." This is how the system of international law functions, and how the morality of the law is explained. The diplomacy of the United Nations Charter is actually based on the strength of guns. A clear example of this is the protection granted by the powertionist government of the United States and its allies following the destruction of the Iranian Embassy by the Zionist Israeli regime. The powertionist governments did not condemn the most serious obvious violations of the system of international criminal justice; rather, they condemned the acts of self-defence carried out by the Iranian armed forces.

For example, the criminal government of the United Kingdom condemns Iran while conspiring in the commission of crimes against Palestinians that have led to 45,000 Palestinians being killed by Israel's aggressive armed forces.[38] Regrettably, the system of monopolisation has become an imperative force in opposition to the theories proposed by the German philosopher Kant.[39] Thus, the principle of morality, which must be respected by all means, and the principle of peremptory international law, which is supported by the provisions of the Vienna Convention concerning the inviolability of diplomatic protection, have all been ignored in the arguments of the states that claim to protect human rights. In short, in Western countries' minds, the attack on the consulate did not constitute a violation of international law, however the Iranian response to the violation of its territorial rights did. This is how the system of authoritarianism of the United Nations functions.

---

[37] Examine Farhad Malekian, *Hypocrisy in International Criminal Justice* (New York: Nova Science Publishers, 2025).

[38] Then, one can just wonder why the Western governments have the right to help Israel intercept the Iranian rockets before reaching Israel. Then the next question will be: Why do Western governments not protect Palestinian children, families, and civilians from Israeli rocket attacks? This is a much more significant question, as the criminal British governments gave the Palestinians land as a gift to the European Jewish refugees. Moreover, we should not forget the fact that Iranian diplomats and military officers were killed by the Israeli strike. Yet more strange is that when Hamas or the military force of Palestine kills 1200 people of an occupying force (who were also killed by the Israeli military forces), Israel responds by murdering probably more than 36,000 (most are under buildings) or more civilians with daily bombardment and cutting off food, water, and all the necessities of life for nearly 2 million people for nearly six months straight without hospitals. Are these not enough of the disproportionate measures of Israeli seventy-six-year criminal governments? More sparingly, Rishi or the criminal minister of the British criminal government does not condemn Israel's bombing of Syria or Gaza?

[39] Farhad Malekian, The Mirage of International Criminal Law: Kant Metaphysics of Mens Rea (Cambridge: Cambridge Scholars Publishing, 2018).

This illuminates the double standards within human rights and criminal justice, and also indicates the violation of moral principles of justice. The virtue of this argument is clear and obvious to any lawyer who has pursued a career in law out of a respect for the morality of justice and not due to immorality and injustice. There is consequently no notion of equal rational virtue in the inner structure of the arguments and reasoning of the big powers. *The validity of the principle of morality in the context of the provisions of international human rights conventions is not at all supported, and it does not presume that it has a particular desire or intention to protect people from the guns of the Security Council. Since the hypothetical imperative power of the gun has endless power over an effective principle of morality and clear steps for the big powers to achieve a specific end of their objectives, speaking about the high value of human rights principles becomes futile.*[40]

6. Utipolitianism Colonializing the Vassal Court

Regardless of whether or not the rules and principles codified in Chapter VII of the Charter have particular motivations, it is obvious that the utipolitianist colonisation of the system of international criminal justice is occurring. As a matter of fact, this utipolitianist colonisation of the Charter of the United Nations has been supported by the office of the prosecutor and the prosecutor themselves. This is particularly evident regarding the Statute of the International Criminal Court (ICC). Whether the ICC stands for something specific or not, it is clear that there are agreeable feelings that arise from the monopolisation of its principles and the unfortunate fact that the Prosecutor of the ICC has no right to speak for themselves as long as they working under the imperative orders of the powertionist governments. Thus, every principle of justice that is entered into the Statute of the ICC is hypothetical when it comes to the very reality of the system of international criminal justice and its rules for the prevention of international crimes.[41]

The ICC has no power to enforce its provisions upon any of its masters, as we have seen throughout its history. The applicability of its provisions and the identification of international crimes depend on the order and control of the notion of morality. Thus, from the point of view of certain members of the

---

[40] Farhad Malekian, *Hypocrisy in International Criminal Justice* (New York: Nova Science Publishers, 2025).

[41] Id.

Security Council, if one needs to succeed economically and politically, one needs to prove that they will follow the orders and decisions of certain permanent members. This means that any argument against the superpowers constitutes an argument against the structure of the International Criminal Court as well. This is because the *Vassal Court is the tail of the Security Council. Certain permanent members of the Security Council, such as the United States and the United Kingdom, control the Court of Justice. They desire certain primary goods for their own purposes and call them the morality of all times. These states only see their own arguments as rational and dismiss other arguments as irrational. Thus, any international legal personality is viewed as illegal, unless they approve of it.* My discussions should not, however, be addressed to their nations or people. My finger is pointed at governments, and not their citizens. Even if one may argue that governments are elected by its citizens, my sentiment remains the same because politicians are chosen with the hope that they are going to uphold justice and morality, and it is only when the politicians come into power that they show their true evil nature.

The preference for a strong application of the system of international criminal justice is therefore the principle of independence and its full respect, if the intention is to prevent utipolitianism from tainting its principles and prevent the colonisation of an international criminal court, which is supposed to provide more rational views those of the Security Council. This is why the value of the principle of morality decreases and the most general assumptions about rationality, the conditions of international human rights, and its power of enforceability crumble. Utipolitianist colonialism in international criminal justice refers to the position under which we have sold justice or placed the implementation of criminal justice into the hands of those who are slaves to their positions. This is why throughout this book we will repeatedly refer to Karim Khan, i.e., the vassal prosecutor of an international criminal court that only follows the orders of its British and American masters.[42]

This is, of course, not surprising. Otherwise, Khan would not still be a prosecutor. This is how the Security Council members control international criminal law and the attribution of the principle of accountability or international criminal responsibility to their own crimes. In order to act on the principles of justice and objectivity, one has to act on the real virtue of the

---

[42] Consult also Clara Nieto, Masters of War: Latin America and U.S. Aggression from the Cuban Revolution through the Clinton Years (foreword by Howard Zinn; translated by Chris Brandt, 2003); Farhad Malekian, Powertionism in International Criminal Justice (New York: Nova Science Publishers, 2022).

theory of categorical imperatives, which means that if the powerful governments desire to see rational principles, they should first change their own actions accordingly. However, the problem is that the principle of the categorical imperative will never be implemented and the monopolisation of the Charter remains a fixture of the international legal system. In particular, this is more obvious when our aims are in the opposite direction. Promoting principles of morality and establishing them is simply impossible as long as we continued to give a free pass to utipolitianism. The value of the essence of international criminal justice decreases, and this cannot be successful without the direction and indirect slavery of certain individuals in the name of serving justice.

This is why the prosecutor of the ICC has a special position concerning the implementation of certain wishes of the powertionist governments. We may also note that the motivational hypothesis of moral justice loses sight of its goals, and the notion of autonomy in international criminal justice ultimately weakens. Due to this, certain powerful governments come up with other reasons to explain current situations by blaming other nations, individuals, and leaders who are fighting to protect their rights. For example, millions of people have been killed under the hegemony of American and British governments, and yet the ICC has remained silent concerning the obvious commission of international crimes, instead supporting supported the vacations of the big criminals.

7. Utipolitianism, the Core of Egocentrism

Righteousness in the system of international human rights, and even within the procedures of international criminal justice, is not only a dream, it also contradicts the basic understanding of the essence of universal morality—if such morality even exists.[43] Now we can add that the assumption of immoral disinterest is based on the very nature of illegality and the endless interest of utipolitianism in the sphere of international politics and, therefore, the monopolisation of international criminal justice.[44] This is the old system of colonialism just in new clothes acting as human rights principles being directed and interpreted by the Security Council. This also indicates that there

---

[43] See Farhad Malekian, Concreting Righteousness in International Criminal Justice (New York, Nova Sciences Publishers, 2024).

[44] Farhad Malekian, The Monopolization of International Criminal Law in the United Nations, A Jurisprudential Approach (Stockholm: Almqvist Wiksell International, 1st ed., 1993).

is no freedom concerning the choice of a system of justice and no hope that the Prosecutor of the ICC and their team will be objective.

This assumption of utipolitianism has been recycled to describe the situation of the international criminal court. As a result of the situation and the reality of the most significant matters of the given time being ignored, the system of the court has strayed in the wrong direction, and more principles of justice are being severely hindered and abused. A clear example of this is the commission of various crimes in Gaza. Certainly, the problems of morality in the structure of the ICC are hidden and raise doubts about the existence of such morality and the assumption of impartiality. Therefore, a clear conception of the principles of justice has not come to fruition, and the values of the system of international human rights conventions have become a dream. We have also seen that international criminal justice has not even worked in the case of Julian Assange, and the Prosecutor of the ICC is responsible for not arresting those who have accused Assange and taken his life away. Assange has been the victim of criminal powertionist governments, including his own government of Australia.

A further example of this lies with Payam Akhavan, the Special Advisor to the Prosecutor of the International Criminal Court. Akhavan is a Canadian citizen who claims to be a specialist in genocide and human rights law, and yet has remained silent concerning the genocide in Gaza.[45] Furthermore, he has also been receiving large amounts of financial aid and academic assistance from the American, Israeli, and British governments. In his long arguments and struggles for justice concerning the systematic massive murder of the Bhai in Iran, he proved that genocide had been committed, but could not bother to do the same for the Palestinians. This is how the morality of the system of international criminal justice and international lawyers works. Good justice is thus limited in its scope and does not even really exist. Lawyers are sold, and thus, justice is for sale in the courts.

---

[45] On genocide consult William A. Schabas, Genocide in International Law, the Crime of Crimes (2000); William L. Hurlock, 'The International Court of Justice: Effectively Providing a Long Overdue Remedy for Ending State-Sponsored Genocide (Bosnia-Herzegovina v. Yugoslavia),' 12 American University Journal of International Law and Policy (1997); George J. Andreopoulos, (ed.), Genocide: Conceptual and Historical Dimensions (Philadelphia, 1994); Machteld Boot, Genocide, Crimes against Humanity, War Crimes: Nullum Crimen Sine Lege and the Subjective Matter of Jurisdiction of the International Criminal Court, (2002); Christopher Browning, The Path to Genocide: Essays on Launching the Final Solution, (2002); Christian P., Scherrer, Iraq: Genocide by Sanctions (2011); Richard Falk, Slouching Toward a Palestinian Holocaust, www.transnational.org/Area.../Falk Palestine Genocide.html, 20 October 2010.

Due to this, any assumption of morality in the systems of international human rights and international criminal justice most contend with utipolitianist challenges, i.e., principle of greed and the use of the system of justice to serve and prioritize powertionist governments. The disinterest in or disregard of the powertionist governments in the Security Council is the original position that proves the basic foundation of the theory of why justice is paralysed.[46] We postulate that governments around the world have opposing positions regarding the system of justice that is taking shape under the criminal assistance of the prosecutor of the ICC, Karin Khan. If he is not biased, then why he did he hesitate to take action against the twenty-first century's Holocaust? It was too late when he finally did take action. If his conduct and decisions are restricted because of his close bond and relationship with the big powers' system of justice, then he is complicit in the commission of genocide in Gaza. The facts of the Gaza case prove that he does not care, and even if he did, he is not free from the notion of accountability due to the promises and oaths that he has to the world under the system of international criminal justice.

Moreover, since we are arguing about the role of the ICC in the development and promotion of injustice by the methods of colonialism and utipolitianism under the inaction of the prosecutor, the evil politicians of the powertionist governments strongly support the criminal conduct of the governments that commit international crimes. The humanitarian purposes of the system of international criminal law cannot be fulfilled with various argumentations and simply believing that the crimes will end. Since the argument of immorality in the system of the Security Council has been supported, only governments that support the criminal actions of Israel are safe, and therefore the freedom of speech has been restricted such that displaying humanity towards the rights of victims is considered to be criminal conduct and therefore against the wills of the powertionist governments of the Security Council. As the argument now runs in the Security Council, the principles of justice are covered with the principles of utipolitianism, which benefits those who are obeying the orders and decisions of the criminal governments.

At this point I must say that every interpretation of the righteous and truthful imperative principles of justice has been monopolized and is unfortunately the result of interpretations made by individuals following their

[46] Farhad Malekian, Paralysing International Criminal Justice (New York: Nova Science Publishers, 2021).

masters.[47] This reflects the current state of the principle of moral justice within the present political conditions. Even though we evidence to support our arguments, we must address the problematic existence of colonial ideology within all of the provisions of the United Nations Charter. It is unimaginable that the powerful governments could arrive at the truth on their own because they are the ones protecting the utility of the system of international criminal justice and befriending prosecutors to cover up their own crimes, as we have seen with the proxy war in Ukraine and the killing of almost 400,000 soldiers. This means that moral law has become the instrument of certain powertionist governments with the hope of removing the Russian president from power and dividing Russia into different countries under the control of the United States of America. If Russia is divided, then the US government will create conflicts between all parts of the newly divided Russia. This is how we implement and respect the justice of an international criminal court.

8. Crucial Arguments About the Values of the Vassal Court

There are several problems that should be addressed when discussing the utipolitianist history of colonial powers and how they have established seats of injustice for themselves in the Security Council. As long as one assumes that they must be guided by a master in the decision-making process, then the monopolisation of power under the authority of the Security Council will benefit them. However, utipolitianism may be more dangerous and humiliating for governments that uphold a consistent set of principles and substitute reactions for the maintenance of norms of morality. The creation of a free and equal rational body between the natural law theory and those who enforce the theories of utipolitianist governments will be a difficult task. It raises doubts about the Security Council's ability to uphold justice and peace for its members. However, acting on any consistent set of elements could have a destructive outcome not only for all members of the organisation, but potentially for all governments as well. This is because all governments naturally resist the imposition of power and the monopolisation of their rights.

All such actions, including self-defence, represent the practical definition of morality and not violations of principles of justice that include the established norms of international human rights law. This indicates that when

[47] Examine Farhad Malekian, Concreting Righteousness in International Criminal Justice (New York, Nova Sciences Publishers, 2024).

the system of international human rights laws is violated, the commission of international crimes has already occurred. As a result, we do not need to wait to witness the violations of the provisions of international humanitarian law during armed conflicts. Consequently, if a government realises that the true face of justice does not exist and the presented decisions or norms hinder its freedoms and actions, it may begin to fight for the establishment of the violated rights, as we have seen the Palestinians doing. The Palestinians have continued to struggle self-determination and against utipolitianist corruption even after 78 years of occupation. The missing part of our argument relates to how the majority of governments in the world are mistreated. This is because utipolitianist governments ignore legal arguments and the notion of morality. The moral law expresses our nature in perceptible and identifiable ways when powertionist governments act contrary to the principles of moral law or the opposite principles of international human rights and do not fulfil the reality of the given promises of positive law and morality. This is a flaw in the system of justice and presents a form of injustice.

We need a constitution that unequivocally prevents the cultivation and development of utipolitianist institutions and provides equal voting rights for all governments in order to stop wars from occurring. The present situation with the system of legislation and voting in the United Nations shows that there is no wise standard of communication of rules within the practice of the organisation. Even if we search for any positive legal or political norm, the outcome is not satisfactory, and it can jeopardise the existence of any government that protests the legal and political system of the Security Council due to its system of utipolitianism and hierocracy in Chapter VII of the Charter.[48] Consequently, the principles of the Charter that contain equal norms

[48] "The question is even more complicated when one or several of the permanent members of the Security Council are involved in the preparation, participation in, or commitment of certain international crimes. Thus, while the concept of international criminal responsibility may exist for the criminal actions of certain highly protected individuals of all states regardless of their political, military, and economic situations, the laws are not enforceable for certain reasons. For example, in the IST, Hussein has no right to express his history of juridical and political power as in an international criminal tribunal those actions are guided and directed under the supervision of the United Nations by international judges. While it seems clear that the system of international criminal responsibility is an integral part of the international criminal justice system, it may not be incorrect to say that both systems have been divided into separated jurisdictional issues. The consequence of this is that the difficult questions of international criminal law such as the question of appropriate implementation of international criminal law in an appropriate international criminal tribunal is still one of the serious problems of international criminal law. Of course, the significant question is not the constitution of the ICC but the prevention, elimination, abolition, and abandonment of international crimes as well as the implementation of international criminal law to every

and distribute moral law must be evaluated in light of true speculations about the system of justice.

However, we are aware that there is not only one solution to this very complicated situation under the principles of inequalities under Chapter VII of the Charter due to the given circumstances. Nevertheless, it is normally required that we tackle the problems that are created by the very unjust system of utipolitianism and the modification of the original position of the concept of morality, which should be respected in order to establish a complete respect for the merit of international human rights conventions. *The problem is that utipolitianist theory and conduct desire to express control over any idea of equality in the realm of morality, freedom, justice, and violations of the principles of equality.* The question is how and why should a majority of the population of the world accept the monopolisation of their codified expressed rights?

Whether we speak about the equality of arms with consideration for the various principles of international human rights, or we speak about the monopolisation of rights under the United Nations Charter, we are still forced to respect basic principles of natural morality. *We must then again decide which principles are the principles of equality for all nations when consciously pursued and acted upon and which principles guide the majority of governments like lambs to the slaughter. In other words, we must be able to make a distinction between the immoral diplomacy of the organisation in the name of the implementation of international human rights in order to monopolise the power of the system of international criminal justice and the very significant question of accountability for the commission of international crimes in the rooms of the Court.* This means that we are trying to realize the difference between free and independent international criminal justice norms and the very nature of the impolitic character of the Statute of the ICC.

9. Semi-Legal Subjects of the Vassal Court

The nature of negotiations and discussions that occur continuously within the scope of the United Nations Charter demonstrate that if any argument about universal morality or humanity is presented in its meetings, including those of

---

individual who has committed international crimes, regardless of nationality." Farhad Malekian, 'Emasculating the Philosophy of International Criminal Justice in the Iraqi Special Tribunal,' Cornell International Law Journal, 58/5 (2005), p. 719.

the General Assembly and the Security Council, it will face harsh criticism and be attacked by utipolitianist authorities if it does not align with the basic immoral philosophy of utipolitianist demands. Such arguments are immediately objected to by the representatives of utipolitianist governments and their allies. However, we are aware of the fact that, in some respects, the idea of utilitarianism or its doctrine demand rights that are a valuable advantage for a minority of governments. The argument in favour of the doctrine is strong. However, there is limited space for exceptions. Those who seek to abolish the principle of equality through any means also aim to abolish the legal legitimacy of moral law. In other words: the principles of fair justice are not allowed to apply to all members of the United Nations. The description of the original position of the principles of equality and human rights, and in particular, the equality of the international legal personality of states, resembles the significant position of the principles of universal validity of the rights of all nations for true justice and thus should not be ignored. The evil nature of the principles of the organisation becomes more obvious when certain governments resort to the doctrine of utipolitianism in conjunction with their imperialist, authoritarian powers. They act on the principles they choose, which are useful for the expansion of their economic, military, and political power and, beyond all, confirm the right of occupation of other nations. A clear example of utipolitianism in practice is the war currently being waged in Gaza against the Palestinian nation.[49] Consequently, the powertionist governments exhibit their power through their aggressive military conduct.[50]

---

[49] During his time as a member of the United Kingdom's cabinet, Lord Curzon expressed dissatisfaction with the content of the Belfour Declaration. He presented the critical situation facing the Palestinians by stating: "The Palestine position is this. If we deal with our commitments, there is first the general pledge to Hussein in October 1915, under which Palestine was included in the areas as to which Great Britain pledged itself that they should be Arab and independent in the future ... Great Britain and France - Italy subsequently agreeing - committed themselves to an international administration of Palestine in consultation with Russia, who was an ally at that time ... A new feature was brought into the case in November 1917, when Mr Balfour, with the authority of the War Cabinet, issued his famous declaration to the Zionists that Palestine 'should be the national home of the Jewish people, but that nothing should be done - and this, of course, was a most important proviso - to prejudice the civil and religious rights of the existing non-Jewish communities in Palestine. Those, as far as I know, are the only actual engagements into which we entered with regard to Palestine." Cited in Palestine Papers, 1917-1922, Doreen Ingrams, page 48 from the UK Archive files PRO CAB 27/24; see also Farhad Malekian, 'Judging International Criminal Justice in the Occupied Territories,' International Criminal Law Review 12 (2012) 827–869, at 830.

[50] Id.

This is demonstrated not only during war, but also in the ways that other governments acknowledge their strong military position.[51]

The above policy then needs to accept the strong power of powertionist military organs and follow their given orders concerning certain important matters if the immoral nature of the theory of utipolitianism is not going to be employed in practice. For that reason, any desire to act justly means following the orders of the political masters or owners of the United Nations. Otherwise, we would be endangering our nation. The United Nations is, to put it simply, a vassal organisation, and will remain one until the Security Council is dissolved. I believe that the current state of international criminal justice, including the system of international human rights, is a complete failure when it comes to fulfilling their duties in line with moral principles. The existence of the Statute of the International Criminal Court, as well as all international human rights agreements, is a shameful reflection of our contemporary justice system. This should bring feelings of guilt to all governments in the world, particularly those that take advantage of the systems of international criminal justice and human rights law.

This inappropriate version of utipolitianism has actually been gaining power, and this immoral power is appearing within more international legal systems. This indicates that the authority of the system of international criminal justice is driven by the underlying power, which is immoral and fails to express the values of our natural essence as free and equal rational beings. Consequently, the decisions of the utipolitianist governments attack our self-respect, violate our values, infringe on our dignity, and overstep the legal and moral depictions of our *somebodiness*. This means that we are mistreated by various intrigues, and our sense of united interests decreases because of the will and the imposition of the force of immoral and unjust decisions by certain governments that are in love with power. They are in love with greed and with killing the populations of other nations.[52]

---

[51] Id.

[52] Muchnik Pablo, Kant's Theory of Evil: An Essay on the Dangers of Self-love and the Aperiodicity of History (Lexington Books, 2010); Farhad Malekian, Judgments of Love in Criminal Justice (Switzerland: Springer: 2017, 2018); Farhad Malekian, 'The Heaven of Justice with Love,' The Journal of the Henry Martyn Institute (2017), pp. 5-29. Farhad Malekian, 'The Canon of Love against the Use of Force in Islamic and Public International Law: Part II: The Anatomy of Love Against Violations,' 15 International Criminal Law Review, 2015), pp. 861-895; Farhad Malekian, 'The Canon of Love against the Use of Force in Islamic and Public International Law: Part I: The Chamber of Love within Legal Discipline,' 15 International Criminal Law Review, 2015), pp. 591-628; Mendus Susan, 'The Importance of Love in Rawls's Theory of Justice' 29 (1) British Journal of Political Science (1999), pp. 57-75.

This occurs either by the force of law or the force of guns. Due to the unlimited power of the controlling system of utipolitianism over the system of the International Criminal Court and its monopolisation, governments no longer have full independence as legal subjects and are instead semi-legal subjects with fewer rights in practice. This indicates that utipolitianism ignores the rights of the weaker parties, even in court. According to utipolitianist policy, the deaths and forced relocation of millions of people by powerful governments is permitted and the ICC is not permitted to issue arrest warrants for them. The exercise of jurisdiction in conformity with the rules of the Court is never seen. *Due to this, legal slavery is a reality within the system of international human rights and United Nations rules.* The result is that the system of international criminal justice does not function as it should in the courts. This indicates that the vassal Court submits itself to the control of power of the authoritarian governments to serve the powertionist or utipolitianist orders. This is similar to the old system of feudalism, a sort of slavery and mastery of a certain power.[53] No notion of morality exists.[54]

The Court therefore cannot prosecute or identify real criminals as it is supposed to. Thus, we have a system of justice that is treated by the law a criminal or transgressive. It is at this stage that we have confirmed that the power of law is weaker than the power of lies, and the power of lies is the power of justice. The power of justice in this case indicates how we can control the system of international criminal justice. This means that the law and justice of the United Nations impose the idea of monopolisation with the purpose of controlling the wealth of all nations in the world by having the old colonial powers wear new clothes of justice in the name of international human rights law. This situation leads not to the presentation of the morality of the law, but rather to an austere command of morality by the powertionist governments. Accordingly, the original position of the system of international criminal justice can then be viewed as a utipolitianist interpretation the presents the conception of autonomy and its methods under the political and legal philosophy of utipolitianist powers.

---

[53] Farhad Malekian, Powertionism in International Criminal Justice (New York: Nova Science Publishers, 2022).

[54] Examine also P. M. S. Hacker and J. Raz, (eds.), Law, Morality and Society: Essays in Honour of H. L. A. Hart (1977); Farhad Malekian, Classical Morality in International Peremptory Criminal Law (Newcastle: Cambridge Scholars Publishing, 1st ed. 2018, 2nd ed. 2021); Joseph Raz, Ethics in the Public Domain: Essays in the Morality of Law and Politics (Oxford: Oxford University Press, 1994); Joseph Raz, The Morality of Freedom (1986).

Chapter 3

Hazardous Unanimity of Utipolitianists for Criminal Justice

1. Unreasonableness of Utipolitianism

In this chapter, I will focus on the practical effects of the theory of utipolitianism and its attack on the institution of morality. I will begin by saying that the principles of true justice have been monopolised by the doctrine of the political economy of the super powerful states as well as by the doctrine of waging war against any nation that does not submit itself to the rules of powertionist utipolitianist governments around the world. This is particularly evident in the case of the United States government, which is the master of creating wars between nations around the world. The philosophy of the categorical imperative within the structure of the system of international human rights law that calls for an equal application and interpretation of the norms does not function and will never function. This does not mean that I am cultivating passive views about international criminal justice. Rather, this is the real contemporary position of all legal systems, and has long been seen since the existence of human civilisation, with the difference that the method for the monopolisation of nations has changed overtime.

While it is true that the principles of morality have been referred to in a considerable number of legal and philosophical arguments, when the principle is needed, it fails to function. In other words, the situation encourages the consolidation of the theory of utipolitianist colonialism and the development of the idea of one-eyed justice. Therefore, the theory of utipolitianism means justice, which looks at the given case with no sense of objectivity. Those that would be chosen and dealt with under this theory are those that have not let their political, economic, and legal diplomacy fall under the control of utipolitianist governments and are therefore condemned by them. The description of this situation no longer permits us to explain how justice must be seen and how the principles of morality must be talked about. These principles are thus rejected under the power of the utipolitianist governments. As a result of this, we have departed from naturalist, moralist, and positivist views in several aspects. *Utipolitianist governments choose the melody for the sound of justice, which then establishes how all states must follow the dancing music of the law or instead choose to be killed along with their children.*[55] *This means that there is no collective choice, only powertionist selection.*[56]

The value of being equal to the law and the level of enslavement to the master of the law increases. Since states are assumed to be equal and should be treated with the same procedures of international criminal jurisdiction, this theory will lose its value and cannot be enforced because of the position of one-eyed justice. This is why we emphasise that the values of moral or legal justice will not reach their intentions in the structure of our interpretation of utipolitianist colonialism and international criminal justice. This is due to the existence of the evil norm of selectivity in the theoretical body of utipolitianism. This indicates that the problem of equality within the international principles of moral ethics cannot function under the principle of selectivity. Therefore, we should try to define a clear sense of international criminal justice that is free and not tied to the impolitic, inappropriate, misguided, or utipolitianist ideologies of powertionist governments. Morality, peace, and equality must be treated with full wisdom in order to promote a unanimous agreement for their application.

For example, the killing of Palestinians and forcing them out of their sovereign territory is a tragedy that has been organized and orchestrated by the ideology of the utipolitianist governments against the very idea of utilitarianism, which encourages pleasure and happiness for all. The theory of utilitarianism does not try to ignore the rights of all people. This is because utilitarianism does not promote universal rights for all men. When we override the interests of other nations or the established rights of other states, we actually infringe upon their sovereign independence by making criminal and selfish decisions, which in turn represent a selfish imposition of the utipolitianist theory of justification. We assume that the governments that support the utipolitianist system being imposed on the population of Gaza

[55] Examine Farhad Malekian, Kerstin Nordlöf, The Sovereignty of Children in Law (Cambridge: Cambridge Scholars Publishing, 2012); Farhad Malekian, Kerstin Nordlöf, Prohibition of Sexual Exploitation of Children Constituting Obligation Erga Omnes (Cambridge: Cambridge Scholars Publishing, 2013);.Farhad Malekian and Kerstin Nordlöf, Confessing the International Rights of Children: The Basic documents with Analysis (Cambridge: Cambridge Scholars Publishing, 2012); Farhad Malekian and Kerstin Nordlöf,'International Legal Status of Children' in Jay S. Albanese (ed.), The Encyclopaedia of Criminology & Criminal Justice (United States: Wiley-Blackwell (5 volumes, 2013), vol. III, pp. 1173-1178.

[56] Id.

understand that the justice being promoted is not real justice, nor do the actions represent the power of the principles of the United Nations. Rather, they reflect the very unlawful and brutal imposition of powerful state barbarity of guns over a handful of unarmed individuals over the course of several decades.

Thus, justice as fairness is a theory that does not exist in the Charter nor in the theory of utipolitianism. Consequently, the value of the freedom of pure intelligence is not based in the theory of the Security Council, which pursues matters based on the principle of selectivity. In this case, we are really outside the range of the theories of international human rights conventions. Consequently, if we want to apply all of the rational ideas of justice to every government, we are forced to see the problems with the existence of the United Nations Security Council and the International Criminal Court concerning their policy of utipolitianism and the existence of corruption within the institutions of international human rights. The old colonial powers of the world should not be involved in determining the principles of international criminal courts, nor should they determine which parties should be prosecuted or granted impunity. If we continue on this path, we will never achieve justice. The Court will remain the same—a private company controlled by the leaders of utipolitianist governments.

For example, the occupation of the Palestinian territories has been carried out primarily due to the policies of the British imperialists, which is why a solution has not yet been found for the conflict. *The justice of civilisation will always be entrusted to the shameful, hypocritical force of law, which will make all nations of the world the victims.* Certainly, if Nazism had not ended, and they had continued to murder Jews, we would have felt more shame and suffering. The difference between justice as fairness and justice as unfairness is so narrow that the current doctrine cannot recognize it when it comes to the very humiliating and organised criminality of the utipolitianist governments regarding the abhorrent genocides during World War II and in Gaza today.[57]

[57] Consult John D. van der Vyver, 'Prosecution and Punishment of the Crime of Genocide,' 25 Fordham International Law Journal (1999), p.286; Mary Robinson, Genocide, War Crimes, Crimes Against Humanity, 25 Fordham International Law Journal (1999), p.275; Matthew Lippman, 'Genocide,' in International Criminal Law, Vol. I (M. Cherif Bassiouni, ed., 2008) pp.405-455; William L. Hurlock, 'The International Court of Justice: Effectively Providing a Long Overdue Remedy for Ending State-Sponsored Genocide (Bosnia-Herzegovina v. Yugoslavia),' 12 American University Journal of International Law and Policy (1997), p.299; Beth van Schaack, 'The Crime of Political Genocide: Repairing the Genocide Convention's Blind Spot,' 106 Yale Law Journal (1997), p.2259; Examine also the statements of Bertrand Russell and the Russell International War Tribunal held in Stockholm, Sweden, May 2-10, 1967 and Roskilde, Denmark from November 20 to December 1, 1967. The Tribunal was essentially created because of different meetings in

We should not permit the effect of dualist theories to enter into the philosophy of justice and morality and divide it into necessary norms and conditional norms as this may be harmful in the end.

2. Utipolitianism Eliminating Rights

The utipolitianist mentality can be particularly seen in the decisions and practices of the United States, Israel, the United Kingdom, and France.[58] This does not mean that there are no other states that practice the policy of utipolitianism, i.e., control and monopolise the rights of other nations. *In short, utipolitianism can preliminarily be defined as a form of decision, conduct, action, inaction, vote, or abstention, seen in the policy of the state in question. These terms are just symbolic examples and are non-exhaustive. Utipolitianism may refer to and contain all these terms and may apply to different standards of decisions that intend to protect the evil views of certain governments against certain victims.* The theory of utipolitianism arose from the monopolisation of the United Nations and refers to the ownership of certain members over others. *All arrangements and policies under the policy of utipolitianism are essentially based on dictating priority over others and pursuing economic interests and gaining political and military privileges.* It is even clear that the term "veto" suggests that the implicit hidden moral conception is under the control of utipolitianist policies. Therefore, its connotations are very broad. The term "veto" actually represents the entire definition of monopolisation of law, economics, and politics in certain situations. This in turn indicates the existence of utipolitianism.

The theory of utipolitianism does not include the interpretation of the common good of humanity, but rather the contrary. This theory acts against the form of justice that was established in the United Nations Charter, particularly as it concerns the duties of certain members under the provisions of Chapter VII of the organisation. A good policy of political and legal legislation of the United Nations Charter should invoke criteria for the just division of international advantages for all nations in order for its works to be recognized as valid. However, the utipolitianism of the system of the United

London in 1966. J. Duffett, Against the Crime of Silence (New York, London, 1968). W. Michael Reisman, 'Legal Responses to Genocide and Other Massive Violations of Human Rights,' 59 Law and Contemporary Problems (1996), p.75.

[58] Study John J Mearsheimer and Stephen Walt, The Israel Lobby and U.S. Foreign Policy (New York: Farrar, Straus and Giroux. 2007).

Nations and, again, certain methods of utipolitianism within the brutal policies of certain governments, stress that justice as fairness neither exists nor applies to the basic structure of the system of international law. This is particularly evident concerning international criminal justice. *The theory of utipolitianism is a method for pitting and subjugating a few governments against the will of the majority governments of the world.* The theory may therefore be described as a closed system that restricts and eliminates the natural rights of other nations and gives them to other nations instead.

Additionally, there may be certain arguments concerning all decisions of utipolitianist governments with their background of colonialism and occupying the power of the soil of the law. This soil of the law refers to the law's essence, which is fundamental to its recognition, and all states suppose that even though the occupation of certain powers is an evil policy within utipolitianist theory, there is still a certain limitation to this unjustified control or occupation of the law. This is why there are certain arguments regarding the behaviour of the utipolitianist governments, which are hungry for power and wealth. Thus, those who argue against the evil powers of utipolitianist governments believe that certain arrangements are fundamental and should not be removed from the practice or decisions of powertionism governments.[59] We are primarily discussing governments that actively abstain or veto resolutions of the Security Council that intend to defend and establish the rights of the victims.

In fact, the cumulative effect of the system of international human rights provisions indicates that the system of morality in the United Nations has been mistreated and that the political legislation of the Security Council does not

---

[59] "Powertionism relates to the preferences, desires, inclinations, and predispositions of individual governments which form the basis for these governments to pursue their malicious intentions by killing and destroying other nations. Powertionism also relates to the powerful desires of governments to reduce the power of other governments indirectly, even if it means putting another nation in danger of facing death and devastation in order to aggressively pursue their interests and take power away from another powertionist government. Some of the most notorious powertionists of the world work collectively to promote the interests of their strongest leader in the name of working for NATO. This does not mean that all NATO members are strong on their own, however they wish to be seen as strong by standing alongside governments which have a long history of promoting devastation, genocide and death in the world. Such governments are green, or as the Germans say: one can certainly see the grün hinter den Ohren of certain NATO members. Only a simpleton would believe that any word out of the mouth of a powertionist government is correct. The elephant here is primarily the United States and NATO and other countries are their puppets. The greed, lies, cheating, and theft carried out by powertionist governments have no sovereign boundaries." Farhad Malekian, Powertionism in International Criminal Justice (New York: Nova Science Publishers, 2022, p.vii.

specify that the basic structure or the soil of the laws should not be sold for the ethical inspiration of moral justice. Moreover, the international legal system is supposed to shape the wills and aspirations that its various nations want to meet and naturally have. Consequently, a legal system of United Nations standards should not be paralysed due to the interests of the utipolitianist governments. How the system of international law appears to work in the organisation should not eliminate the rights of others, but it should satisfy their presentation for the reestablishment of their dignity. Thus, when we have voted against the rights of Palestinians or South Africans in the Security Council, we seriously have ignored the substance of morality and violated the established needs of all laws.

3. Deliberating Injustice Provisions

The desires of the utipolitianist governments affect and eliminate the rights of nations, and thereby violate the principles of international criminal justice. This is because there is a strong connection between certain fundamental violations and certain basic rules of the Statute of the ICC. Such violations against the fundamental rights of other nations are so serious that they also go against the principles of international criminal law.[60] Although, of course, they are perfectly obvious and have always been recognized as violations, vetoing proposals that would restore the rights of the Palestinians and their homelands implies the approval of genocide. This is particularly significant regarding the military and financial aid given to the Israeli government. In reference to Israel, the aggression of genocide is an example of violations of morality, justice, and judgments by the big utipolitianist government.

It is not without reason that one can argue that the prioritisation of utipolitianist theory indicates the serious sickness of the system of international criminal law and indicates how the real features of the

---

[60] For international criminal law examine Georg Schwarzenberger, 'The Problem of an International Criminal Law,' 5 Current Legal Problems (1950) 265; Edward M. Wise, 'Prolegomenon to the Principles of International Criminal Law,' 16 New York University Law Review (1970) 562; Farhad Malekian, International Criminal Law: The Legal and Critical Analysis of International Crimes (2 vols. 1991); Farhad Malekian, Principles of Islamic International Criminal Law: A Comparative Search (2011); Farhad Malekian, The Monopolization of International Criminal Law in the United Nations: A Jurisprudential Approach (2nd ed., 1995); M. Cherif Bassiouni (ed.), International Criminal Law (5 vols., 1999); Farhad Malekian, International Criminal Responsibility, in M. Cherif Bassiouni (ed.), International Criminal Law, (1999), p. 155.

mechanism of justice within the provisions of the United Nations function. The fact is that this ill and immoral measure of the United Nations was actually enforced by the United States government when the Charter was going to be adopted as independent law with a complete international legal personality. The United States had already made it clear that if the organisation did not institute the veto right, they would not join. This condition was also put forward by the same government concerning its membership in the League of Nations. Thus, all members of both organisations were forced to accept the conditions put forward by the United States; otherwise, neither organization would have ever existed.

Without the participation of the United States government, it would have been practically impossible to create the United Nations. This means that utipolitianist theory was already present in the cornerstones of the Charter. The representative of the United States of America actually did not sign the Charter until the veto right was written into Chapter VII. That is why the veto right became the most significant principle of the Charter, and all members then signed, ratified, and affirmed its existence. The veto right is a result of utipolitianism. In other words, members officially accepted a right that promotes the utipolitianist standard of justice and the use of immoral force as legal force within a system of powertionist governments. This indicates that utipolitianist theory became the law and prohibitions on the use of force in international relations of states lost all meaning. Those leading members actually meant the use of immoral, unjustified, and illegal force became justified. If this interpretation is wrong and an exaggeration, then we are still confirming the use of force and aggressive, brutal decisions behind the veto rights of the provisions of the Charter as morally right. Here, we are speaking about a government that brought the Declaration of Human Rights into the organisation.

This means that we actively affirm the evil ideological and political reality of the theory of utipolitianism, implying the most dangerous and genocidal power of the United States, the United Kingdom, France, Germany, the Netherlands, and even Switzerland. Although the system of international human rights dictates that decisions must be made based on moral and human rights norms, the practice of the utipolitianist governments has been quite different. We often acquiesce to the monopolisation of the rules of justice that destroy the entire existence of the system of international criminal justice without even thinking about the morality inherent in the status quo. Consequently, while abandoning justice for the established injustice principles of the United Nations Charter may seem rational in the beginning, it will eventually end in genocide. Utipolitianist theory is therefore based on convincing other governments or nations that their policy and administration of judgments are based on the development of the rules of pre-existing law or constitution of the Charter and are not able to be imposed by internal authorities.

4. Cannon Methods of Utipolitianists

The notion of justice, which is the most intricate question of international jurisprudence, including the natural laws, is one of the most essential pillars for realising the virtue of pure morality. Even if we suppose that the provisions within the body of the United Nations and the Security Council that promote the monopolisation of the rights of others are the result of misinterpretations, the principle of morality in the mind of man, should not be disregarded, if it even exists. Moreover, it is best to take a very short glance at what has occurred throughout the history of the United Nations and the General Assembly. All the evidence proves that several governments, including the United States, the United Kingdom, and Israel, were against the abolition of slavery and apartheid. This in turn indicates that they were in favour of fighting, killing, and eliminating the rights of the black population of South Africa that was trying to achieve freedom and equality as promised by human rights conventions.

The obvious point is that these nations had strong economic control over South Africa and controlled the rights of its citizens. In fact, certain members of the Security Council presented and supported the theory of utipolitianism during meetings.[61] Thus, the theory that is integrated into the Charter of the United Nations and the provisions of the Security Council was employed for decades against the rights of people. These rights have long been recognised and identified under the Universal Declaration of Human Rights and, naturally, all other human rights agreements concerning the right to self-determination. At first glance, it may appear that the inspiration of the international human rights system and the opinion of men create doubt concerning the rights that are already established with moral values. One might reason that this conception of justice, which relies on the intentions of

---

[61] Richard Falk, The Accountability of Leaders: A Challenge to Civil Government and Society in Jeremy Brecher, Jill Cutler, Brendan Smith, In the Name of Democracy: American War Crimes in Iraq and Beyond (American Empire Project), (New York: Metropolitan Books, Henry Holt and Company, 2005), pp. 301-307.

the utipolitianist theory, is correct, since they know politics, the law, and they have great military strength. This encourages us to promote exploitation, apartheid, discrimination, and genocide as good ideas, since we believe that they will not occur.

If we suppose that that is true and that such governments know the law and politics, then we are promoting violence within democracy rather than a wise method that does not tolerate the use of weapons. In other words, we are trying to see a wise man's reasoning not as a priority, but as an alternative to the use of guns and the murder of individuals. It might seem as though there is no alternative but to follow the evil and unjust theory of utipolitianism, except judging how the system of international institutions works is not a matter of privacy or inheritance, as many children claim they should be kings because they have inherited the position. We should remember that international criminal justice and the elements of international human rights do not function due to the legacy of power that has ended in the killing of millions on many occasions. Consequently, in the light of a supreme conception of the philosophy of law and morality, one has to search for prosperity in the principles of wisdom and morality instead of promoting the evil utipolitianist ideas of governments.

We should not forget that the United Nations was originally supposed to be established based on the ideas of rights, justice, freedom, equality, and, above all, the right to self-determination. These ideas have just been suggested as the permanent pillars of international criminal law in order to prevent crimes against subjugated populations.[62] However, they serve the opposite function or only serve to highlight the crimes of non-Western actors instead of uncovering the hidden actions of utipolitianist governments. Thus, only non-Western nations are seen as committing international crimes and not understanding the theory of human civilisation. Therefore, *utipolitianist* theory is clearly a reduction of the value of man, not only in the United Nations Charter, but also in the corridors of the International Criminal Court. We must

---

[62] Examine Farhad Malekian, The Monopolization of International Criminal Law in the United Nations: A Jurisprudential Approach (2nd ed., 1995); M. Cherif Bassiouni (ed.), International Criminal Law (5 vols., 1999); Farhad Malekian, International Criminal Responsibility, in M. Cherif Bassiouni (ed.), International Criminal Law, (1999), p. 155; Georg Schwarzenberger, 'The Problem of an International Criminal Law,' 5 Current Legal Problems (1950) 265; Edward M. Wise, 'Prolegomenon to the Principles of International Criminal Law,' 16 New York University Law Review (1970) 562; Farhad Malekian, International Criminal Law: The Legal and Critical Analysis of International Crimes (2 vols. 1991); Farhad Malekian, Principles of Islamic International Criminal Law: A Comparative Search (2011).

examine the very unusual nature of the monopolisation of man under the authority of an organisation that is essentially a private entity that cannot function if the veto rights are used against its fundamental principles. Furthermore, the veto right indicates the termination of the power of justice, whether it is called the United Nations or the International Criminal Court. We thus reject the institution of justice of the United Nations and the scope of all adopted principles regarding peace and the rights of states. As a result, only the most effective voice remains— that of utipolitianism. These assumptions were made and orchestrated in accordance with the aims of great political parties or the clues of clubs of powertionist governments, cut into small cubes.

5. Utipolitianist Supremacy Over Vassal Courts

The capacity of the system of international criminal justice is bound by comprehensiveness and capacity for freedom. The broadness of utipolitianist ideology is mainly influenced by various interests, including the occupation of the rights of others. This is then justified with a desire to hunt down terrorists and call upon their allies.[63] That is why utipolitianists not only work with vassal governments that follow their orders, but also with vassal prosecutors who stealthily enter into a relationship of protection with one or several utipolitianist governments. Once this occurs, the relevant vassal prosecutor gains legal power but loses independence and the self-confidence to act or make their own decisions.

In order to ensure that their theories are successful and their interests are protected, utipolitianist governments accuse any nation of anything they can in order to take their rights. The idea is to occupy the power of the Charter and the power of law, which means justice is under the control of utipolitianists. This presumption does not mean that the theories are tied to a particular pattern of international human rights or international criminal justice interests, but

[63] A clear example of these policies is the events of September 11th. David MacGregor, 'September 11 as 'Machiavellian State Terrorism,' in Paul Zarembka, The Hidden History of 9-11-2001 (New York: Seven Stories Press, 2008); Paul Zarembka, The Hidden History of 9-11-2001 (New York: Seven Stories Press, 2008); Thierry Meyssan, 11 September 2001: L'effroyable imposture (2002); Arthur Naiman, 9/11: The Simple Facts - Why the Official Story can't Possibly be True (US: Soft Skull Press, 2011); John Farmer, The Ground Truth: The Story Behind America's Defence on 9/11 (New York: Riverhead Books, 2009); Don Paul and Jim Hoffman, Waking Up from Our Nightmare, the 9/11/01 Crimes in New York City (New York: I/R Press, 2004); Paul Zarembka, The Hidden History of 9-11-2001 (New York: Seven Stories Press, 2008); Michel Chossudovsky, War and Globalisation: The Truth Behind September 11 (Global Outlook, 2002).

rather to a particular arrangement of institutional level that is planned and carried out for the purpose of obtaining supremacy over all other states. The theory of justice undeniably takes for granted the philosophy of good faith for equality and achieving rights without any particular prejudice. If the principles of justice are based on the promoting good for every nation, there is no doubt that the power of the utipolitianist governments decreases, which is why the powertionist governments cannot accept such principles in practice. There is no value in justice, in particular international human rights or international criminal justice, if the system of utipolitianism discourages the promotion of morality.

Furthermore, we must take the delinquency of the system of international criminal justice that prevents the big international criminals from being held accountable into account. A just system of international human rights, in particular international criminal justice, must generate its own policies of prevention and support for victims of international crimes. However, the practice of the ICC reflects the opposite. This means that it must organize itself to bring the states committing international crimes under the jurisdiction of the Court. It must also have a desire to act in accordance with its principles and intentions to promote and achieve justice. Thus, the requirement of stability and the criteria of the court depend not only on the provisions of its statute, but also on the efficiency of its prosecutor or judges, including their sincerity toward the real master of the Court.

This is the situation regardless of the fact that certain utipolitianist governments are not even members of the Court and yet still have control over its judicial power.[64] Consequently, the reasons why the principles of justice do not function and are paralysed must be seen from various perspectives that concern the virtue of justice under the authority of those who participate in the system and interpret the principles independently. In this sense, the principles of international criminal justice can be defined as a partial ideal of the notion of morality that does not reach its real intentions. As the argument for embedding ideals into our systems of international human rights and international criminal justice does not just sound good and accurate to principles, they have, in other words, to be free from all forms of intrigue.

Although the provisions of international criminal justice define an ideal elementary structure for the establishment of the rights of others, the enforcement of such rights in the building of the law is indeed powerless, and

---

[64] Farhad Malekian, Paralysing International Criminal Justice (New York: Nova Science Publishers, 2021).

we cannot assert that the provisions are fair if they have not been enforced on all criminals without discrimination. For example, we should not free the leaders of the United Kingdom or the United States from their criminality only to prosecute African leaders with European judges and prosecutors in the offices of the ICC instead. The Statute of the ICC sets up an international legal system in which no discrimination concerning the nationality of criminals has any legal validity. This includes its written documents and the practical implementation of those documents.

6. Utipolitianist Bamboozling Explanations

An ideal form of justice therefore includes institutions of human rights or criminal justice that foster the virtue of permanent justice and discourage desires and such policies of aspirations of justice that are fundamentally incompatible with the principles of morality. Of course, a number of other matters may be listed for the implementation of a perfect system of justice, which actually depends upon the given time and conditions as well as the policies of certain governments. *We mean that the system of international criminal justice, which is not based on free conscience and respects the power of utipolitianism has no free structure or platform on which justice acts freely and independently.*

The fact is that in the conception of justice, the general form of a just international criminal court should not stray from the common interests of states. This is because although idyllic justice may not exist, morality does, and it has been vital to the system of international criminal justice and functions independently and consistently with the standards of international human rights law. *There is no question about whether justice is right or wrong, but rather if justice has been independent or not. If it has been, then authentic justice may be more feasible. In the process of justice, we should not play the role of superior or inferior in order to specify and write its final words. In sum, the way the system of international criminal justice functions today is a reflection of the autocratic institutions imposed by the utipolitianist processes upon the majority of states in the world.*

Even in the European Court, justice has been seen as a colony of those old colonial powers, and therefore the Court has functioned as a vassal court in certain situations in order to fulfil the requirements of the autocratic state. A clear example of this situation is Ireland, where the British government brutally tortured Irish prisoners and deprived them of sleep. This case demonstrates the influence of utipolitianist rules on the system of international human rights and international criminal justice. This has been seen on occasion without any limitations about the mystery of evil powers. It should be noted that utipolitianism's perception of human rights practices might not be so upsetting and may not show that the liberty of conscience has been terminated.

The theory of utipolitianism acts as reasonably as possible with the intention of monopolising the economic and political gains of technocrats, which in turn demonstrates the rise of authoritarian elites in the government.[65] *Thus, while it shows that this basic national and international freedom is justified, it also colonizes all personal, institutional, or governmental freedoms.*[66] *This indicates that utipolitianism is the manifestation of supremacy and functions within the United Nations Charter and the International Criminal Court. Utipolitianist governments own the vassal court as their servant, as has been seen in the practice of the ICC, which never takes action against its chief masters, i.e., the United States and the British governments. As a result, the Court is wholly dependent on court's superior orders.*[67]

In a vassal state, it may be perceived as a sign that governmental authorities are sacrificing their fundamental rights to promote peace and justice at the national, regional, and international levels. This is precisely the practice of certain Western governments with invisible diplomatic arms.[68] These governments are like foxes and use the genocide of other nations to guarantee their own freedoms. Evidently, my explanations presume that the overall assumptions concerning which the principles of international criminal justice should be chosen and applied to the perpetrators of international crimes are correct. This means that the pre-determined principles are adopted for the interests of all men and are not purely decorative. Certain principles must therefore have institutional forms and should be embedded within the statutory conception of international criminal justice.

---

[65] Consult Farhad Malekian, *Hypocrisy in International Criminal Justice* (New York: Nova Science Publishers, 2025); Farhad Malekian, *International Crime of Blackboard-Barbarism* ((New York: Nova Science Publishers, 2025).

[66] Id.

[67] Id.

[68] Id.

7. Vassal Instrumentality in Criminal Justice

The fact is that the utipolitianist system of imposing international criminal justice is shared with non-conscientious governments, which turn into supreme utipolitianist governments and prevent the implementation of the provisions of international criminal justice in the office of the prosecutor of the ICC by all means. This indicates that the prosecutor of the ICC has already been sold to the policies of the superpowers. In other words, *the office is controlled by, and belongs to, the utipolitianist governments, and therefore the prosecutor acts and takes decisions under constraints that align with the existing desires of its masters. A clear example of this is, as we have mentioned, Karim Khan. In this respect, the system of international criminal justice, as an example of equality of rights, which contains the nature of an idealistic theory of international criminal responsibility, has already changed its imperative substance to protect justice and functions in opposition to the system of utilitarian norms.*[69] *This indicates that the task of the prosecutor is to carry out the will and desires of utipolitianism within the ICC.*[70] *This includes the image of the morality of the Court and, naturally, the utipolitianist governments. This completes the idea that utipolitianists are the masters, and the vassal prosecutor or vassal judges are the servants.*[71]

The most significant and irritating matter in the system of international criminal justice is that the prosecutor is made to only carry out the orders of the big, powerful nations and is not supposed to point out any criminal objections or accusations to the conduct of the utipolitianist governments. Now it may appear that since the original basic idea of utilitarianism is equality, any distinctions between the quality of the desires of utilitarianism and utipolitianism seem to be artificial. Thus, both theories and their practical tactics reach a stage that is neither useful for the minority nor the majority of the nations of the world. This is because any notion of utility speaks about certain satisfaction and, therefore, the elimination of certain rights of others.

---

[69] Examine also Mark J. Osiel, 'Why Prosecute? Critics of Punishment for Mass Atrocity,' 22 Human Rights Quarterly 118 (2000); A. Bellamy, Responsibility to Protect: the Global Effort to End Mass Atrocities (Polity Press, Cambridge, 2009); David Wippman, Atrocities, 'Deterrence, and the Limits of International Justice,' 23 Forham International Law Journal 473 (1999); Farhad Malekian, Powertionism in International Criminal Justice (New York: Nova Science Publishers, 2022), pp.231-237; Farhad Malekian, Tour de force of Moral Virtue in International Criminal Justice (New York: Nova Science Publishers, 2022).

[70] Consult A. Bellamy, Responsibility to Protect: the Global Effort to End Mass Atrocities (Polity Press, Cambridge, 2009).

[71] Id.

However, the gap between wills is very significant when it comes to utipolitianist theory. Due to this, the criterion for choosing between both theories is very similar, although utipolitianism drives the entire engine of international criminal justice and its court in The Hague. The utipolitianists always say that following their orders and words guarantees security for other governments, and that they can promote their economic, political, and military conditions if those governments follow the lead of utipolitianist governments. This shows that the International Criminal Court enters into close relationships with the new model of old colonialism in certain situations.

According to this theory, all alternative arrangements and success will be arranged by the masters of law, i.e., powertionist governments. On this basis, utipolitianist theory selects between the ideals of utipolitianism's original ideology and of the colonialist idea itself and presents a less compatible common utility of interests. Generally speaking, utipolitianism means control over three important factors: international human rights, international criminal justice and the very notion of morality. All three collectively represent the standard of the moral virtues of the utipolitianist theory and those dispositions that are the operative desires of its political, financial, and military needs. Consequently, it would be wrong to claim that the basic principles of utipolitianism in the system of the United Nations are not wrong and are not monopolised under the provisions of the Security Council.

The reality is that the elements of utipolitianism do not provide common interests, and there is no possibility of having clear vision concerning various pure principles of international human rights within the structure of the utipolitianist theory. This indicates that it is difficult to accept and value the system of a theory that was chosen by powertionist governments and that changes based on their desires. Such a system also creates circumstances that jeopardize the rights of other nations due to the principles of international human rights. These initial conditions of the will of utipolitianism may seriously affect the formation of human good and force the entire mechanism of justice into indefinite injustice that could end with the commission of genocide. Clear examples of such scenarios include the killing of the populations of Gaza, Syria, Lebanon, Afghanistan, Iraq, and Ukraine. The situation in Ukraine is the result of the criminal conspiracy of the US, the UK, France, and other NATO members.

The basic structure of justice differs greatly from the desires and inclinations presented in accordance with the theory of utipolitianism, which essentially discourages the existence of rights to the equality of arms, and, as a result, equality among the subjects of the United Nations as well as the systems of international human rights and international criminal justice eventually disappear under such circumstances. The difference between utipolitianism and independent justice is that justice, equality, and fairness are the basic foundations of an independent ideal of peacefully settling disputes and not killing civilians. Clearly, with the notion of utipolitianism and the original idea of utilitarianism, we cannot be certain what the result of the principles of international human rights or criminal justice will be and how they are going to meet the theory of justice as fairness and its essential values for the entire international human civilisation as a whole. Since there is no appropriate principle in the idea of utipolitianism of the Security Council because of veto rights, we will always face a conflict between a proper idea of justice and the improper demands of authoritarian powers.

8. Poisonous Vassal Dealing with Utipolitianism

The notion of justice within the United Nations Charter, and particularly in the ICC, treats the lies of the politicians as justice and the truth presented by the victims as lies. This indicates a clear exchange between utipolitianist governments and vassal subjects. Consequently, we need to face the basic truth, prioritize the principles of morality, moral law, moral principles, and ensure that all men receive their rights and have their personal integrity upheld. This implies that the very unjust principles of inequality in the Charter of the United Nations should be abolished, despite the fact that we have been accustomed to these unfair principles of the utipolitianist theory for over seven decades. The theory of justice consists of various landscapes with various features that are not dependent upon the existing desires of the paternalist governments, but rather on the value of all subjects of the law with the same gavel of truth.[72]

Utipolitianist ideology involves the continual exchange of justice among vassal states, governments, and courts. The conception of a just basic structure in the system of international criminal justice or its courts is not necessarily

[72] Mary Margaret Penrose, 'Lest We Fail: The Importance of Enforcement in International Criminal Law An Essay on the Nature and Immutability of Truth,' 15 (2) American University International Law Review (1999), pp. 321-394; Steven Luper-Foy, 'Introduction: Global Distributive Justice' in Steven LuperFoy (ed.), Problems of International Justice (London: Westview Press, 1988), pp.1-24; see also Muhamed Sacirbey, 'International Criminal Tribunal Born as Bastard?' The World Post, https://www.huffingtonpost.com/ambassador-muhamed-sacirbey/ international-criminal-tribunals_b_3344169.html (visited on 4 November, 2017).

based on the provisions of its statutes being in harmony with its intentions of establishment, but rather on the very notion of the independent power of such statutes, which can serve as a framework of customary rules of law for appraising the existence of its institutions. This means that justice and truth should not be exchanged or traded. In order to identify the correct principles of justice, we should therefore not be obliged to follow the wills of certain utipolitianist governments that act as the owners of the systems of international law. What is really more sensitive in the system of international law is not necessarily their dependent or independent characters, but rather the motivations behind that independence or dependence. By assuming certain general desires of the big political governments in the Security Council and respecting those desires, we are making a deal that puts our values of justice on the line. Morality disappears, and corruption occurs.

We should try to always direct the use of force in the direction of righteousness. Thus, the primary good of justice is essentially our resistance against any use of force or monopolisation.[73] Once we accept injustice, we are expected to tolerate it, which is neither healthy nor recommended. We may successfully obtain the requisite independence from the existing circumstances of utipolitianist governments under the provisions of Chapter VII of the Charter if we trust that the principles of international human rights must be respected and any provisions that threaten these principles should be declared null and void. The original intention was characterised by the possibility of the principle of harmony between the means and the end, and not between the wills of the old colonialist governments, as outlined in the United Nations Charter. *Moreover, the judgments delivered in the resolutions of the United Nations Security Council are mostly fertilizer for the norms of imperialist powers, which are primarily influenced by one-eyed justice. They poison the principles of equality in the basic structure of law. For example, if we believe that the old British imperialist power has ended its colonialist habits and is acting justly within the corridors of the Security Council and its meetings, we have to say that the race of political wolves has ended and will never return. This is a legal, political, and moral lie, since the criminal British governments have proven to be the main authoritarian governments, and their*

[73] Examine further Farhad Malekian, Condemning the Use of Force in the Gulf Crisis (Almqvist & Wiksell International, 1st ed. (1992), 2nd ed. (1994); Ramsey Clark, The Fire This Time: U.S. War Crimes in the Gulf (Thunder's Mouth Pr., 1992); Ramsey Clark et. al., War Crimes: A Report on United States War Crimes Against Iraq (Maisonneuve Press, 1992); Jeremy Brecher, Jill Cutler, and Brendan Smith (eds.), In the Name of Democracy: American War Crimes in Iraq and Beyond (Metropolitan Books, 2005).

poisonous arrows have touched nearly every human civilisation. Their actions have resulted in the harm and distortion of the entire concept of royal justice.

It would therefore be very difficult not to mix all these United Nations laws, human rights, and international criminal justice with political-criminal arguments here. This is because any arguments relating to the principles of human rights law and international criminal justice are connected to the fundamental principles of legal, military, and political morality, which represent both the beginning and end of the same philosophy of justice. This means that when moral consensus does not exist in the basic structure of the largest organisation in the world, we can believe that the principle of morality can be reached and respected within human rights instruments. It may be very difficult and problematic to believe that the assumption of unanimity in the structure of the political philosophy of the United Nations and its establishment is truly right and not just false idealism. However, *there is no belief in the characteristic values of the Charter and particularly in the International Criminal Court from the philosophical legal point of view, except to say that the Charter is a bed coach of political arguments in which all political parties deliver their judgments, and yet are still subjected to utipolitianism as a result of the votes or vetoes of the utipolitianists. The legal philosophy of the Court becomes a vassal that is for sale like cargo.*

9. Utipolitianism Leading Criminal Norms

The dirty and very baseless systems of international human rights and international criminal justice serve to brainwash populations globally. This situation is part of the procedural conception of the corridors of the United Nations, international human rights institutions, and, naturally, the system of international criminal law as presented in the basic structure of the International Criminal Court. In this way, the system of international criminal law shapes the content of the theory of justice, which is suitable and acceptable to the needs of the utipolitianist government of the United States. For instance, the relevant government is not a member of the ICC, rescinded its signature, and has never ratified the Statute of the Court. However, it uses the Court's jurisdiction to carry out their utipolitianist policies. As a result, the Court is threatened both openly and behind closed doors, including by American presidents, diplomats, and Republican legislators.[74]

With the help of its allies, the ICC succeeded in putting the present Russian president on the list of wanted criminals, however the vassal prosecutor is still silent about all of the crimes that have been committed by the British, Israeli, American, French, Canada, German, and Australian governments. Recently, the office of the prosecutor made even more disappointing decisions concerning the case. This is what should be called the utilitarian dominance of the power of international criminal justice. For the most part, the metaphysical tradition, including the classical utility presented by certain British philosophers, supposes that there exists some applicable proper perspective concerning the influence of morality on the nature of all law. However, the actions of the League of Nations, the United Nations, and even the International Criminal Court have demonstrated the complete opposite.

As a matter of fact, the norms of morality, human rights, and humanitarian aid have enabled governments to cheat civilisations. Therefore, any notion of unanimity on moral questions may create artificial circumstances that help the superpowers achieve their various economic and political intentions. Even if we suppose that there is a form of unanimity and express consent from nations concerning certain acts, these remain instrumental as long as disparities between judgments and decisions of the ICC or resolutions of the Security Council have the first word. Consequently, different moral theories arise from different deductions from the system of international human rights without any particular effect on the victims of international crimes. In this sense, any impression of unanimity about the system of international criminal justice and its activities behind the barrier amounts to inherent lies cultivated in the basic structure of jurisdiction. This indicates that the traditional notion of moral philosophy fails in the sphere of jurisprudence of international criminal courts.

It must be expressed that what distinguishes international criminal justice as fairness is its capacity to take action against selectivity or utipolitianism instead of promoting international vacations for the most serious international criminals. The theory of justice should present a natural procedural adaptation of the concepts of autonomy in its legal structure and decisions, not the contrary. This is known as international criminal justice because fairness constitutes the central institution for the value of international human rights in

---

[74] US lawmakers slam ICC prosecutor's Israel arrest warrant requests, https://www.aljazeera.com/news/2024/5/20/us-lawmakers-slam-icc-prosecutors-israel-arrest-warrant-requests.

the international community as a whole. However, when that does not function properly, the problem of rational choice concerning the implementation of international criminal principles on criminals or their accountability before international criminal courts becomes completely nonsensical. This situation demonstrates the vassal nature of the Court in various cases. If the values of international criminal justice are ignored, then the theory of criminal justice or human rights justice cannot succeed. Consequently, we need an account of the major good of self-respect for the moral needs of the international community if the theory of utipolitianism is going to be prevented and abolished within the structure of the United Nations.

Chapter 4

Standards of Utipolitianist Morality in International Criminal Justice

1. Heritage of Criminal Violations

It is essential to keep in mind that our main discussions deal with utipolitianist theory, which in turn concerns the monopolisation of three major subjects of human civilisation, namely: the United Nations Charter, the system of international human rights, and the body of institutions of international criminal justice. Monopolisation in this case refers to the control of these subjects and forcing them into the position of a vassal subject. Thus, our three main topics of discussion deal with the question of justice that are under the full control of powerful nations. These topics are also evaluated with regard to the notion of morality and whether they have any notion of morality and if they can explain why it does not function and why they are the tool of monopolisation and promote a utilitarianist power of control. The theories of international human rights and international criminal justice that we are dealing with have some serious moral problems regarding their political, military, and economic natures. The position of the relevant subjects raises the question of what is really hidden in their characters. The intention of this question is not to explain and disclose the power of hidden evil policies in controlling the direction of the aforementioned subjects, since their malicious employment by utipolitianists must be clear to any rational international lawyer or government.

Attempting to prove their real nature therefore seems unnecessary and would obviously be outside the scope of elementary questions of ethical justice. Illustrating the content of the principles of international criminal justice is simply a repetition of incorrectly employed norms. Moreover, speaking about the doctrines of international human rights or international criminal justice and what their intentions were and how these intentions are misused and mistaken in other practical applications, represent other perspectives concerning the priority of certain utipolitianist governments. This is why we try to keep the theory of justice safe, and no harm is done to its ordinary intentions. However, as we know, interpretations of international human rights principles and international criminal justice principles claimed in the Statute of the International Criminal Court depend upon the general facts. There is nothing except control over their mechanisms by the authoritarian states. Consequently, the theory of justice presumes an explanation of the prior interpretations of its norms by the given authorities of the utipolitianist governments. It may therefore be essential to understand the hidden power behind the mechanism of justice, and how to recognise their lies and prevent the effects of those lies in the scrutiny of moral conceptions for the sake of all governments.

It is a true and very obvious fact that when the system of international criminal justice operates without morality or violations of the most significant principle of justice, the theory of pure justice loses its legal and ethical force, and any assumption of righteousness in such a legal system seems unlikely. At first glance, this may not be very significant, and it may not matter too much if the systems of international human rights and international criminal justice do not speak about the existence of morality. However, continuous violations of the contents of the principles of justice bring their quality into question and uncover the real nature of why the rules of justice are not fulfilling their purposes. This means that we may refer to a wide range of arguments and examine a number of legal and political issues in order to reach acceptable conclusions. This indicates that since the law and regulations are already present in the content of agreements or statutes, the questions of moral philosophy may take priority over any other theory. The reason for this is that the systems of international human rights and international criminal justice have been violated since their inception. In other words, the reason for their creation, formulation, and adoption was to bring the notion of morality into practical use with full respect and dignity.

2. Missing the Notion of Morality

We are obligated to recognize the practical application of international criminal justice as fairness, and discover the reason why it has not worked in the United Nations and the ICC. My intention is to make it clear that all of the resolutions of the Security Council and the judgments of the ICC ought to fit within a certain framework in order to avoid any misunderstandings. Furthermore, this framework should promote the moral ethic and its effects on all decisions. Under this framework, any resolution that permits people to kill is illegal, unjust, and also seriously immoral, as we saw during the Gulf War with the occupation of Iraq. This is also the case in the process of justice in the ICC, whereby in providing impunity to the criminals, we ignore the values or reasons of morality for the establishment of the ICC. Some of the most significant problems with the increased violations of the standards of justice in the world are therefore institutionalised in various sectors that we have adopted for the implementation of proper justice without a proper standard of responsibility for the perpetrators and owners of the utipolitianist theory of injustice. Simply put, the law protects the big criminals.[75]

All of these matters concerning the system of international criminal justice and the United Nations should satisfy the principles of international human rights conventions. However, since they fail to do this, we have to find another solution to the very serious problem of violations of the system of international criminal justice by the powertionist governments and their alliances. To begin with, it may be possible to distinguish between the different characteristics of the powers in the Security Council, in the General Assembly, and under the international personality of the ICC. All the governments in the Security Council and the General Assembly have different powers, and their legal authority is not equal in practice, even if it should be according to the UN Charter. This means that our system is far from understanding the significant function of morality for its authentic implementation.

Although the voting rights seem to be equal for all state parties, the hidden power reflects a different reality. This can particularly be seen in the veto rights of certain members under the provisions of Chapter VII of the Charter. The result is a significant imbalance of power, which can lead to both legal and political powers accomplishing their objectives. Thus, the Charter of the United Nations is clear about the creation of a hierarchy of power, categorising the value of decisions, and permitting the notion of immorality. This is clear authorisation for certain governments to do whatever they want when it comes to important issues of international criminal justice and violations of international criminal conventions. All this has to do with the ownership of the means of legal and political power. This is exactly what the classical

---

[75] On international criminal responsibility see Nina Jørgensen, The Responsibility of States for International Crimes (OUP Oxford 2000); A. de Hoogh, Obligations *erga omnes* and International Crimes: A Theoretical Inquiry into the Implementation and Enforcement of the International Responsibility of States (Kluwer The Hague, 1996); J. Crawford, S. Olleson, 'The Continuing Debate on a UN Convention on State Responsibility' 54 ICLQ, (2005), 959–7.

distinction imposed upon the victims of the colonial powers of European criminal governments in the system of international law do.

The extent of the monopolisation of power in the Security Council is inherent and was entered into the Charter under the colonial system of injustices. The examination of this historical development demonstrates the underlying reasons for the existence of imbalance in the system of power and, consequently, a significant increase in the violations of the system of international criminal justice and the killings of millions of individuals in the name of justice. This is why our voting system is the way that it is, and why voting is pointless in the Security Council due to the existence of veto power. States with the veto power make the decisions about who lives or dies and to what extent the morality of the law can be violated. A clear example of this is the current situation in Gaza and the killing and displacement of millions by the utipolitianist criminal actions being carried out in the name of saving the savage principles of humanity. As a matter of fact, the utipolitianist government of the United States has succeeded in killing all of the resolutions in the Security Council that have sought to address the ongoing genocide of the Palestinians.

3. Defending Moral Methods of Utipolitianism

The utipolitianist governments present a form of political-legal force in the vocabulary of the system of international organisations, such as the UN, that claims to be the main source for its establishment and prevention of the use of force is indeed barbarity.[76] There are therefore various ways to evaluate the nature of justice and its power of applicability based on the extent of its of indivisibility and the size of the evil nature of continuous brutal criminal

[76] That is why I have clearly stated "In other words, if the use of force is prohibited by all means, it cannot be permitted by any means. If the application of capital punishment is abolished, it cannot be justified in any situation, as is the case in Article 6 of the Covenant. If the norms of legality are correctly divided into primary and secondary rules, then we cannot deprive them of their high human values. Likewise, if Islamic law is a permanent brotherhood, then it cannot be removed from this significant principle. If the communist idea is to share greater common interests of humanity, then it cannot be isolated from other theories. The norm of love is built on the strength of justice and our ability to understand that if every human being has the inherent right to life, freedom of speech and marriage, this is a collective inheritance, and therefore no human being should be isolated from this right by any means. Particularly, the above rights are an integral part of peremptory norms of international law." Farhad Malekian, Trading Virginity of International Criminal Justice (Nova Sciences Publishers, 2020).

violations of the system of international criminal justice that are designated as being necessary for the preparation for peace, humanity, and the protection of victims of war. The notion of massive immorality has completely distorted the indivisibility of forms of justice that establish the essence of morality. These are presented in various arguments calling criminal conduct acts of self-defence.

The most surprising thing is that the same utipolitianist governments that violate international human rights and international humanitarian law also claim to respect all matters concerning the provisions of international human rights law and international criminal justice. This is its moral standard of justice. These governments go further and assert that the Israeli government has been very careful to respect international humanitarian law in armed conflicts, despite killing Palestinians in Gaza. Moreover, the American government is continuously evaluating the acts of the Israeli government to ensure that they do not violate the humanitarian law of armed conflicts. The massive killings are thus also based on humanitarian moral justice.

These are indeed the most outlandish and absurd statements that are continuously being made by American politicians such as Antony Blinken, who should be prosecuted under the jurisdiction of an independent international criminal court— of course, if such a court existed and was not a vassal of a super powerful state. *This is why we insist that the system of morality, which should be the main channel of the philosophy of international human rights and international criminal justice and which should be engrained into all provisions of the United Nations Charter, has long been dishonest and tarnished by the creators of the organisation and been replaced by the political powers of utipolitianism with the constitution of its morality.*

We are not distinguishing between the traditional form of morality and the form of morality that has been established by the UN. Morality a notion of immorality, irrationality, inhumanity, and a number of intricate points within the philosophy of monopolisation of the Charter of the UN and the practices as presented and seen in the exercise of power and occupation of the rights of others. However, the main idea is that any notion of international good or bad, right or wrong, just or unjust, should be controlled and decided by the Security Council and its permanent members. Permanent members refer to the United States, the United Kingdom, and France, which have been behind many massacres and wars, including those in Vietnam, Syria, Iraq, Yemen, Korea, Afghanistan, and Palestine. The Gulf War was one of the most brutal wars ever waged under the purview of the United States of America with the assistance of NATO members.[77] The actions of the permanent members explain why there are many violations under the present law of the United Nations that may be called the law of power.[78]

All these arguments indicate the existence of a strong notion of utipolitianism and its power to control the law and the resources of nations, which should not be separated from their rightful owners, yet are through the political processes of the monopolised organisation. Since there is no strong military power to put an end to this brutal distribution of politics in the sense of preventing unjust definitions and barbaric utipolitianism, the immoral use of the law of the UN has become a mainstay. Consequently, the member states of the organisation do not receive the same amount of respect nor do their legal personalities have the same value. In fact, the definition of the international legal personality of member states and their equal arms reflects the cultivation of rosy flowers that have no power to resist the long winter of inequality, which has been created by the utipolitianist power of the United States and its allies.

4. Rotten Roots of Utipolitianist Arguments

Various features of international human rights norms that basically derive their motivations from the moral characteristics of the Universal Declaration of Human Rights include all temptations with rotten roots. This is because whatever a utipolitianist government does, it greatly contributes to the increasing number of victims globally and the destruction of other countries. If there is any protest against the impolitic standards of injustice, those protesting are threatened with sanctions. This form of politics thus contributes to justice and the implementation of human rights standards. The language of the provisions of Chapter VII of the UN speaks about their binding force; this semantic language has more of a psychological function rather than a legal one. Therefore, it follows that arranging for an appropriate meeting between the political parties of the UN would not be helpful, and it may bring about another force because of the non-binding rules of the Charter.

---

[77] See Farhad Malekian, Condemning the Use of Force in the Gulf Crisis (Almqvist & Wiksell International, 1st ed. (1992), 2nd ed. (1994); Ramsey Clark, The Fire This Time: U.S. War Crimes in the Gulf (Thunder's Mouth Pr., 1992); Ramsey Clark et. al., War Crimes: A Report on United States War Crimes Against Iraq (Maisonneuve Press, 1992); Jeremy Brecher, Jill Cutler, and Brendan Smith (eds.), In the Name of Democracy: American War Crimes in Iraq and Beyond (Metropolitan Books, 2005).

[78] Id.

Even if the majority or all of the members of the UN were willing to vote against the utipolitianist theory in the organisation, they would presumably be up against vetoes or the use of nuclear weapons. The governments would force all of the members of the organisation to pay for the crimes of utipolitianist governments. Thus, once the members of the organisation agree to collectively act against certain powertionist governments, their membership is terminated, leading to the end of the organisation's duties and tasks. As a result, any action against utipolitianism is not only condemned, but could also lead to punishment under the procedures of the International Criminal Court.

Moreover, utipolitianist governments and their allies may label permanent governments of the Security Council as vassal governments. This has been seen with Macron "labelling Russia as a 'vassal state,'" which went viral in China. However, the French government has hidden its vassal position from the United States government.[79] This situation reflects the proxy war in Ukraine, which was planned by the American government and started with the accusation of the Russian president with the hope of destroying the political power of Russia. That is why the sense of justice under the provisions of international human rights law and international criminal justice puts the world into an unsafe position.

Of course, in order to promote justice schemes, we need to understand the structure of an unwise and corrupted democracy, including the circumstances that contribute to the lack of assurance that binding rules can be effectively enforced and eliminate the legacy of inhumanity in the nature of the big political powers of the organisation.[80] It therefore seems that the use of coercion is perfectly rational for utipolitianist powers, and they do not disgrace themselves. Dishonestly against the law of morality is considered to be today's standard of honesty. A substantial number of traditional criminal activities of colonial powers are thereby justified.

This is not my personal statement, but reflects the truth that one can see and understand in the fresh new clothes of old colonialism with the patterns and outlines of the provisions of the Charter and its developments. Consequently, the need for the enforcement of the notion of pure morality for

---

[79] Analysis: Macron's labelling of Russia as a 'vassal state' goes viral in China; Xi Jinping tries to obscure the G-7 summit by sending envoys to Ukraine. https://asia.nikkei.com/Editor-s-Picks/China-up-close/Analysis-Macron-s-labeling-of-Russia-as-vassal-state-goes-viral-in-China.

[80] Richard Falk, The Accountability of Leaders: A Challenge to Civil Government and Society in Jeremy Brecher, Jill Cutler, Brendan Smith, In the Name of Democracy: American War Crimes in Iraq and Beyond (American Empire Project), (New York: Metropolitan Books, Henry Holt and Company, 2005), pp. 301-307.

all nations has to be promoted by the same sense of justice within the fairness for all populations of the world. The characteristic features of the essential imposition of the provisions of the international criminal court are therefore unavoidable if firm assurance is going to be given to all nations of the world that are honoured as a healthy civilisation of human beings that should at least be equivalent to the unarmed civilisation of human animals.[81] Preventing dishonesty and fostering a flood of truthful morality requires this approach.

5. Dismissing Morally Multilateral Confidence

Another aspect of the utipolitianist monopolisation of the system of international criminal justice is the daily increase in its power.[82] We have seen that the governments producing weapons have benefitted the most from the current system. This means that the whole system of the United Nations works against any government that protests the sale of weapons to the perpetrators of genocide. This theory is supported by the moral principles of utipolitianist governments. The difference between powerful governments and victim governments is that the former are the masters of the weapons, while the latter are hindered by the Security Council. It is evident that the necessity of collective power, collective agreements, and collective force does not exist because of the threats made by utipolitianist governments and the possibility of war being against such a collective force. A clear example of this is the ongoing genocide and the Holocaust in Gaza and throughout Palestine.

> Long ago, Napoleon Bonaparte I ordered his diplomats to exact certain rights from their enemies. They replied that gaining possession of such rights would be very difficult at the negotiation table. He told them, you should lie. They replied, they will lie too. He told them to lie more. They replied, they will lie more. He answered and said to them, you should lie as much as necessary until you are granted the rights. With the provisions of Resolution 1373, planned long before 11 September 2001, the permanent members of the Security Council used their political, military, and legal power under the provisions of Chapter VII of the Charter of the

---

[81] Farhad Malekian, Trading Virginity of International Criminal Justice (Nova Sciences Publishers, 2020).

[82] Examine Farhad Malekian, Powertionism in International Criminal Justice (New York: Nova Science Publishers, 2022; Farhad Malekian, The Monopolization of International Criminal Law in the United Nations, A Jurisprudential Approach (Stockholm: Almqvist Wiksell International, 1st ed., 1993, 1995).

United Nations to gain full decision-making rights in order to prevent violations that could be identified as terrors. The reasons for the adoption of Resolutions 1368 and 1373 were therefore the events of the September 11 terrorist attacks in the United States in New York in 2001. The position is rightly stated by Professor Michel Chossudovsky of the United States in his excellent book The Globalization of War: America's "Long War" against Humanity. The realistic position of the book has even been confirmed by many well-known officials, e.g., by the Canadian Department of National Defence or by the Assistant Secretary of the USA. Resolutions 1368 and 1373 recognized and reaffirmed "the inherent right of individual or collective self-defence in accordance with the Charter." If the right had already been affirmed, why should it be reaffirmed again? The Security Council intention was to take a detour to avoid the Charter's provisions, the whole of which was and is a game with the aim of achieving legal permission to wage oil wars, to murder "BinLaden: the forbidden truth," and to secure the oil pipelines in Afghanistan and Syria. 11 September was actually the day in 1922 on which the League of Nations had proclaimed the British Mandate in Palestine. It denotes the power of the Balfour Declaration for the creation of Israel. The declaration has been a critical point in relations between both of these respected nations.[83]

Consequently, the collective force is now unable to combat utipolitianist governments. If states attempt to collectivize, they risk triggering a third world war and the use of nuclear weapons against them. Stating that the UN principles are solely based on the morality of the propensity for self-interest and injustice of a utipolitianist government is not a shallow view. The reason for this is simply because the world has seen a number of wars since the establishment of the UN. The actions and decisions of the UN have led to the greatest wars rather than the greatest peace and justice. Some people may have different arguments regarding the protection and support of the works and decisions of the prominent members of the organisation. They may thus argue

[83] http://davidduke.com/the-big-lie/ (accessed 8 May 2016); UN Security Council Res 1368 (2001) (n 95) paras. 1, 3–4; UN Security Council Res 1373 (2001) (no. 95) paras. 1–3; Bin Laden was one of the men in Afghanistan who had full information about the criminal activities of the United States during and after the Cold War. His assassination was therefore a mystery for justice in order for the world to face the truth in the relevant region. See also Wayne Madsen Jean-Charles and Guillaume Dasquie, Forbidden Truth: U.S.-Taliban Secret Oil Diplomacy, Saudi Arabia and the Failed Search for bin Laden (2002). Farhad Malekian, The Mirage of International Criminal Law: Kant Metaphysics of Mens Rea (Cambridge: Cambridge Scholars Publishing, 2018), pp.138-139.

that the actions taken by the authorities of the utipolitianist governments have been correct. Such opinions are expressed by governments that believe that their political and economic situation can be changed through the use of force and aggression that may be used against them by the leading powers in control.

They therefore prefer to adhere to the orders of utipolitianist governments instead of promoting the rights of victims and struggling for their reestablishment. In the United Nations, a large community that is the collection of numerous governments around the world and apparently represents their voices, the degree of morally multilateral confidence in one another's truthfulness and words is not as strong as it should be. The reason for this is essentially the non-existence of trust in the words, actions, and decisions of the utipolitianist governments, the intentions of which are solely to be convinced by lies and, if this is not possible, by guns. This reality reflects their own political and legal interests. This renders the proper enforcement of the system of justice impossible, despite it being promised in the Charter. Consequently, this creates superfluous relations between the states of the international legal community as a whole. This is, of course, to be expected from the nature of the decisions and conduct of the utipolitianist governments.

In a well-ordered international organisation, particularly to the standard of the United Nations Charter, one would believe that sanctions will be used against the utipolitianist governments, which are the most essential reason for the commission of international crimes such as crimes against humanity, war crimes, genocide, apartheid, aggression, torture, and acts of holocaust as seen in Palestine. However, not even mild sanctions have never been imposed on powertionist governments. Nonetheless, sanctions have been applied against any nation or state that has failed to follow the orders of utipolitianists concerning certain matters relating to the rights of self-determination. Despite the existence of such sanctions dealing with the punishment of utipolitianist governments, even in the case of their serious crimes such as genocide, war crimes, and crimes against humanity, no action can unfortunately be taken because of their political influence and roles in a case.

This is why their crimes always go unpunished, which in turn becomes a real dilemma for international criminal justice. The question then concerns how criminals should be identified under the system of international criminal courts, when there is no doubt that the crimes are committed by the separate or collective motivation of certain governments. Such situations can only be explained as involving vassals. Additionally, the horrible international crimes committed in Abu-Ghraib per the utipolitianist theories by the powertionist governments of the NATO members are a clear example of the impunity of certain governments and the controlling force of the United Nations and the International Criminal Court. That is why the assurance of justice under the system of international criminal courts and the United Nations itself is different. Here, the purpose is to make clear that the provisions of the UN do not function with moral standards of impartiality, and that we need to adopt other policies to insure that these standards are met. The fact is that such a powerful legal standard of justice does not exist in the provisions of Charter VII or the provisions of the General Assembly.

6. Aggressiveness of the Immorality of Utipolitianists

Maintaining international confidence in the scheme of international human rights or international criminal justice that can be useful for the rights of weak nations or victims of international crimes by utipolitianist governments is a utopian dream. The situation arises from the absence of moral power in both the UN and the ICC. It is here that the mere existence of an effective international organisation that has moral, legal, and practical power over all governments, including the utipolitianists, appears necessary and unavoidable for the protection of prosperity and the moral baggage of peace, justice, humanity, and love. This is necessary even if the general faith in the legal characteristics of the United Nations and ICC has already been damaged. The establishment and existence of an organisation that is beyond all political powers is therefore a crucial step for justice.

This indicates that there is a necessary connection between the increasing number of victims of international crimes and the brutal establishment of the rights or powers of utipolitianists within the system of international criminal justice and the United Nations. In other words, all matters have become a game between powerful criminals and powerless individuals, groups, and nations. As a result, it is no longer a case of what powertionist governments' gain and what the powerless governments, nations, or victims lose. Instead, it is a question of integrity. This means it is not just the question of the wealth and resources of other nations that are being stolen, but rather the very essential fundamental question of the integrity of *somebodiness* of nations, the values of having international legal personality, and the violations of traditional classical rights of a nation to be treated equally in the course of the provisions of the law and under its practices.

Thus, we are violating the very essence of *somebodiness* in a nation and forcing them into the position of *nobodiness* with the idea of utipolitianist theories as dictated by Chapter VII of the Charter. When the Prime Minister of Israel clearly stated that the genocide of Palestinians constitutes a "war of civilisation against barbarism," the victims were put into a position of purely *nobodiness*. The Prime Minister's statement reflects the deep immorality of the leaders of the Zionist government. Here we are speaking about the worst genocide in the history of mankind. Despite this, the existence of the genocide has been ignored and instead viewed as a legitimate response to the resistance efforts of the Palestinians, including those of Hamas. The Israeli Defence Forces (IDF) along with the American and British Armed Forces are not labelled as terrorists.[84] Instead, resistance groups fighting for freedom and the end to an occupation are. This is despite the fact that the struggle for self-determination is an integral right of any nation under occupation and is an established *jus cogens* norm. This is particularly applicable when the struggle has been going on for over seven decades.

This demonstrates the clear double morality within the utilitarianist system of the United Nations. It also demonstrates the dependent system of international human rights and international criminal justice, in particular in the office of the ICC prosecutor, Karim Khan. It actually means that the interrogation and displacement of millions of Palestinians over the decades have been legitimate. Utipolitianist powers are therefore the definition of the unlimited use of force against victims without any consequences. Moreover, when the French resistance army was fighting against dictatorship and the Nazi occupation, it was viewed as being completely legitimate and lawful by all European governments, however the acts of resistance by Palestinians are labelled as illegitimate acts of terrorism. However, we know that the system of international law permits and recognizes resistance struggles as legal forms of defence.

---

[84] For some definitions of terrorism see Ahmed, N. Mosaddeq, "Terrorism and Statecraft: Al-Qaeda and Western Covert Operations after the Cold War," Zarembka, P. (Ed.) The Hidden History of 9-11-2001. (Research in Political Economy, Vol. 23, 2006), Emerald Group Publishing Limited, Bingley, pp. 149-188. https://doi.org/10.1016/S0161-7230(06)23005-0; David MacGrego, 'September 11 as 'Machiavellian State Terrorism,' in Paul Zarembka, The Hidden History of 9-11-2001 (New York: Seven Stories Press, 2008); Louis Kos-Rabcewicz-Zubrowski, The Creation of an International Criminal Court, in International Terrorism and Political Crimes 519 (M. Cherif Bassiouni ed., 1975); M. Cherif Bassiouni, (ed.), International Terrorism and Political Crimes (1975); Johannes Husabø Erling, Ingvild Bruce, Fighting Terrorism through Multilevel Criminal Legislation: Security Council Resolution 1373, the EU Framework Decision on Combating Terrorism and their Implementation in Nordic, Dutch and German Criminal Law (Martinus Nijhoff Publishers, 2009).

It is in the nature of utipolitianism to designate acts of resistance as acts of aggression, savagery, brutality, barbarity, cruelty, and ultimately—as acts of terrorism. However, utipolitianism's humanitarian assistance, implementation of human rights, and rules of international law reflect true terrorism. Utipolitianists then go on to call their own nations civilised and other nations uncivilised or underdeveloped, implying that such states lack the proper knowledge of Western civilisation. This is the real feature of the system of international law and the provision of international human rights as promoted by Western powers. Killing millions of people is permitted and seen as civilised. It has even led to Barack Obama earning a Noble Prize and Tony Blair being made a member of the Order of the Garter by the Queen of England. Thus, utipolitianism awards those who massacre millions and kill, execute, torture, imprison, and banish all those who threaten their policies. This is the current situation for millions of Palestinians. All this reflects the scope of morality of immorality in utipolitianist theory.

The entire population of Palestine has been imprisoned at some point. They have received a short sentence, a long sentence, torture, rape, or a life sentence, and it is still called the implementation of international human rights law. Under utipolitianist rules, receiving a particularly heavy term of seventy-eight years' imprisonment for a nation means nothing. This is why one of the world's most intelligent people, namely Julian Assange, was condemned to 240 years' imprisonment. Whatever arguments we present concerning the logical understanding of the question of justice in utipolitianist theories, it becomes a serious dilemma that is almost impossible to solve or adjust its direction of basic morality. We must confess that the system of international criminal justice and its human rights principles under the conventions of human rights laws challenge serious difficulties. Therefore, the most reasonable course of action for solving these difficulties lies with the utipolitianist judgments in the Security Council of the United Nations.

7. Superiority and Inferiority of Moral Arguments

Rational decisions are defined by utipolitianism as following in the footsteps of injustice. Nonetheless, with the globalisation of human rights, the intention is to promote a system of international human rights that can stabilise and share knowledge of justice among all members of the United Nations. However, such justice has been hindered or banned in the utilitarian plans of utipolitianists. As a result, the problems created by governments cannot be solved, and both utipolitianists and victims remain in their current positions of superiority and inferiority respectively. Even though we could create more human rights provisions, doing so would not have much of a positive effect, if any.

While speaking about these shortcomings of the system of the United Nations Charter, which has made the bodies of all human rights instruments and the vassal Statute of the International Criminal Court, which is controlled by certain utipolitianist governments, we have to unfortunately keep in mind the murders of the victims, the seizure of their property, and the infringement upon their sovereignty and independence. This not only includes destruction of military equipment, medical facilities, universities, and schools, but also the seizure of natural resources. We have seen this with the United States' pursuit of the oil and gas resources of Arab states, including Iran. This means that other governments should accept the utipolitianist judgements about the resources of other governments and their use as dictated by the United States government and its close friends including, France, Britain, Israel, the Netherlands, Germany, Canada, and Australia. The utipolitianist policy is not to purchase natural resources at the price that is sold by certain governments, but to officially own those resources for the lowest price possible.

All these matters still depend upon certain questions and the resistance of a nation against the barbarity presented and imposed by the institutional logic of the governments, including in what way the institutions of the powerful nations are respected by the resistance. Any other political, cumbersome, and restrictive measures carried out by the victims are interpreted as endangering the plans of the utipolitianists, and thus the victims face sanctions. In fact, imposing sanctions on governments that do not follow the political guidelines of powerful utipolitianist governments is a rejection of the utipolitianist policy of interests. Therefore, becoming a greater voice than what is presumed by the utipolitianist plans means breaking the hidden cover of politics, which is not permitted under the collective decisions of the relevant powertionist governments. It will bring anger, frustration, and war. It is therefore only under the command of utipolitianist theory that the system of international criminal justice and its vassal Court should be interpreted and applied. A clear example of this is the current case involving the Israeli Zionist government that is before the ICC and the condemnation of Israel's brutal crimes against the Palestinian population. The president of the utipolitianist government of the United States and their allies are threatening the ICC office since it has overstepped and violated its inferior position with this case.

There is no freedom of expression within the United Nations Charter. This is based on the fact that all words of freedom, equality, humanity, morality, and justice are only symbolic as long as the power of the organisation is determined by its Chapter VII. Even though a state is permitted to defend itself under the provisions of Article 51 of the Charter, it is the Security Council that ultimately decides which actions constitute self-defence or not. This has been with the situation in Gaza, where the acts of self-defence have not been recognised, nor has the Palestinians' right to statehood. As a result, all hope of a two-state solution has passed.[85]

The basic feature of utipolitianism is the extension of its power, which can be assembled into various international economic markets or the rules and provisions of the United Nations, and then chosen, interpreted, imposed, and demanded by its politicians, of course, with the assistance of national or international lawyers.[86] The fact is that the theory of utipolitianism is controlled by those who control the markets and investments. Therefore, there is no common or collective opinion concerning which provisions of the Charter should be used in particular situations to face the problem of justice. *We mean that the systems of the United Nations, human rights, and the ICC are presented like goods and tools throughout political markets, not for the elimination of untreatable injuries or harm to the victims, but more for the welfare of future generations of a particular given nation. Nonetheless, we should not forget the fact that all these tools of injustice are coloured by the notion of morality and the inspiration of humanity.* This means taking a collective decision may not be possible in the meetings of the Security Council and in the will for the empowerment of moral justice or to put the truth on the desk. In both the General Assembly and the Security Council, there is great concern regarding the prevention of irreparable harm to the rights of victim nations, but the fact is that stabilising and demanding such a connection between right and wrong is basically both practically and theoretically impossible and predatory because of the unlimited power of utipolitianist theories.

Under certain conditions in Chapter VII of the UN, there is no way to improve the methods of voting in the Security Council, and, as a result, there

---

[85] According to Julian Assange, the president of true democracy, telling lies is the ultimate tool used by utipolitianist government to protect their interests.

[86] Farhad Malekian, Conscience of Lawyers in International Criminal Law, the Burden of Doppelgängers (New York: Nova Science Publishers, 2021); Farhad Malekian, Conscience of Judges in International Criminal Law, the Heart of Judgements (New York: Nova Science Publishers, 2021); Farhad Malekian, Conscience of Prosecutors in International Criminal Law, the Heart of the Matter (New York: Nova Science Publishers, 2021).

is a contradiction between the thousands of provisions in the Charter and the veto right. Saying it is a political right really diminishes its horrible nature. *The veto is actually a legal power as well as a form of utipolitianism and legal barbarism. If this were not the case, then we could ignore this evil power. The question is: how can the theories of international justice and international criminal justice be integrated into one word—veto? The veto is a manifestation of the discrimination and humiliation within the systems of international human rights and international criminal justice. It would have been more advantageous if we had not permitted veto rights to exist within the UN system. While the entire intention of the United Nations is to serve the majority of states parties, the intention of veto rights is to take away the voting integrity of all members and delegitimize their international legal personalities.*

8. Zero Tolerance for Morality

In order to ensure that justice survives, it is important to respect the appropriate conditions of the principle of morality as dictated by the philosophy of equilibrium. Moreover, any failures, inadequacies, or misinterpretations of justice are equivalent to the loss of life. However, as the American political lawyer Madeleine Albright was asked in 1996, "We have heard that half a million [Iraqi] children have died. I mean, that is more children than died in Hiroshima. And, you know, is the price worth it?" She replied, "*I think that is a very hard choice, but the price, we think, is worth it.*" This is a very clear position that demonstrates the theory of utipolitianism. This denotes that monopolistic rules are permitted and are even an integral part of the Security Council's games.[87] However, those rules are not guaranteed for any member of the organisation except the royal members of the United Nations that claim to have the highest morality. The fact is that the principles of their morality have evil foundations.

At the end of the day, there is no reason to speak about inequality in the UN and the inconsistent treatments of its members. This is because every matter seems to be in order, and any inconsistency of rights cannot be recognized by the fake colour of human rights and morality. Every rule of the organisation is imposed without due regard for our views. They have 'self-

---

[87] Farhad Malekian, 'Emasculating the Philosophy of International Criminal Justice in the Iraqi Special Tribunal,' Cornell International Law Journal, 58/5 (2005), pp. 675-725.

utipolitianist' characters. This means that even though we engage in a war of rules over which view is correct and which one does not conform to the moral or legal substance of the law, such speculations are not comprehensive because all our movements are controlled by the utipolitianist standard of rules and theories. Members of the United Nations are not free to make their own independent decisions. By recognizing this, our intention is not to promote unchecked provisions of the Charter, but rather to insist on the fact that it is essential to distinguish between the functions of normative rules and the functions of hierarchical authoritative rules.

The former is connected with their reference to the equality of arms in achieving legal and moral ethical efficiency, and the latter with their dictating power of monopolisation of rights. It is permitted and enforced in accordance with the provisions and desires of the utipolitianist regimes in order to establish their dominance. Indeed, this process of justice in the United Nations Security Council means we must try to take the elephant out of the office of the Council even though it has already been there for over eight decades. The effectiveness of these unjustified provisions regarding veto rights persists even if the provisions are removed. The only distinction is that the Council's provisions establish legal superiority in any situation, whereas their absence encourages automatic implementation. This means that there is no need for any warning. Nonetheless, it does not follow that there should be prerequisite rules since the orders and wills of politicians are not based on any particular regulation, but rather on what powertionist governments want and have planned in advance.

This indicates that taking a constructive approach to the system of international human rights or international criminal justice is extremely problematic and potentially not even possible. Thus, we can see that the notion of morality has been killed by utipolitianist theory. Consequently, drawing up an efficient schedule for when the immoral provisions of the Charter will be eliminated is a utopic dream and not possible in practice. The world is currently faced with a very cold form of morality, which has long been frozen and may soon perish. It is thus necessary to recognise that *the institutions of human rights are working in accordance with the requirements of justice that are presented and demanded by the utipolitianist powers and not with the wisdom of appropriate justice. There is no qualified response to the questions of justice, morality, and understanding of human needs since every matter greatly depends upon the tradition of the utipolitianism of the superior powers.*[88]

The current theory of justice does not address the imbalance between the Charter's words and their application in practices. It would be ironic to request the application of moral justice when setting out the needs of justice from a moral perspective has already been hindered. The international criminal judgments will then determine which variation is most likely to bring the real criminals under its jurisdiction in any given case concerning international accountability. The utipolitical occupation of true justice ultimately results in justice not being able to function.[89] We are then left with a form of criminal justice that is not only wholly undemocratic, but which can ultimately lead to the end of the existence of justice itself.[90]

The fact is that justice is nothing more than a reflection of a nation's strength. That is why no assessment can be comprehensive. Justice is only the result of different political parties fighting. However, the concept of justice in the system of international criminal courts is now instead the platform on which victims and witnesses should be able to help the system of international criminal courts function properly and emphasize that its existence is essential for peace, humanity, and the notion of morality. The best case scenario would be for utipolitianist governments to give up their political monopolies within international criminal justice and not act like hidden snakes to legitimise their criminal conduct. For example, in the Gaza case, the Western vassal states,

---

[88] The guilty conscience of the permanent members of the Security Council is revealed by the following statement: "We're selling arms to just about everyone on the planet. The more conflict, the more insecurity –the bigger the market place for arms. And certainly I don't think there is any interest in the US government whatsoever to reduce the opium crop that comes out of Afghanistan every year. That money from the sale of drugs, from the sale of opiates, particularly out of that part of the world, is eventually laundered and entered into s system and becomes legitimate. There are many governments on the planet, including the US, that benefit from those deposits once they are cleaned, so to speak… What they are doing is continuing the gravy train for many Washington bureaucracies and it increases insecurity around the world… Fundamentally for the US there has been a great deal of benefit for people in government over the last 15 years based on what we have done in Afghanistan: people have gotten rich, companies have made a lot of money, the Pentagon budget has never been larger, and there are no questions in Congress. Congress rubber stamps every budget request that they ask for. These are government benefits, and of course the cost is paid by people in Afghanistan and the people around the world, who suffer insecurity as a result of our policies." The retired US Air Force Lieutenant Colonel Karen Kwiatkowski, https://www.rt.com/op-edge/340391-us-benefits-taliban-terrorists/ (visited on 01 September 2024).

[89] Carefully consult id.

[90] Id.

such as Germany, Sweden, Australia, Canada, and France, have all supported the utipolitianist criminal position.

Chapter 5

Utipolitianist Modifying the Objectivity of Criminal Justice

1. Precarious Elements of Criminal Justice

One should not ask what is legitimate in utipolitianist international criminal justice or international human rights.[91] There is a clear tendency in the theory of utipolitianism that every matter is legitimate, even the commission of genocide. Taking out the organs of prisoners during times of war is also legitimate and was an integral part of Nazi policy during the Second World War. That is why the utipolitianist power of the Zionist government in Israel is doing the same thing with the Palestinian prisoners during the ongoing war against self-defence and self-determination in Gaza. Thus, according to its fundamental theory, utipolitianism is about pursuing interests and desires, even at the cost of millions of civilian lives. *The primary definition of utipolitianism in international criminal justice is that criminal justice should follow the interpretations and deductions that have been drafted and asserted by the powertionist authoritarian governments. Contrary to the opinion of many philosophers, justice should not create happiness according to its virtue, but rather according to the desires of superior governments.* This reflects the appropriate notion of distributive justice under the system of international criminal law due to the understanding of utipolitianist governments such as the criminal Israeli Zionist government. Such a conception means taking a distance from the reasonings of fair justice and ignoring any notion of moral

---

[91] See Issues in Contemporary Legal Philosophy: The Influence of H.L.A. Hart (Ruth Gavison, ed., 1987); Heidi Hurd, 'Challenging Authority,'100 Yale Law Journal 1611 (1991); G. Hughes, 'Validity and the Basic Norm,' 59 California Law Review 695 (1971); H.L.A. Hartart, Essays in Jurisprudence and Philosophy (1983); Joseph Raz, The Morality of Freedom (1986); J.W. Harris, Legal Philosophers (2nd edn.,1997); Johan Austin, The Province of Jurisprudence Determined and the Uses of the Study of Jurisprudence (1954); Gerald J. Postema, Bentham and the Common Law Tradition (1986); Julie Dickson., Evaluation and Legal Theory (2001); H.L.A. Hart., The Concept of Law (1961). H.L.A. Hart., The Concept of Law (2nd edn, P.A. Bulloch and J. Raz eds., 1994).

substance that seems to be necessary for the proper definition of justice as a whole.[92]

However, utipolitianism, which sees international criminal justice as the control of power, rejects any notion of the original position of elements of justice. There is thus no original principle in the philosophy of justice, except that it has to follow and be seen by utipolitianist governments.[93] There seems to be no way of demanding the essential elements of justice, which are naturally understood within any definition of the term "justice." This means that the requisite standard of justice is ignored in utipolitianism and international criminal justice in practice, thereby denoting the violation of primarily principles of international jurisprudence. These principles include the equality of arms, impartiality in the procedures of justice, and the respect for the truth.[94]

Moreover, the notion of the virtue of justice may fail if there is no moral or legitimate exercise of the norms of international criminal justice and if the prosecutor or judges of the court are not completely objective in their conduct and decisions. When these official personnel of the ICC are working in the vassal atmosphere of an international legal personality, then justice is not present in any space.[95] It is true that any claims made by the big political powertionist governments and any attempts to reject the truth and replace it with lies, imply the unjust distribution of fair justice along with dishonesty. We should therefore not put aside the fact that men are entitled to the equality of arms in the process of justice, and since this equality does not exist in the structure of the system of the Security Council, trust in the system of justice, which is the presentation of utipolitianism in the cloth of justice, is impossible to accept as fair justice in the mechanism of International Criminal Court.[96]

Utipolitianist international criminal justice is therefore a false procedure of justice, which is mostly an untrue spectacle that appears to respect international human rights law and the rights of the victims. However, the reality is that it acts contrary to the basic principles of the Statutes of the International Criminal Court and the regulations that demand the victims' rights be protected during all procedures, which does not occur. With the monopolised law of the Charter, more fundamental rights are rejected. The principles of international criminal justice that are supposed to regulate the

---

[92] Id.
[93] Id.
[94] Id.
[95] Id.
[96] Id.

basic structure of duties and obligations of judges and prosecutors do not mention moral principles within utipolitianist theory. Therefore, there is no motivation for distributive justice. This contention is unfortunately accepted by the majority of governments around the world. This is why we are seeing the return of the brutal criminal acts of Nazism from the Second World War in the territories of Palestine today.

The forceful monopolisation of the legal vocabulary is not a concern for utipolitianist governments. The strength of their weapons is the basis for their monopoly on international legislations, which are considered a form of natural rights. Additionally, there are no common-sense principles for collective protest against such monopolisation among governments. Governments are unable to unite due to their fears. Even if governments try to be released from utipolitianists' monopoly of power, it will not work since states differ concerning their political policies and their various political interpretations of international law. Surely, all governments are morally stable and cannot be separated from one another if justice is respected with the moral virtue of international human rights. Similarly, no government in advance asserts that we should or should not violate the system of international human rights or international criminal justice. This is because they believe that they are on the right side of the provisions, which becomes more dangerous and ironic when utipolitianism comes into power and ensnares Western governments in its criminal plans.

Thus, utipolitianism actually means utipolitianism-making power, which is unfortunately synonymous with treaty-making power. The former term relies on the definition of monopolisation of the basic structure of law by force, while the latter relies on the rules of law in accordance with negotiation and various meetings for the ratification of treaties based on the full consent of all parties. All of this makes it perfectly obvious that justice has to be established in our moral judgments, that no government deserves to be treated unjustly, and that no nation in the world deserves to be subjected to genocide. Moreover, none of the guidelines of justice should intend to be immoral due to discrimination or power politics. This is the fundamental lesson of the virtue of justice.[97]

[97] Id.

2. Judging the Colour of Criminal Conducts

Utipolitianist international criminal justice is not a question objective judges determining what crimes have been committed and what the punishment is. Rather, the most essential question is how to colour the crimes of criminals with human rights provisions. Doing this results in the mistreatment of nations since the purity of justice has already been sold and decisions have already been made. The initial legacy of natural justice falls from its platform onto other platforms of justice that have been created because of corruption and stealing wealth from other nations. From a moral point of view, the precept that should be called the root of justice is occupied in the name of one government that knows more than another, and as a result, wisdom for justice disappears and becomes the property of utipolitianism.[98] Once again, we face new interpretations of justice. This is because the principles of justice of utipolitianist governments occasionally change depending on their advantages and their political, economic, and military interests. We should thus not forget the fact that the definition of justice under utipolitianism has no basic principles and does not follow the just principles of international criminal law. Thus, any effort to go in the direction of the right definition of justice is somewhat impossible and therefore impractical.

Beyond all, utipolitianist justice is the presentation of justice by the NATO members, most of whom are afraid to be on the side of the truth, and as a result, they are unable to respond to the immoral decisions of the powertionist governments. Such states prefer unjust decisions, inequalities, and injustices. Additionally, it is very clear that any member of NATO should know that rights in the basic structure of the Security Council or the United Nations are generally wrong. And certainly, the precept of international criminal justice, which should be based on and emphasize morally right principles, is essentially ignored. This means that the principles of justice, which are essential for the balance of power, entirely fail to achieve these objectives. The same conclusion may be reached concerning the system of international human rights, which is essentially the basic reason for the existence of international criminal justice. In the ongoing remarks on the

[98] Consult Farhad Malekian, 'Judging International Criminal Justice in the Occupied Territories,' 12 International Criminal Law Review (2012), 827–869; Farhad Malekian, 'The Canon of Love against the Use of Force in Islamic and Public International Law: Part II: The Anatomy of Love Against Violations,' 15 International Criminal Law Review, 2015), pp. 861-895; Malekian Farhad, 'The Canon of Love against the Use of Force in Islamic and Public International Law: Part II: The Anatomy of Love Against Violations,' 15 International Criminal Law Review, 2015), pp. 861-895.

notion of justice, one must therefore concentrate on the value of the essence of humanity and not the definition and strength of power.

The fact is that the notion of moral worth, which often refers to the arguments of morality and Kant's opinion, not only refers to the moral duty of man to be righteous, but it also indicates that it is a personal responsibility of any person or authority to always act in good faith, not because they have responsibilities stemming from their position, but because people should be morally competent and not harm anyone. Thus, acting in good faith is the value of humanity, and it has nothing to do with the expression of sympathy from a moral point of view. Being good should not only be considered a duty, but it should also be recognised as human nature. This point is particularly significant concerning states that have the legal or political authority under the provisions of the Charter of the United Nations to be good. However, the utipolitianist governments infringe upon the notion of moral worth and claim to have legitimate legal rights under the system of the Charter. They then defend this notion of morality and human rights in their political speeches, particularly those of their evil criminal representatives such as John Kirby, Antony Blinken, or Lloyd Austin, all of whom support the brutal mentality of the utipolitianist theories.[99]

We can only compare a well-ordered international legal and moral aspiration with the present international legal society, which has been completely corrupted by the views and support of utipolitianism. There is no effective desire to comply with the existing rules of international human rights justice or international criminal justice with the actions governments that are violating the international legal system. This means that utipolitianist governments carry out the most brutal policies of utipolitianism to serve their own political and economic policies. The graveyards from the genocide in Gaza that have been found near hospitals with thousands of Palestinians that were buried alive, a large number of whom were doctors, workers, and patients who can no longer be identified are a clear example of this.[100]

It is evident that the human rights philosophy of utipolitianist governments has not only committed crimes against the population of Palestine, but it has also committed genocide against the notion of equal moral

---

[99] Kirby and Blinken are the masters of lies and evil without any notion of human personalities. The policies of all three have been rejected by wise Americans.

[100] Consult Anatomy of a Genocide - Report of the Special Rapporteur on the situation of human rights in the Palestinian territories occupied since 1967, Francesca Albanese (A/HRC/55/73) (Advance unedited version), https://www.ohchr.org/sites/default/files/documents/hrbodies/hrcouncil/sessions-regular/session55/advance-versions/a-hrc-55-73-auv.pdf.

worth of the inhabitants of the world, for which the United States government has primary criminal responsibility.[101] Although the main point is that the notion of moral worth does not deliver the first objective purpose of the United Nations, it is important when it is discussed in conjunction with the theory of other principles of the Charter, which are connected with the theory of moral worth. This is because they cannot properly work out the moral virtue of the principles, provisions, norms, or elements if they are not discussed in relation to the concept of morality.

3. Several Vassals of Utipolitianist Governments

The fact is that the long list of crimes committed by the utipolitianist governments against the principles of justice expressed in the Statute of the International Criminal Court indicates that the utipolitianist ideal currently dominates and occupies the entire philosophy of human rights concerning the rights of individuals. *If the ICC is not a vassal court, then what is it? A vassal court is a court that loses its independence. The mass graves of individuals indicate the vassal position of the ICC or its fake legal character as well as the repeated violations of the basic principles of humanity despite its existence. This means that once these significant principles or justice are violated, the notion of moral worth loses its sense of speaking and supporting justice and can be characterized as the evil desires of the powertionist governments to eliminate any notion of moral worth.*

The Gaza case may be analogous to the relation between the substantive principles of humanity within the legal characters of human rights norms and the evil nature of the brutality of superpower politics to achieve its goals. [102]

---

[101] Id.

[102] Mark J Osiel, Obeying orders: Atrocity, Military Discipline, and the Law of War (Transaction Publishers, 1999); Timothy L. H McCormack, The Law of War Crimes: National and International Approaches (Brill, 1997); Rene Provost, International Human Rights and Humanitarian Law (2002); William A. Schabas, War Crimes and Human Rights: Essays on the Death Penalty, Justice and Accountability (Cameron May, 2008); Steven R. Ratner, Jason S. Abrams, and James L. Bischoff, Accountability for Human Rights Atrocities in International Law: Beyond the Nuremberg Legacy, (3rd ed., Oxford Press, 2009); Eric Stover, My Neighbour, My Enemy: Justice and Community in the Aftermath of Mass Atrocity (Cambridge University Press, 2004); Benjamin B. Ferencz, New Legal Foundations for Global Survival: Security Through the Security Council (Oceana Publications,1994). See also Farhad Malekian, 'Judging International Criminal Justice in the Occupied Territories,' 12 International Criminal Law Review (2012), 827–869; Farhad Malekian, Trading Virginity of International Criminal Justice (Nova Sciences Publishers, 2020).

Since international criminal justice has permitted legal domination in power politics, utipolitianist governments have had no reason to protect the concept of justice, and everything comes back to the brutality of victims. Therefore, they release themselves from any notion of accountability.[103]

However, in an equal international organisation, all governments should enjoy the same standard of rights by having the same voice in different bodies of the organisation. The legitimate expectations that may be required are the elements of objectivity, fairness, and the duty to uphold just negotiations for the sake of protecting moral substance. We have to comply with the scheme of what justice requires and treat all subjects accordingly. The legitimate expectation is that reference to the rules and precepts has to reflect the correct version of the distribution of moral humanity and not immoral humanity. When the notions of power, morality, justice, and the gavel of international criminal justice are taken away and given to the Israeli Zionist government for example, then all notions of morality and humanity die. The fact is that utipolitianist governments have sold themselves to the economic power of Zionism, and as a result, the commission of genocide is viewed as the protection of the evil Zionist political policies.

The principles of justice for the institutions of humanity cannot succeed if they are cultivated in the hearts of evil governments. It should also be noted that even if a government has unjustly taken the gavel of justice into its own bloody hands, this does not mean that the existing rules of justice concerning morality and humanity should also be destroyed to serve the dirty political needs of such a government. In other words, losing the definitions of equality and humanity under the force of a superpower does not indicate the end of our own qualities or our own skills. Therefore, the losers should actually win in the interpretation of justice and humanity. Morality should thus not be subjected to contingencies that come from the interpretations and actions of certain political parties.

With all this, we are centralising the intention of this chapter on the non-objectivity of the principles of international criminal justice when it comes to the question of applicability. When the question of the accountability of certain criminals arises and their prosecution becomes necessary, then the provisions of the Vassal International Criminal Court either do not function or are ignored. Utipolitianists monopolising the elements of objectivity in international criminal justice leads to more imperfect and defective outcomes. It is not an exaggeration to claim that the utipolitianist system of international

[103] Id.

criminal justice deviates significantly from the systems of international criminal justice and human rights. This is because the utipolitianist governments are more intent on pursuing their interests and work outside the ordinary requirements of the International Court of Justice, the International Criminal Court, and the Security Council in order to do so. This is clearly evident in their actions and use of military force against other nations, as we have seen in Iraq and Syria.

The notion of humanity then loses its defined statute and becomes a term that is referred to by utipolitianists to promote their intentions. There are thus several ways to acquire a vassal court, a vassal judge, a vassal prosecutor, and a vassal state. All these intend to have certain objects controlled by certain powers in order to help the vassal object survive. It refers to a give-and-take under the power of the controlling state. This means that there is no way for the vassal to regain independence. A vassal subject does not get the option of voluntarily carrying out certain acts or decisions unless it first fulfils the conditions set by the utipolitianist government. This indicates that the vassal Court of the ICC can only be given the opportunity to take decisions according to the hidden diplomacy between it and its master. However, if the ICC chooses to not to respect the decisions of the utipolitianist government, then it would be the ultimate form of protest against its masters, as we have seen with the prosecutor of the ICC and the US government.[104]

4. Complicities of Governments with Utipolitianism

We can distinguish between the criminal conduct that has been committed in Syria and Iraq and the criminal conduct that is currently being carried out in Gaza. The latter involves the most barbaric government of our time and it is committing international crimes with the power and support of the United States government. The gravity of the crimes implies the savagery of conduct and the implementation of the system of utipolitianist human rights under the guidelines of the Security Council provisions. How the principles of human rights law have been cast out and the claims that have resulted from the ideologies of morality and humanity show the evil mentality of certain governments that direct and use the utipolitianist system of the Security

[104] Examine Farhad Malekian, Powertionism in International Criminal Justice (New York: Nova Science Publishers, 2022); see also Clara Nieto, Masters of War: Latin America and U.S. Aggression from the Cuban Revolution through the Clinton Years (foreword by Howard Zinn; translated by Chris Brandt, 2003).

Council to commit their barbaric crimes. Even if there is no desire to wage war and commit crimes, utipolitianists promote it among various nations.

There is no doubt that certain governments support a form of international criminal justice that is under the control of one or a few states. This means that they do not look to find any reason to match moral worth, at least in the context of international criminal jurisdictions. The reason for this is simply because they are safe, and that is the only reason for their human validity, human rights law, and human morality. They believe that as long as the super-evil political governments do not have anything to do with them, there can find safety under the fake theory of human rights law. The notion of a superior moral character in human rights agreements is not taken into account by governments who follow the orders of unjust governments. The practice and political position of a number of Western governments imply this fact. More notably, even if the international humanitarian conventions are completely violated, they still believe that they have greater advantages over the sense of justice that is presented by the utipolitianist system of the United Nations Charter. *My statements are not connected to the opinion of any form of justice, but rather to giving justice a chance to be free from individual or collective madness, antagonism, and the bitterness of hostility directed against its existence by our own governments.*[105]

In an international legal system that judges the character of the United Nations Charter and the nature of international criminal courts, justice must be pure. Our goal is to find a system for truth, even if we are not in pursuit of it, otherwise, the entire system of international human rights law and criminal justice would be a mirage. We mean that punishing certain individuals under various national systems for petty crimes or murder is a joke if we continue to

---

[105] For instance, Professor Chossudovsky clarifies that "America's New War' consists of extending the global market system while opening up new "economic frontiers" for U.S. corporate capital. More specifically, the U.S.-led military invasion -in close liaison with Britainresponds to the interests of the Anglo-American oil giants, in alliance with America's "Big Five" weapons producers: Lockheed Martin, Raytheon, Northrop Grumman, Boeing and General Dynamics. ...The 'AngloAmerican axis' in defence and foreign policy is the driving force behind the military operations in Central Asia and the Middle East. This rapprochement between London and Washington is consistent with the integration of British and American business interests in the areas of banking, oil and the defence industry. The merger of British Petroleum (BP) and the American Oil Company (AMOCO) into the world's largest oil conglomerate has a direct bearing on the pattern of Anglo-American relations and the close relationship between the American President and the British Prime Minister. In the wake of the 1999 war in Yugoslavia, Britain's giant weapons producer, British Aerospace Systems (BAES), was fully integrated into the U.S. system of defence procurement." Michel Chossudovsky, War and Globalisation: The Truth Behind September 11 (Global Outlook, 2002), p.64.

set other criminals that have committed abhorrent international crimes free. Here, *I am not trying to set the national criminals free, rather my intention is to illustrate what the ethical and philosophical function of our logic is when we execute someone for killing one person, while we are encouraged and applauded when we let people who have killed millions go free. Clearly, if the concept of justice is correct and described without any prejudice, it must apply to anyone who commits a crime.*

My finger is particularly pointed at the international criminals who have successfully killed millions of individuals in other nations. This is because the purpose of the system of international criminal law and justice is to uphold the basic natural rights of all victims and call for people who have engaged in the commission of genocide, crimes against humanity, war crimes, torture, aggression, and rape to be held accountable. However, such individuals still receive impunity for their criminal conduct—which is against all civilisations of humanity. It would be better if the acts proscribed by the system of international criminal justice were in accordance with the system of national criminal justice. Even if this were the case, it would have no legal enforceability. Otherwise, it would be far better if national criminal jurisdictions were as equal as international criminal jurisdiction is. This would mean impunity for all criminals. Of course, I fully realize that my statement is not correct and contradicts the philosophy of justice and penal statutes of all governments in the world. Nevertheless, this statement clarifies how frustrating international criminal justice systems are. This also applies to the system of the United Nations Charter, which respects all criminals under its Charter, and yet we disrespect all national criminals under our national legal systems. This indicates that we have different forms of moral substance and policies.

The propensity to commit grave international crimes has increased in recent times, and the notion of a just international society has rapidly waned.[106] This may be due to the development of the weapons industry and the will to find good international markets for our products. This is the reality for all states participating in the dangerous weapons industry.[107] It is clear that the distribution of economic advantages between various societies has made the function of international human rights and international criminal justice very blind, which is particularly obvious when we look at the politics of Western governments.[108] The very unfortunate fact is that all wars are waged in regions

---

[106] Id.
[107] Id.
[108] Id.

far from Western countries. This again indicates that the utipolitianist theory of the United Nations Charter and the International Criminal Court are granting full support for wars to be waged in other regions of the world.

This alone reflects the violations of the entire system of international human rights law. How can we speak about universal human rights law and its significant original ideologies concerning the protection of the dignity of man but not about the rights of victims? The basic rights of man and his practical motivations are entirely different. These statements are not the opposite of the system of international human rights law and international criminal law and justice. The function of the unequal distribution of rights and freedoms for men should not be treated differently. Thus, we cannot speak about all nations of the world on one hand while also attacking these nations with our guns and bombs. This is an indication of the non-existence of international human rights law and the violations of all principles of morality as a whole.

A clear example of this is Swedish political diplomacy, which claims to be based on democracy. However, this same democracy has delivered heavy weapons to the Israeli government to be used in the genocide against the Palestinian population.[109] The same is true about the criminal policies of the British and French governments, as well as the Indian government to a certain extent. These are just a few examples of how we protect and support the philosophy of international human rights law and international criminal justice behind the hidden doors of our offices and how we humiliate and kill other nations with other pretend neutrality. The aforementioned governments operate with double diplomacies, which are motivations for dirty terrorist conduct. However, we condemn other nations and call them terrorists if they exercise their right to self-defence as equal as self-determination. Thus, the motivations behind certain governments' policies and their criminal contributions to the commission of international crimes such as genocide or crimes against humanity are categorised as acts of self-defence, or self-protection. They claim to carry out these acts to free themselves from resistance groups, which are incorrectly designated as terrorists by NATO utipolitianist governments.

---

[109] Richard Falk, The Accountability of Leaders: A Challenge to Civil Government and Society in Jeremy Brecher, Jill Cutler, Brendan Smith, In the Name of Democracy: American War Crimes in Iraq and Beyond (American Empire Project), (New York: Metropolitan Books, Henry Holt and Company, 2005), pp. 301-307.

5. Utipolitianism as the Owner of the Court

Assuming that every government accepts the significance of the existence of the provisions of the system of international human rights law, each one still has to decide whether criminals have carried out their crimes on their own or with the help of others. This is a demonstration of our attitudes towards human rights and how we evaluate the system of international criminal justice. In a well-ordered international organisation there would be no need for a cowardly or vassal international criminal court. Due to this, we are always dealing with the problem of violations due to the existence of the utipolitianist theory within the most important international organisation. Thus, it is necessary to see the problem of justice from the perspective of its violations and then calculate whether acts committed by other nations are acts of terrorism or acts of self-defence against our own terrorist acts.

In the procedures of international criminal justice the arguments of criminality are always directed at the weakest parties and the strong remain protected from any arguments around their criminal activities. This is how the system of international criminal courts is established and driven by military strength, or the vassal theory of justice. *The question of international criminal justice belongs to the political authorities of the utipolitianists for the most part and the theory of protection of their arguments by those lawyers who have learned law in order to earn an income instead of to bring truth to the desk of justice.* Due to this, complying with the law of the Statute of the International Criminal Court is controversial, whereas the justification of which rules or principles should be the subject of discussions belongs to the authoritarian power in some way.

Any theory concerning the accountability and attribution of international criminal responsibilities is completely misleading and suggests no strict criminal responsibilities when the notion of criminal responsibility is a tool in the personal possession of the utipolitianist governments.[110] Any alternative

---

[110] Consider, for instance, the case of Ariel Sharon, who has been accused of committing acts of genocide. In discussing Sharon's international criminal responsibility for his actions in the occupied territories, our assessments are grounded not only in the principles of *de lege lata* and *nullum crimen sine lege* but also in the principle of equitable application of international criminal justice to all individuals who infringe upon the fundamental tenets of international criminal law. In 1982, Sharon perpetrated acts of genocide against Palestinians and Lebanese at the Sabra and Shatila refugee camps. The Belgian authorities sought to indict Sharon for these criminal acts; however, in 2003, U.S. President George W. Bush urged the Belgian government to discontinue its prosecution of this case. See Nicholas Blanford, Sharon May Be Off Hook as Belgium Revisits Law, DAILY STAR (Leb.), July 14, 2003, available at http://lebanonwire.com/0307/03071417DS.asp; Francis A. Boyle,

justification for the accountability of the super-terrorist *governments* will be in *their* own hands, and, naturally, justice does not function as it is should. This has been seen repeatedly since the establishment of the ICC, and various other *ad hoc* international criminal tribunals have not even taken any action against the real violators of international criminal law.[111] While I am writing this book about the use of the system of international criminal justice by governments, it is also true that the principles of justice in utipolitianism sometimes go hand-in-hand with the theories of utilitarianism that call for extreme pressure. The utipolitianist theory posits pressure beyond pressure in military, economic, and political matters. This helps to cannibalize and destroy the legal system. It also points out the characteristic vassal positions of the United Nations and the International Criminal Court.

There thus exists a combination of utipolitianism and utilitarianism that attacks the idea of equality. This does not mean that utipolitianism is the same as utilitarianism. They are different theories with different intentions. However, the theory of utipolitianism is both, with the difference that it aims to gain international control over the utility of resources under its own monopolised order—especially since all utipolitianist governments have the intention of seizing power rather than presenting more reasonable principles of justice. This at first seems lawful since their arguments are based on the implementation of the system of international human rights law and are thus valid. However, in reality, that is not the purpose of utipolitianism, and therefore, with these explanations, utipolitianism succeeds in convincing its audiences and taking control of not only the resources of the victims, but also the system of international criminal justice to a certain degree.

We must not forget the fact that utipolitianist policies may not only be opposed to by most governments in the world, they may even be opposed to by national movements and citizens of the same utipolitianist government. A clear example of this is the great movement among brave students, some professors in the United States, and certain universities against utipolitianist power. This movement reflects that views expressed by such governments may create serious conflict between the public and the policies of governments. In other words, utipolitianist ideologies may be firmly rejected through demonstrations and protests. The result of this is that utipolitianist

---

Barak Appoints War Criminal Yaron, https://www.derechos.org/human-rights/mena/doc/boyle2.html (last visited October 31, 2005); Farhad Malekian, 'Emasculating the Philosophy of International Criminal Justice in the Iraqi Special Tribunal,' Cornell International Law Journal, 58/5 (2005), p.719.

[111] Id.

theory loses value, or if it succeeds in lying and convincing its own population, it is viewed as the secondary theory that is rejected and seen as belonging to certain political groups or wealthy groups that control the economy and politics of the world. In the end, the systems of international human rights and criminal justice both lose their original definitions and are organized or controlled by the utipolitianist theories of justification of law and morality. *The reason for this is very simple. Utipolitianism is a new form of international criminal law, international human rights, international humanitarian law, and international criminal court that exists to enable monopolisation. This is the new method of monopolising the morality of criminal justice and scrutinising its usefulness against the will of the utipolitianists.*

As a result, if justice as fairness is one of the main objectives of international criminal justice, it becomes the instrument of classical colonialist doctrine. In the end, the international human rights law establishes a new method of monopolisation that dominates nations worldwide. Moreover, given the importance of the principles of international criminal law and justice against those who have treated the provisions and principles of international human rights law badly, we do not have any aspirations, and our remarks concerning conceptions of equal justice, fairness, and respect for the rights of victims will not be manifested. *The fact is that under the utipolitianist theory, no minimum standard of justice will be seen, and there will be no guarantees for the basic human rights principles at any level on a positive platform.* Therefore, the strong arguments from the points of equality, justice, and morality will not be seen and will lose their original purposes. This is why we have constantly been told that we need to scrutinise the reasons behind the provisions or principles of the United Nations Charter, and we need, in the end, to abolish those rules or entirely abolish the Security Council.

It may even be a good idea to create a new international organisation that is completely free from all forms of monopolisation that have been enforced by the utipolitianism of the Security Council. The view arising from the various principles of injustice and immorality of the Charter is thus the reason for insufficient latitude in the determination and achievement of the concept of the minimum standard of justice under the procedures of the organisation and under the authority of the international criminal court. Moreover, going too far to claim that the theory is useful for the maintenance of the balance of justice is like asserting that the system of international human rights is powerful without any courts.

6. Indisputable Self-Indulgent Norms

Equality will not be achieved if justice principles are borrowed from the concept of fairness and the character of justice presented by the utipolitianist strategic system. Therefore, by using the differences that exist in the judgments of utipolitianism and principles of judgments of pure international human rights or international criminal justice as examples, some other standards that are not equivalent and give different results that conflict with the scope of definitions and applications. Additionally, it is true that this concept of justice, which was introduced by utipolitianism, may still be recognised as perfect and vital. This means that utipolitianism, with the assistance of its allied powers, orchestrates such evocations and insists that their conclusions are not only authentic, but also beneficial to every nation in the world.

As a result of this interpretation of the standard of justice, the system of international criminal justice is discounted and the statements of the politicians of the world are given priority. The leeway behind the prospects for the strength of character of the system of international criminal justice decreases and, as a result, the volume of the interpretation of international human rights law loses its power of definition, interpretation, and demands. This indicates that the arguments around the system of fair justice are permanently unsettled, and agreements concerning equality among states and members of the United Nations are controversial and have unwanted consequences.

We must not forget the fact that there are different principles concerning the arguments presented within political-legal judgements and utipolitianist dreams. Both argue for the existence of rights. However, one promotes the existence of pure equality, while the other promotes the contrary. Both also speak about human rights, albeit with the difference that their basic backgrounds and reasonings are not the same. One speaks about equal rights and their enforcement, while the other speaks about human rights with greedy conclusions. This variety of mixed views is the main reason why the system of international criminal jurisprudence has lost its intrinsic conceptions of criminal justice and criminal procedures, which direct all members of the United Nations to the same end. However, different political views in the applied Charter present different aspects of justice, morality, and humanity.

Although the criteria for a formative definition of justice and equality are clear, the system of utipolitianist interpretations evaluates them differently. The fact is that the big super-political governments that are strengthened by military guns, in particular nuclear arms, impose their unconditional and indisputable self-indulgent norms. It must be acknowledged and recognized that hardly any fair arguments arise concerning the discussions and values promoted in utipolitianist policies. There is therefore no form of justice that has been reasonably evaluated and presented by utipolitianist governments. They are often content with their own happiness at the price of the lives, happiness, and resources of other nations. The utipolitianist governments arrive at different conclusions when it comes to specific decisions that involve listing a common-sense philosophy of ethical precepts. These include certain policies for the prevention of wars, barbarity, genocide, holocaust, and crimes against humanity. Then, the utipolitianist governments demand that all members of the General Assembly or the Security Council fully comply with their statements.

In particular, regarding questions of international criminal justice and international human rights law, there are different understandings about the judgments of international courts and whether they have any basic validity. That is why the whole structure of the system of decisions within the United Nations, and particularly the resolutions of the Security Council, continue to permit wars—utipolitianism cannot survive without waging wars and creating conflicts among various governments or nations of the world. This is why the ICC fails to function when it is supposed to. The sole reason why we introduced its Statute is to take advantage of its vassal nature, which makes it dependent on the orders of the masters.[112] Thus, despite the fact that the different principles of the United Nations seem to support equality, peace, humanity, justice, and morality, offhand influences have been very effective in the policy of the organisation and, as a result, the rights of victims have not been respected and the number of victims increases daily.[113] This means that the system of international criminal justice faces an increasing number of violations, and more and more governments develop double moralities due to the unequal distribution of power.[114]

However, it may still be the criterion that causes the background and control of the weights of fair justice to fall and the judgments of the governments to not match the various notions of equality expressed in the system of international human rights, including the United Nations Charter as

---

[112] Examine the views of Richard Falk, John Mearsheimer, Avram Noam Chomsky, Jeffrey Sachs and Richard Wolff including colonels Douglas Macgregor, William Scott Ritter and Senator Richard H. Black. See John J Mearsheimer and Stephen Walt, The Israel Lobby and U.S. Foreign Policy (New York: Farrar, Straus and Giroux. 2007).

[113] Id.

[114] Id.

a whole. Due to this, the moral values and substances of norms are modified and rely on the intuition of humanity, which brings much lower standards of equality and more problems of injustice with it. This is, of course, very acceptable under a system of international organisation that is solely guided by the principle of utipolitianism. Any hope for the existence of more basic principles of human justice and morality becomes fleeting and explains the legal boldness and aptitudes of our judgments about the distribution of international human rights and criminal justice—that is, the decision and development of uncertainty in the system of justice. There will therefore always be conflicts between the consequences of our human rights and criminal justice and those of our approaches that call for equalities of voice.

7. Pandemic of Inevitable Injustice

Certainly, none of the falsified principles of humanity should prevail or be imposed on the nations or populations of the world.[115] However, this is not a judgment cast to be free from the effects of utipolitianism, rather a fact that has to be respected at all times and under all circumstances. We should remember that the principle of humanity and provisions of international human rights for the protection of the system of international criminal justice are not bargaining chips, and that their methods and substance are already fixed. Otherwise, all principles of the system of human rights would not be fully acceptable and would have to be redrafted to protect the immoral rights of the utipolitianist powers.

Therefore, we must make significant changes to the views stated and defined within international conventions. We should officially categorize the principles of utipolitianism and the occupation of the resources of other nations as fully visible principles. We must leave any question concerning the problem of balancing the essence of equality and the specification of our conception of justice in a vacuum. While the principles of justice expressed by utipolitianism may not appear to be pitted against our principles of equality, they are actually working as destructive tools against humanity.[116] Therefore, a relatively concrete principle of humanity that is expressed and stated by the system of international human rights may be condemned and imprisoned in

[115] Ramsey Clark, War Crimes – A Report on United States War Crimes against Iraq (Maisonneuve Press, 1992).

[116] Id.

the prisons of political jurisdiction, i.e., utipolitianism, and theories of occupation of rule by the force of guns.

Thus, while the difference between the principles of true international human rights and the untrue principles of human rights of the utipolitianist governments does not strike us as strange and reflect the shortcomings of the previous representatives of governments with those of the present, we are still compelled to speak the truth. When it comes to violations of the system of international criminal law under the theory of utipolitianism and committing a range of international crimes against the victims, the result will be that the crimes will, of course, be protested by many, in particular by the victims of utipolitianist governments. This situation reflects the judgments of various populations of the world and governments that dare to object to the immoral conduct of utipolitianist policies. Furthermore, we may see that the political authorities of many societies unfortunately overlap their policies of pretend democracies with the utipolitianist criminal decisions, conducts, and reactions.[117]

While the purpose of democratic societies is to appeal to the common interest of all citizens and the purpose behind the establishment of the United Nations and the International Criminal Court in The Hague is to achieve a mutual and multilateral understanding of the problems of international society, these are viewed as being completely unnecessary by utipolitianism. No utipolitianist government unwaveringly admits to forcing the basic principles of democracy in the wrong direction, and this is actually a sickness in the processes of all international legal gatherings, including the United Nations and the ICC. Consequently, the advantages and disadvantages of the existence of any democratic views come under serious question within the jurisprudence of international law, which seeks to establish a fundamental balance between the means and the end. We require something beyond the efficiency of the principles of democracy that do not present and support the theory of democracy and instead promote the will and evil interests of the utipolitianist governments. Otherwise,

> A good will is good not because of what it effects, or accomplishes, not because of its fitness to attain some intended end, but good just by its willing, i.e., in itself; and, considered by itself, it is to be esteemed beyond

---

[117] Richard Falk, The Accountability of Leaders: A Challenge to Civil Government and Society in Jeremy Brecher, Jill Cutler, Brendan Smith, In the Name of Democracy: American War Crimes in Iraq and Beyond (American Empire Project), (New York: Metropolitan Books, Henry Holt and Company, 2005), pp. 301-307.

> compare much higher than anything that could ever be brought about by it in favour of some inclinations, and indeed, if you will, the sum of all inclinations. Even if by some particular disfavour of fate, or by the scanty endowment of a step motherly nature, this will should entirely lack the capacity to carry through its purpose; if despite its greatest striving it should still accomplish nothing, and only the good will were to remain (not of course, as a mere wish, but as the summoning of all means that are within our control); then, like a jewel, it would still shine by itself, as something that has full worth in itself.[118]

The question then is: do we really believe that democracy is present within the UN Charter? Do Western countries actually care about social justice and equality in other parts of the world? Or do those utipolitianist governments use the term "democracy" to pay lip service to detractors and legitimize their prolonged global dominance in order to satisfy their greed? There are a considerable number of other questions relating to the morality and human rights of the Western powers, which, with their methods of committing crimes, speak about democracy for other nations via the trade of their weapons. In return, they commit many more international crimes to establish and enforce their own dominant objections. This is the notion of international criminal law authoritarianism.[119]

Since it is impossible to maximize the implementation of the principles of international human rights, the theory of consistent equal liberties, freedom, and fair opportunity between all nations becomes ridiculous to refer to because of its ties to the unjustified controlling roles and rules of powertionist governments. It seems that the policies in the system of justice expressed by the Security Council are a reasonable extension of the conventions of human rights with the aspiration of democracy face up to the inevitability of adapting and adopting themselves to a rationally complete conception of justice. Therefore, the practical values of humanity, democracy, and peace must fight against the fake notion of democratic values. These concepts identify implausible standards of justice and judgments, and ultimately affect the jurisdiction of international criminal courts.

---

[118] Kant in his Groundwork.

[119] Consult also Richard Falk, The Accountability of Leaders: A Challenge to Civil Government and Society in Jeremy Brecher, Jill Cutler, Brendan Smith, In the Name of Democracy: American War Crimes in Iraq and Beyond (American Empire Project), (New York: Metropolitan Books, Henry Holt and Company, 2005), pp. 301-307.

8. Final Frontiers of Utipolitianists

When the standard of equal and fair opportunity for all governments disappears from the structures of international bodies, then chances of equality among nations being achieved decline, eventually increasing inequality of rights, whether in civil or criminal procedures. In this instance, the necessity for the protection of different principles of humanity loses legal protection and value. This is how utipolitianist plans are decided along with how we should accept their judgments. The balance of law is thus replaced with the balance of guns and the latter with the extreme forms of inhumanity, injustice, and humiliation of the rights of victims. It is actually the role of monopolisation of the law and justice that is more productive than the role of authentic conscience and the extension of purely comparative human rights rules.

As a result, when criminal justice is not objective, the system of international human rights latches onto the terminal tackle like a fish. This tackle is actually used within the structure of the rules of the United Nations and therefore it is not so strange to see the entire systems of international human rights and international criminal justice functioning like a tackle box, which has various tools for bringing governments under its order and controlling of their reasoning, interpretation, and judgments. These tools can be used, interpreted, and applied with a variety of powers and perspectives with the intention of pretending that the tools are relatively harmless to convince governments that a strong government, such as the United States, is trying to protect the basic principles of international human rights—even though they are actually completely destroying them.

Moreover, such a government pretends that it is fighting against all injustices against other nations, and therefore its policies should be supported by other governments. Here, we are particularly referring to the double morality of certain Western governments, particularly the Criminal British governments and the German government, which is still perpetuating the same polices of the Holocaust against children.[120] This group of governments and

---

[120] "The Harvard University Medical Report from the first Gulf War documented the deaths and injuries of children as a direct result of the use of force. Accordingly, over 550,000 children suffered because of medical shortages caused by the Security Council's inhuman and illegal sanctions.25 I will not mention in detail here the permanent members' indirect responsibility for the poisoning of Kurdish children under Saddam Hussein's authority or the bombing of Palestinian children because of certain permanent members' political and military support of the Israeli military forces." Farhad Malekian, The Mirage of International Criminal Law: Kant Metaphysics of Mens Rea (Cambridge: Cambridge Scholars Publishing, 2018), p. 171.

their criminal conduct can be identified by their historical records and the continuation of such criminality, particularly on the part of the British governments. Thus, their policies of criminality and their implementations cannot be compared with the law of utipolitianism alone and must also be compared with the entire monopolisation of utipolitianists with the intention of the complete destruction of any notion of morality.

Consequently, it is essential to evaluate the theory of utilitarianism and the principles of utility within the framework of democratic organisations to struggle against any unjustified force. However, this must be done with a comprehensive understanding of the complexities involved, including the slow-moving nature of governments, which may encourage fatal impediments. The system of international criminal courts can also hold these governments accountable for their criminal acts that violate the provisions of international criminal law.

This means we not only lose the objectivity principle of criminal justice in the Court, which transforms into a vassal subject, but we also lose the objectivity of being human and instead witness the deaths of millions of innocent individuals under the provisions of international human rights law for economic gain. This is a shame for the system of international jurisprudence and an irreparable wound in the lives of victims and nations. This is precisely how it was planned by the United States and Israeli governments and their allies concerning Gaza, with the claim that they are fighting against the resistance army called Hamas, all with the intention of banishing them from their own territories. This means that the aforementioned governments are killing millions of people and using the international criminal justice system to serve their own interests.

There are a number of significant messages that must be kept in mind in order to avoid misunderstandings about the principles of the International Criminal Court. We should realize the fact that it is the capacity and the preference for more righteous methods of jurisdiction that cause justice to survive, not the various hazardous conducts and decisions of the utipolitianist governments. The Nazi movements were criminal movements, as has already been established. Even if we asserted that the establishment of the International Criminal Tribunal for Nuremberg was wrong, we would still condemn the savage and barbarous acts of German Nazism against the innocent Jewish population of Europe.[121] This is the same concerning the

[121] Farhad Malekian, 'Comparative Substantive International Criminal Justice,' in Ronald C. Slye (ed.), The Nuremberg Principles in Non-western Societies: A Reflection on their Universality, Legitimacy and Application (2017), pp. 10-44.

crimes that are currently being committed against the population of Gaza. If it is a useful theoretical notion to follow the utipolitianist theory, then the system of international criminal justice should prepare itself to see much more human suffering.

As the German philosopher Kant stated, we should be very careful with our actions to avoid autocracy, monocracy, authoritarianism, or the dictatorship of certain utipolitianist governments becoming the guiding principles of our corrupt international democracy.[122] Many related matters require further explanation. It is clear that the plans of utipolitianist governments pose a threat to the security of peace and humanity in general. Their plans of action are not neutral. This can be seen in the implementation of their criminal conduct all over the world. This indicates that the goals achieved by the plans of the utipolitianist governments are the result of their criminal conduct and perpetual lies. They are always inclined to describe their criminal conduct as righteous and productive.

9. No Error of Utipolitianist Misconception

When a utipolitianist government decides what to do and what the scope of its present or future plans will be, it works to occupy the sovereignty of other states and their resources. The utipolitianist government's choice to pursue military action will lead it to acquire land, properties, and resources, even if millions have to be slaughtered for that to happen. It is evident from all our arguments that some states believe that what the utipolitianist government's desires are necessary since there exist other super powertionist governments

[122] For Kant theories consult Immanuel Kant, 'Religion within the Limits of Reason Alone,' in Religion and Rational Theology, ed. and transl. Allen Wood and George di Giovanni (Cambridge University Press, 1996); Immanuel Kant, 'Religion within the Limits of Reason Alone,' in Religion and Rational Theology, ed. and transl. Allen Wood and George di Giovanni (Cambridge University Press, 1996); Immanuel Kant, Answering the Question: What is Enlightenment? (1784); Immanuel Kant, Critique of Judgment (1790); Immanuel Kant, Critique of Pure Reason (1781); Immanuel Kant, Groundwork of the Metaphysic of Morals (1785); Kant Immanuel, Metaphysical Foundations of Natural Science (1786); Immanuel Kant, Opus Postumum (1995); Immanuel Kant, Perpetual Peace, and Other Essays on Politics, History, and Morals (1784); Immanuel Kant, Perpetual Peace: A Philosophical Sketch (1795); Immanuel Kant, Practical Philosophy (editor: Mary J. Gregor, 1999); Immanuel Kant, Prolegomena to Any Future Metaphysics (1783); Immanuel Kant, Religion within the Bounds of Bare Reason (1793); Immanuel Kant, The Critique of Practical Reason (1788); Immanuel Kant, The Metaphysics of Morals (1797); Immanuel Kant, The Only Possible Argument in Support of a Demonstration of the Existence of God (1763); Immanuel Kant, The Science of Right (1790).

that threaten the existence of peace. At any given time, rational governments decide between what is beneficial or harmful for all governments. This is the normal expectation in valuing the function of the rules of law and their effects in conjunction with their present major desires of the utipolitianist choice of criminal actions and rational choice based on moral law. Nonetheless, all arguments collapse when faced with the basic power of the Security Council.

The sole hope here is that the General Assembly of the United Nations adopts resolutions against utipolitianist criminal conduct even though the final implementation of such resolutions still remains in the hands of the same authoritarian utipolitianist member of the Security Council. Any aspects of General Assembly decisions that seem peculiar to the utipolitianist government will be considered, not with the purpose of modifying its criminal direction, but with the purpose of completing and preventing any political or legal movements that threaten their interests. This occurs within different bodies of the United Nations. In these cases, no rational criteria can prevent the criminal decisions and conduct of politicians, while the rational decisions of certain governments may be useful for the majority of governments in the world.

Although our judgments often rest on self-evident proof, they cannot change the minds of criminals and the perpetrators of crimes against humanity, war crimes, apartheid, or genocide. Thus, any definition of satisfaction here means maximising the expected needs and plans of the utipolitianists through a hedonistic confirmation of their wills. Every matter is clearly left in the hands of the utipolitianist government and they have to decide what is best for them, regardless of the huge amount of suffering that may be inflicted on others. There is no real judge or court to judge the relative importance of the existence of the principle of international legal personality. In another words, if the prosecutor of a Court does not act or delays taking action, then they are a vassal.

As a matter of fact, the utipolitianist government can remove the international legal personality of a nation state and give it to another group to form a nation with a new name, i.e., Israel. This process is called the implementation of human rights, even though it is carried out through the implementation of irrational norms of colonialist power. Here, my reference is to the criminal British governments throughout history. Additionally, because of the greed of the utipolitianist governments, the outcome of all their criminal conduct is viewed as natural and not a violation of the system of international criminal justice.

This means that there are no errors of reasoning in the theory of monopolisation of the system of international law or the Court and there should therefore be no misunderstandings concerning the criminal conduct of the utipolitianist government. This is based on the fact that it is lawful and permitted to commit crimes according to its final decisions, which are solely based on its own vote and veto power. The international legal system therefore encompasses the basic values of international legal personality in the nature and values presented by the use and threat of force, even though Article 2(4) of the Charter of the United Nations prohibits its use. I must not forget the fact that such prohibitions are not against the intention of the utipolitianist governments, but rather against those that are against any utipolitianist power.

There are obviously true beliefs and false beliefs about the system of international criminal justice and its monopolisation. However, the fact is that the evidence of criminality also implies the existence of lies. One who may assert that the Holocaust of the Jews and the Holocaust of the Palestinians did not happen or are not currently happening? Those people or authorities are like spiders with eight limbs and with fangs of weapons, able to inject war, horror, and massacres and poison into the victims. Still, the Zionist government permits the commission of genocide by referring to the Holocaust. American Professor Norman Finkelstein rightly stated: "The biggest insult to the memory of the Holocaust is not denying it, but using it to commit genocide against the Palestinian people."[123]

---

[123] Pietro Stefanini, 'Palestine and the Mirage of International Criminal Justice – Can the ICC improve the Security of the Palestinians,' available at http://platform.almanhal.com/Files/2/90090 (Visited on 1 November 2017); Statement of ICC Prosecutor, Fatou Bensouda, respecting an investigation of the Situation in Palestine (Statement: 3 March 2021), https://www.icc-cpi.int/news/statement-icc-prosecutor-fatou-bensouda-respecting-investigation-situation-palestine; Statement of the Prosecutor of the International Criminal Court, Karim A.A. Khan KC, on the Situation in the State of Palestine: receipt of a referral from five States Parties (Statement: 17 November 2023), https://www.icc-cpi.int/news/statement-prosecutor-international-criminal-court-karim-aa-khan-kc-situation-state-palestine; Statement of ICC Prosecutor Karim A. A. Khan K. C.: Applications for arrest warrants in the situation in the State of Palestine (Statement: 20 May 2024), https://www.icc-cpi.int/news/statement-icc-prosecutor-karim-aa-khan-kc-applications-arrest-warrants-situation-state.

Chapter 6

Corruption in the Office of the Vassal Prosecutors of the ICC

1. Cardinal Measures of Utipolitianism

The term "utipolitianism," although my own invention, has existed throughout the history of human civilisation and has occupied a very significant place in the national, regional, and international courts of criminal justice. Thus, the framework of the term has always existed, even if the term had not been coined to encompass the expression of manipulation, monopolisation, colonialism, powertionism, and the use of unlawful force in the name of the use of legitimate force.[124] In other words, utipolitianism refers to the occupation of the philosophical and humanitarian notion of the International Criminal Court and the transformation of its international legal personality into a vassal Court. The problems and reasons for speaking about utipolitianism therefore confront the control of the power of the law and the imposition of its desires by various sanctions. Thus, the question of utipolitianism is so deep and the approximations are so insufficient that they severely conflict with the systems of international human rights and international criminal justice values. The notion of morality disappears and is replaced with barbarity and greed, as we have seen in Gaza. The human rights effects of significant rules of morality are unfortunately tempered by utipolitianism.

In other words, when we talk about utipolitianism, we are referring to the most inhuman use of power in the form of legally permitted terrorism under the system of the United Nations that has been employed in order to take the power of the ICC under our control. It is to be kept in mind that although the United States of America is not a party to the Court, it takes control of the vassal Court whenever it deems fit.[125] Some may claim that the military guns

---

[124] Farhad Malekian, Powertionism in International Criminal Justice (Nova Sciences Publishers, 2022).

[125] The fact is that "the international criminal court cannot be effective if it is subservient to the vacillating interests of nationstates. Such subservience delimits the true and illusory adjudication powers of the court. …The lack of coercive power to bring an accused before the court emasculates the legal character of an international criminal body. Merely branding

of the big powers must make the final decision and utilize the systems of international human rights and international criminal justice in order to convince individuals, groups, nations, and governments that things must be this way.[126] No one can say what the underlying principles that account for these basic principles of justice really are. This is because they are frightened by the terrorist power of utipolitianist governments and obey the orders of political powers out of self-preservation. A considerable number of governments understand this policy of monopolisation of international criminal justice but prefer to remain silent because if they speak out, their criminal, political, and economic policies will come under fire. Consequently, it is easier for such governments to follow the policies outlined by the strong, powertionist government. With the term "powertionist" governments, we are referring to governments that are hungry for power and unjustly interested in the natural rights of others without showing their real face to occupy the rights of other nations of the world. Of course, all of this is obvious.

I am not saying anything new about the unfaithful diplomacy of the system of international human rights and international criminal justice, both of which are entirely under the control of utipolitianist governments. Moreover, it has always been recognised that the ethical principles of human rights and international criminal justice are vague and ambiguous when it comes to certain very serious and sensitive questions. The principles are not imprecise; however they are all written and interpreted collectively, and therefore, the presentation of pure human rights and understanding of human integrity becomes very controversial in connection with the principles of the United Nations. The implementation of the principle of fair justice thus becomes very difficult and impossible to achieve.

If justice or pure objective justice cannot be achieved in the office of the most significant international organisation in the world, which was established with the purpose of preventing international crimes and bringing criminals under the jurisdiction of a criminal Court to be punished, then we are no longer

---

an individual as an "international fugitive" is adding little to the success of either Tribunal. As the current situation indicates, international criminal law cannot depend on the acquiescence of powerful nations. Otherwise, international tribunals return to the setting of "victors' justice," which begs the question whether international criminal law is capable of equitable distribution. Without salient enforcement, international criminal law provides only the enticing mirage of justice." Mary Margaret Penrose, 'Lest We Fail: The Importance of Enforcement in International Criminal Law An Essay on the Nature and Immutability of Truth,' 15 (2) American University International Law Review (1999), pp. 321-394, at 363-4.

[126] Id.

in the house of justice, but rather in a corrupt institution that has been created and supported by criminals. The policies of the utipolitianists have even achieved the institution of justice, and not only justice, but also the basic principles of the institution of international criminal courts, which constitutes one of the most significant institutions of world civilisation. The principles of international criminal justice have a lot of potential advantages in the greater intelligibility of their demands and in what needs to be completed to satisfy the natural and legal rights of victims. Here, we are not just speaking about civil crimes or national crimes, but also about the victims of significant violations, or, in the terminology of international humanitarian law, "grave crimes."

It might be thought that the vagueness and complexity in the administration of justice are the essential reasons for the impunity of international criminals. The ICC prosecutor is unable to prosecute criminals protected by their authoritarian power. This is the weakest argument that can be made by anyone, including the office of the prosecutor. Consequently, any argument that the difficulties in identifying international crimes are the reasons for impunity and that the theories of utipolitianism are not influential can be completely rejected. As a matter of fact, calling upon the responsibility of everyone who has clearly violated the provisions of international criminal justice is not only the responsibility of the office of the prosecutor, but also an established legal and natural duty. Moreover, the ICC is responsible for bringing anyone suspected of committing international crimes or anyone who encouraged or aided in the commission of international crimes under their jurisdiction. Hence, the argument that there is difficulty in identifying international crimes is weak at best.

The prosecutor of the Court is not only responsible for preventing utipolitianist influences in their office, but also has an international legal responsibility under international peremptory criminal law to fulfil their immutable duties. Moreover, the principle of utipolitianism can be overcome by a strong justice of the reasoning of international *jus cogens* norms and ensuring the wellbeing of the provisions of international criminal justice.[127] I

---

[127] For *jus cogens* norms examine Czaplinski, Wladyslaw 'Concepts of *Jus cogens* and Obligations Erga Omnes in International Law in the Light of Recent Developments' 23 Polish Yearbook of International Law (1997–1998), p.87; G. Danilenko, 'International *Jus cogens*: Issues of Law-Making' 2 (1) European Journal of International Law (1991), p.42; A. D'Amato, 'It's a Bird, It's a Plane, It's *Jus cogens*' 6 Connecticut Journal of International Law (1990), p.1 AJJ de Hoog, 'The Relationship between *Jus cogens*, Obligations Erga Omnes and International Crimes: Peremptory Norms in Perspective' 42 Österreichische Zeitschrift für öffentliches Recht und Völkerrecht (1991), p.183; E de Wet,

do not plan to stress these notions of the responsibility of the prosecutors of the ICC, since the more imperative objections to the rules and influence of utipolitianism are at another level, as previously discussed. In short, there are several ways of establishing and initiating cases against violators of the system of international criminal justice.[128] The prosecutor may be said to be indifferent concerning several alternatives that belong to the system of international criminal justice; however the prosecutor of the ICC is never permitted to allow the unlawful and brutal system of utipolitianism to use the cardinal measures of the system of international criminal justice against the rights of victims. The cardinal measures of the system of international criminal justice include, issuing arrest warrants, establishing prosecution, and calling for the international criminal responsibility of those who have committed crimes against humanity, war crimes, aggression, torture, apartheid, and genocide. This is how we come to have a small amount of respect for the principle of moral substance in the Statute of the International Criminal Court and violate the international peremptory criminal law.[129]

'*Jus cogens* and Obligations Erga Omnes' in de Wet, E and J. Vidmar (eds.), Hierarchy in International Law: The Place of Human Rights (2012); P Dupuy, 'Some Reflections on Contemporary International Law and the Appeal to Universal Values: a Response to Marti Koskenniemi' 16 European Journal of International Law (2005), p.131; C. Focarelli, 'Promotional *Jus cogens*: A Critical Appraisal of *Jus cogen*s' Legal Effects' 77 Nordic Journal of International Law (2008), p.429; Glennon, MJ 'De l'Absurdité du Droit Impératif (*Jus cogens*)' 110 Revue Générale de Droit International Public (2006), p.529; Robledo Gómez, A El Ius Cogens Internacional (Estudio Histórico Crítico) (1982); Gómez, A. Robledo 'Le *Jus cogens* International: Sa Genése, sa Nature, ses Fonctions' 9 Recueil des Cours de l'Académie de Droit International de la Haye (1982), p.172; L. Hannikainen, Peremptory Norms (*Jus Cogens*) in International Law: Historical Development, Criteria, Present Status (1988); M.W. Janis, 'The Nature of *Jus cogens*' 3 Connecticut Journal of International Law (1988), p.359; A. Kawasaki 'A Brief Note on the Legal Effects of *Jus cogens* in International Law in International Law' 34 Hitotsubashi Journal of Law and Politics (2006), p.27; A.J.J. de Hoog, 'The Relationship between *Jus cogens*, Obligations *Erga Omnes* and International Crimes: Peremptory Norms in Perspective' 42 Österreichische Zeitschrift für öffentliches Recht und Völkerrecht (1991), p.18; M. Byers, 'Conceptualising the Relationship Between *Jus cogens* and *Erga Omnes* Rules' 66 Nordic Journal of International Law (1997), p.211; A. Cassese, 'For an Enhanced Role of *Jus cogens*' in A. Cassese (ed.), Realizing Utopia (2012); C. Chinkin, '*Jus cogens*, Article 103 of the UN Charter and other Hierarchical Techniques of Conflict Solution' Finnish Yearbook of International Law (2008), p.63.

[128] Id.

[129] Id.

2. Privatisation of International Criminal Justice

In establishing criteria to distinguish between criminals, it might be assumed that there is a different standard of international criminal justice, which may be called private or public international criminal justice. One form of justice is that the prosecutor's office prefers to treat cases as ordered by the masters of the court above, which reduces the risk of them losing their jobs. The other is the system of international criminal justice, which provides impunity. This means that there is a difference between concepts of impunity that have been influenced and ordered by utipolitianism and the corresponding rules of the same system that only target those that are not on the same platform of utipolitianism. This means that the idea of utipolitianism in the system of the United Nations Security Council has been influenced significantly and has been effective, meaning that the decisions of the office of the prosecutor of the ICC have to be as well. In comparing alternatives, we ascertain that all degrees and levels of accountability solely belong to the utipolitianist governments. This conception of cardinal utipolitianism causes immeasurable suffering and difficulties concerning the imposition of international criminal responsibility on individuals, groups, organisations, and governments. As a result, we avoid pursuing the question of accountability in favour of granting impunity.

On the one hand, this procedure of impunity not only increases the number of victims of international crimes, as we have seen in Palestine, it also leads to discrimination. On the other hand, granting impunity would mean that we are experiencing more discrimination, which brings unsatisfactory results to the international legal system, and the entire international criminal system becomes more arbitrary and less objective. We should not forget the fact that the system of international criminal justice has many provisions of international human rights in its constitution and was established to protect the rights of the victims of gross violations. In other words, the system has the merits of reconciliation, reparation, understanding, compromise, and full respect for the rights of the victims.

However, the way in which the theory of utipolitianism imposes and monopolise the ethical assumptions contained in the body of international criminal justice and human rights makes the theory of justice very fragile, and the theory of good and pure justice is continually replaced with the theory of bad justice. This indicates that the concept of a correct and sufficient ethical philosophy has disappeared. Consequently, it can be shown that if a serious or massive international crime like genocide is committed, no measures can be taken against criminals because of the existence of utipolitianism—an influential theory in the system of international criminal justice. Of course, the office of the prosecutor may be active and effective if a procedure of deliberation and reconciliation has been ordered by the utipolitianist governments. However, such movements are rarely seen unless they are independent of utipolitianist governments.

However, the prosecutor of the ICC may also take other measures if the involvement theory or request for arrest warrant is in play. A clear example of this was when an arrest warrant was issued for Putin with the support of utipolitianist governments, including the United States, Britain, and France.[130] *All the provisions of international criminal justice support equal maximum utility for every provision of international criminal law and encourage its implementation. This means that there is a significant difference between the various applications of the same international rules at different times, depending on who is going to be identified as a criminal. The rules of international criminal justice, which have been identified as being invalid by the utipolitianist governments, are now used by the utipolitianist theory to determine the concept of wellbeing of the system of international human rights because they support the destruction of other nations with the hope that they can then monopolise their power and seize their natural resources.*

All this indicates that the ordinary notion of international criminal rules appears to allow for variations in the sense that a different interpretation of the concept of international criminal justice is expressed by powertionist governments that satisfies their theory of the utility of the system by all means under their political diplomacy. This explains how the theory of *zero-one law indicating no right* is implemented with the intention of monopolising the commission of international crimes by the utipolitianist governments under their own calculated values. This situation implies that there are people who believe that the international public is unintelligent and cannot understand the differences in policies and variations of international criminal justice. In short, powertionist governments enforce utipolitianist theory with the intention of guiding the prosecutor of the ICC in their own direction.

We must now see and examine the question of international criminal justice from the point of view of multilateralism and consider whether the

---

[130] "Pre-Trial Chamber II considered, based on the Prosecution's applications of 22 February 2023, that there are reasonable grounds to believe that each suspect bears responsibility for the war crime of unlawful deportation of population and that of unlawful transfer of population from occupied areas of Ukraine to the Russian Federation, in prejudice of Ukrainian children." https://www.icc-cpi.int/news/situation-ukraine-icc-judges-issue-arrest-warrants-against-vladimir-vladimirovich-putin-and.

system of international criminal justice was drafted, created, and imposed wisely. This examination is essential, since if we do not know that our system of international criminal justice is not equal and does not promote equality between the state members of the international political-legal community, then we are losing sight of the main goal behind the creation of criminal justice and its ethical values in the process of criminal jurisdiction. It is not necessary to stress the difficulties that we are facing in the process of international criminal justice and the relevant problems that have been raised since its establishment. I am referring here to the system of the International Criminal Court in The Hague and its influence on the development of fair or unrealistic justice. The subjects of the court are individuals, and these individuals are categorized using various terms such as "groups," "nations," "organisation" or "governments."

The difference between governments and other actors is that governments act under the purview of state power. This indicates that government crimes are also state crimes, even if all of the individuals, groups, or populations in the relevant state did not contribute the relevant international crimes. Overall, speaking about wisdom in relation to the conduct of different subjects of international criminal justice means that we are speaking about the reality of our actions and the borders of its definition within the norms of international criminal justice. Therefore, any ethical theory in the consideration and examination of the conduct of the subjects of international criminal courts is connected to the possible commission of criminal actions conducted under the name of the state. This indicates that we examine the question with full consideration of justice as fairness and justice as wisdom. If justice is deemed to be fair, which it frequently is based on the understanding of US governments, but it is not in practice, then the relevant government employed insufficient reasoning in the consolidation of justice into its politics.

3. Utipolitianists Against the Wisdom of Criminal Justice

If the judgments of international criminal courts or philosophical legal systems are to be recognised as fair, then fairness must first prove that justice is wise. This denotes that the basic reasoning of our arguments within our judgments has met the essential point for truth, wisdom, and authentic documents. The problem arises in the present context of the system of international criminal courts: whether they are truly objective and whether the prosecutor of the Court is acting upon the free, reasonable, and appropriate ethical institutions of conscience. The answer to this sophisticated question depends on the degree to which international legal wisdom is interpreted and how it is constructed. The system of international human rights has clarified how generous human fairness should be and what measures adequately define what conscience is and what the requirements for fairness are.

This leads to another question regarding what the definition of wisdom is and how it can be interpreted. This in turn depends on our average expectations concerning the definitions of justice, judgments, and wisdom. However, any response to this may be unsatisfactory. *The relevance of judgment and its reasonableness may determine the definition of wisdom. Although we may adjust the prospects of norms in the system of justice, they are still artificial and do not meet the requirements of wisdom. Our personal intervention may create more disadvantages than advantages in the system and the fact that wisdom may not be seen. The reason for this is that our personal interventions may present artificial facts and synthetic veracity. We should not forget that the requirements of wisdom, justice, and judgment are very simple. There exists only one true truth—one that lacks any obsequiousness or flattery. This means true texts and indices must be good in nature, and a conscience should be free of personal wills and desires that mirror the true substance of wisdom—free of the wills of unwise and wise men. But it should only be a wise truth.*[131]

If we suppose that the size of wisdom and 'justice' is variable, then we should view them in conjunction with a sophisticated form the term justice and its profound need for the expression of 'wisdom,' which in turn could prevent excessive harm to the rights of the victims. This is especially essential when pure norms of justice prefer wise interpretations of their substance, which are sufficiently promoted by the norms of objectivity and outweigh any wrongdoing on the part of those tasked with finding the truth. This may prove that the notion of true impartiality supports a sufficiently large amount of

[131] However, as I have clarified "Radical evil or, let me say in this conjunction with the propensity to radical terror, is the situation when we give priority to our own wills and interests. We do not necessarily think we are obviously correct; we simply choose to give in to the temptation to favour our self-interest in our choice of maxims on certain occasions. This is not because of the existence of bad or evil maxims in our nature, but because we give precedence to certain matters and less attention to others. We choose between good and good and between bad and bad. In fact, our wisdom is the slave of our wills, and our wills are the one-eyed justice of the radical propensity to evil that makes evil deeds inevitable. This may be a matter of self-love and selfinterest or, if we consider international organisations like the United Nations, it is the consequence of our strong military mobility or political power." Farhad Malekian, The Mirage of International Criminal Law: Kant Metaphysics of Mens Rea (Cambridge: Cambridge Scholars Publishing, 2018), p. 87.

impartiality in the office of the prosecutor, as well as with the judges of the ICC. Thus, utipolitianist doctrine may direct the ICC to sacrifice the rights of the victims of international crimes to its own advantage. This is how the concept of vassal state has been identified historically, and now, the term "vassal" is applicable to the prosecutor of the ICC. Obviously, the utipolitianist doctrine promotes the monopolisation of the rights of others, and it seems clear that the system of international criminal justice is unable to come to any practical and useful conclusions or judgments because of the greedy desire to occupy the rights, territories, and resources of other nations.

Although the ICC might make appropriate judgments in certain cases, cases have only been brought against African leaders thus far. All Western politicians and American leaders believe they are modern-day saviours and are not involved in acts of immorality, wickedness, debauchery, evil, or sin.[132] A clear example of this is the current case of Palestine, where utipolitianists have great interest in the occupation of the rights of the victims and thus ignore the statements of the ICC. Even though we accept that the ICC has an independent international legal personality and therefore should not follow the orders of the utipolitianist governments as it concerns Gaza, its actions have proven the opposite. It is not at all independent. Thus, whether we understand the evil conduct dictated by Western wisdom or whether we should fight against the injustices of the utipolitianist theory imposed by the Security Council under the legal power of the International Criminal Court, the position of interpreting such wisdom does not change and remains unwise. Even if fighting against utipolitianism seems impossible we should not obey the orders of the utipolitianist governments in the Court. We should not leave the platform of wisdom and rest on the platform of evil humanity, malicious morality, and the injustice of great powers instead.

Any hope for simplicity within the system of utipolitianist wisdom can therefore lose its value, and the entire system of proportional justice standard of legality and morality, which is led by the classical principle of colonialism

[132] For instance "the system of torture they (the colonisers) devised … mirrored the horror of the savagery they so feared, condemned – and fictionalised … The mimesis between the savagery attributed to the Indians by the colonists and the savagery perpetuated by the colonists in the name of … civilisation. This reciprocating yet distorted mimesis has been … the colonial mirror that reflects back onto the colonists the barbarity of their own social relations, but as imputed to the savage … And what is put into discourse through the artful story telling … is the same as what they practiced on the bodies of Indians." Michael Taussing, 'Culture of Terror –Space of Death: Roger Casement's Putumayo Report and Explanation of Torutre,' in Interpretive Social Science: A Second Look, Paul Rabinow & William Sullivan, eds. PP. 241, 276-278, 245, 262 (1987). Quoted in Mark Osiel, The end of Reciprocity (2009), p.255.

and the greed of authoritarian governments concerning the exertion of their power over other nations, faces the tragedy of gun power. If, theoretically, the power of justice were mixed with the power of understanding, perception, and the sense of values of wisdom, then the theory of justice could gain peace and fairness, and the ideal of the Statute of the International Criminal Court, including the million provisions of international criminal justice, would not collapse. Following a just rational principle for the system of justice does not necessitate many international conventions or many philosophical or ethical rules for understanding the morality of justice and the rules of judgments combined and delivered with wisdom. *Justice, wisdom, peace, and judgment are four inseparable friends.* The only issue that isolates and destroys them is the greed of the authorities. This in turn brings the brutal and unjust theory of control into power, along with the hypothesis of the theory of utipolitianism, which itself is directed, empowered, and ultimately enforced by powertionist governments.

As a result of this, we are left with millions of victims, and their natural and territorial dignity is occupied by the theory of powertionism in international criminal justice as a result of monopolisation and the unlimited unlawful use of force.[133] In the end, this utipolitianist theory also blocks any intention of resorting to self-defence for the establishment of vanquished rights.[134] This also presents the moral idea in the office of the prosecutor of the ICC. There is no way to see a free and independent system of international criminal justice if justice continues to be accompanied by utipolitianist friendships.[135] These statements are entirely true and do not mislead the justice audience. Justice, as a tool of utipolitianism, has been seen throughout the entire system of civilisation, particularly after the establishment of the United Nations, which officially removed the possibility of any negotiations on the question of justice.[136] This indicates that the actions of the Court are being controlled and the Court is now a vassal subject.

---

[133] Consult Farhad Malekian, Powertionism in International Criminal Justice (Nova Sciences Publishers, 2022).

[134] Consult Farhad Malekian, 'Judging International Criminal Justice in the Occupied Territories,' 12 International Criminal Law Review (2012), pp.627-869.

[135] Id.

[136] Id.

4. Utipolitianism Subjugating the Mind of the Prosecutor

In all circumstances relating to conflicts, we should examine the very question of wisdom and see if the system of international criminal justice has met the conditions of wisdom. It is a fact that, one does not want to encounter utipolitianist theory in questions of justice and within the UN and international criminal courts, however, the fact is that in all matters of justice, the victims seek out governments that stand for justice and truth, even though such governments are being controlled by others. Obviously, if utipolitianist governments were willing to save the natural rights of man and the principles of international human rights law, they would have never created the UN Security Council.

Again, the permanent members of the Security Council realise that their existence in the Council is not wise and goes against the fundamental principles of equality for all states parties to the organisation. While operating on the assumption that they are saving generations of human beings, they kill any idea of wisdom and prioritize economic progress instead. They consider their greedy willingness at any given phase of civilisation to be sympathetic, knowing that they are right in their decisions and that wisdom will disappear from the system of international criminal justice and international human rights if they do not interfere. By this very simple, unrealistic logic, they annihilate the very sensitive and essential definitions of the notion of wisdom perception with their military force. The concept of wisdom is a vital part of the subject of morality and its significant role in preventing inhumanity under the power of guns. It is the disappearance of wisdom that brings justice under question.

The just principles of international human rights apply to what is significant for its existence or for the continuation of human civilisation. Thus, we can assume that utipolitianist theory avoids imposing very aggressive behaviour. However, the examination of UN history demonstrates the contrary. In other words, it has behoved our predecessors to keep the wisdom of law and custom under their control if they wanted to control the system of legislation, whether national or international. This has been seen and proven. Therefore, to ask what is reasonable for members of the United Nations and the states parties to the International Criminal Court in The Hague is harmful to the rights of the victims. Consequently, speaking about justice and trying to balance it with the theory of wisdom is impossible given the history of utipolitianism.

When we arrive at the conclusion that justice has lost its true meaning with reference to the commission of international crimes, such as in Gaza, it seems unfair to speak about justice for the victims with the intention of improving their circumstances with lies and the unwise presentation of resolutions in the Security Council. Of course, we can speak about justice and its wisdom by all means, as such justice does not refer to the justice of utipolitianist theories resulting from the establishment of unjust institutions. When the notion of justice is not adopted democratically, then the concept of the basic human rights of victims is powerless. This is because no one knows how to interpret the rights of victims, based on the fact that all matters of justice and the concept thereof are being controlled, and as a result, the system of the International Criminal Court fails to accommodate the rights of the victims.

This is particularly significant with reference to the fact that the prosecutor and judges of international courts may be controlled, whether due to corruption or the power of guns. This means that we cannot reach democratic decisions that serve all states parties to the Court as well as the victims. Moreover, it is obvious that the goodness of all notions of justice being equivalent to fairness and truthfulness remains doubtful. This is particularly significant concerning the knowledge of the techniques and skills of international criminal law, which require more radical truthfulness than any other subject of common justice. It is also a characteristic of a just, basic structure in the system of criminal justice, which gives it the shape of wisdom. In other words, justice is not musical orchestration, but rather the embodiment of righteousness.[137] In this respect, justice as fairness contrasts with utipolitianist theories, and actually remains at war.[138]

The just body of international human rights law can be regarded as an established road between humanity and inhumanity to carry out its fair contribution to the burden of apprehending and preserving an established, just, and practical philosophy for the sake of man, with full attention being given to preventing the influence and demand of utipolitianist theories. At the end of the day, the process of imposing the provisions of international criminal law and international criminal justice is in the control of the powertionist governments of the United Nations, i.e., the permanent members such as the United States, the United Kingdom, and France. This does not mean that the Russian and Chinese governments have no influence in the Security Council,

[137] Examine Farhad Malekian, Concreting Righteousness in International Criminal Justice (New York, Nova Sciences Publishers, 2024).

[138] Id.

however the majority of violations of the system of international criminal law have been committed under the orders of the aforementioned three governments. *The United States government is itself alone the statute of the ICC, or the gavel of justice. Although particular circumstances may be effective in the decision of this self-established monopolised court, which has an invisible character, the final words are always delivered by the United States powertionist government.* Thus, international criminal justice is under the full control of the politicians of the American governments who want to maximise the power of their government over the existing systems of international organisations.

5. Prosecutor under the Control of Utipolitianism

Indeed, the basic principles of international criminal justice do not function and have been monopolised by the invisible provisions of the United States government. This means that the utipolitianist governments of the world have a strong influence on the decisions of the International Criminal Court in The Hague, thereby making it a vassal court. This indicates that the principles of international criminal justice for the protection of humanity, victims, and peace are always controlled by the strong, immeasurable force of the utipolitianist theories of immoral humanity. Even though the use of political force forces people to obey the rules of international law, especially the basic principles of international human rights law, these rules are ignored when the interests of the utipolitianist governments are criticised. Different interests of utipolitianism confront quite different issues of international conflicts, including international criminal justice.

A clear example of this is the utipolitianist government of France and its monopolised, colonial demands in Niger. There are many other examples, including the present Egyptian government, which is a colony of the United States government in practice. All these cases draw on and limit the application of the provisions of international human rights and thus limit the establishment of international criminal justice for serious offenders of international criminal law. Our intention is obviously not to limit the scope of various systems of international law, but rather to draw attention to the fact that the original position of the philosophy of international criminal justice does not work, and that the theory of attribution of criminality is a business within the system of criminal jurisdiction, and particularly in the office of the prosecutor of the ICC.

This means that the previously accepted legal and moral duties are not upheld, and therefore speaking about truthful international criminal justice under the present provisions of the United Nations Charter is a false truth. The problem lies with agreeing over time with the hopes of having a true institutionalised system of justice that does not treat all individuals or governments justly when it comes to serious breaches of international criminal obligations. Consequently, what seems fair to the powertionist governments is completely unfair to international legal legislation and causes harm to the original position of international criminal justice.

The significance of the system of international criminal justice should naturally be based on its objectivity and not its misinterpreted provisions under the theory of utipolitianism. While all states parties fully understand the reality of the monopolisation of the system of criminal justice, they do not seek independence from the system because they are weak and must follow the orders of the powertionist governments. This results in the failure of the system of criminal justice, which leaves states parties alone in this unjustified situation. This means that utipolitianism, as we have mentioned earlier, is found not only in the office of the prosecutor, but also in the mind of the prosecutor as well. On the other hand, the interests of the utipolitianist governments strengthen and become the vocabulary of international criminal order and the platform for international criminal jurisdiction.

The most interesting fact here is that the ICC prosecutor, Karim Khan, did not do anything about the crimes that had been committed out of fear of losing his position. This indicates that he has little faith in justice and that he has failed to uphold the oath that he made to protect the truth and the dignity of the system of international criminal jurisdiction, even when faced with the deaths of 45,000 Palestinians. This situation is indeed a clear reflection of the value of our conscience under the system of international criminal justice and how those who pretend to be working for the security of victims do not care for the lives of victims when their own position is threatened by the theory of utipolitianism.[139]

---

[139] The 1993 resolution of the Committee of Human Rights is the basis for the Special Rapporteur's mandate. The Special Rapporteur is tasked with fulfilling the mandate. Inter alia requires "To investigate Israel's violations of the principles and bases of international law, international humanitarian law and the Geneva Convention relative to the Protection of Civilian Persons in Time of War, of 12 August 1949, in the Palestinian territories occupied by Israel since 1967; To receive communications, to hear witnesses, and to use such modalities of procedure as he may deem necessary for his mandate; and To report, with his conclusions and recommendations, to the Commission on Human Rights at its

Although the prosecutor of the ICC knows that the court is not subordinate to the order of the powertionist governments, we have seen that the independent power of the prosecutor continues to be controlled by others in practice. The character of the ICC, which was conceived to promote fair justice and fair trials, remains governed by the indirect force of guns, and therefore, any conception of justice that can reach to the rights of the victims of massive international crimes such as the Holocaust is not implemented. This consideration may deserve further explanation because of the superfluous oath that has been expressed by the prosecutor of the ICC before the Court.

6. Massive Crimes due to the Delay of the Prosecutor

The International Criminal Court does not require or permit any oath that is based on false pretences. Even if we suppose that the oath expressed by Karim Khan was authentic, it was still missing its basic principles or ignored the fundamental requirements of justice that dictate that justice must be independent, and that the prosecutor of the ICC should not violate this significant function of the independence of the office if justice is to be maintained. The concept of independence is essential for ensuring that the principles of international criminal justice are fully understood and for promoting equality among all member and non-member state parties. It would be a serious mistake to believe that a fair and effective system of international criminal justice can operate under the authoritarian power of utipolitianism and the use of force for terroristic purposes. What the system of international criminal justice wants is eloquent, faithful sincerity to its essence, which requires the objectivity of the office of the ICC, including regarding the crimes being committed in Gaza.

Even though the prosecutor of the ICC, Karim Khan, initiated a case against the Zionist criminal government in Israel, the prosecutor has already contributed to the perpetuation of international crimes against the Palestinian population because of the silent position he has maintained through today. In order to achieve its needs and intentions, the International Criminal Court needs to react immediately to criminals in order to prevent further international crimes from being committed. In fact, it is more likely to be a positive hindrance to the commission of crimes against humanity, war crimes,

---

future sessions, until the end of the Israeli occupation of those territories." https://www.ohchr.org/en/special-procedures/sr-palestine.

aggression, and genocide. It would be a meaningless strategy of the system of international criminal justice if the prosecutor acts when serious violations have already been committed when it is possible to prevent them much earlier.

It is obvious that a humanitarian system cannot be effective because the system of international criminal justice has already been under serious attack by the perpetrators of international crimes. However, this is not a problem for international criminal justice that does not function effectively when the basic principles of the system are facing a completely savage narrative of humanitarian definitions due to the desires and interests of the paternalist-utipolitianist system. This is a system under which the paternalist theories of international criminal justice are enforced with the full intention of monopolising not only the law of the big international organisation, but also following the orders of paternalist governments. Even though the first principle of international human rights and international criminal justice is to establish equality of arms between its subjects, and such principles do not function under the utipolitianism justice system, there is a serious clash between those criminal justice norms. These are the ordinary norms accepted by the majority of states as well as the norms of international criminal justice that are controlled and dictated by the utipolitianist ideology, i.e., paternalism.

As I have discussed in another book, paternalism intends to manipulate every matter that concerns other nations, governments, or states. For these reasons, paternalism enters the system of international criminal justice not with the intention of helping its enforcement power, but the contrary. This in turn violates the principle of fair justice based on the notions of equality, objectivity, and morality. The difference between the principles of paternalism, powertionism, and utipolitianism with reference to the systems of international human rights and international criminal justice is very slight, albeit complex. *In short, powertionism in international criminal justice speaks about the co-opting of other nations' authorities and powers by powertionist states that are hungry for power.*[140] *The theory of paternalism in international criminal justice refers to the theocratic, hierocratic, and authoritative control of other nations in the world. Paternalism is the heir of the traditional colonial rules of control, and its sole intention is to direct governments with dictatorial power. Consequently, paternalism characterises control through sanctions and resolutions. However, the presence utipolitianism in international*

[140] Consult Farhad Malekian, Powertionism in International Criminal Justice (Nova Sciences Publishers, 2022).

criminal justice implies that the legal power of utility is being used to control the interpretations and orders of criminal law.

Thus, we have systematic connections between the systems of international criminal justice that are collectively against the normative international criminal justice that were drafted and established by the majority of the governments of the world for the good of all men. Thus, the three aforementioned systems have the clear intention of occupying the key elements of international criminal justice. *Of course, normative international criminal justice is less favourable for the paternalist, powertionist, and utipolitianist philosophies of justice. Rather, it normally consists of the facts that must be fulfilled, by one means or another, under the merit of its provisions. This means that the only way the international legal community can enforce normative international criminal justice is to accept the political judgment of the policies of those governments that are designed to monopolise the normative international criminal justice.*

This indicates that it is not the standard of objectivity that operates within the system of international criminal jurisdiction, but rather the standard of who-knows-how. By supporting one another's ideologies by various means, the system of international criminal justice finally begins to function, albeit crudely. As a result, the victims of heinous international crimes have the worst outcomes and the paternalist, or utipolitianist governments the best. So much so that, in the brief rough draft of some of the leading structural features of the just presentation of the system of international human rights principles, we are just circling around a chain of objections made by those three systems of modern colonialist powers. We can now see that the system of obligations in the office of the prosecutor of the international criminal court does not work. As a result, the Court is dependent to various degrees and the utipolitianist governments control what the Court is allowed or not allowed to say. Therefore, legal personality is potentially subject to the intentions of the powertionist governments. For example, this vassal court was unable to take action concerning the crimes committed by the United States in Afghanistan.

This is particularly significant when the prosecutor of the ICC or the responsible offices of any governmental or international organisation value their jobs more than their duties. The present prosecutor of the ICC adores his job, and not even the murder of over 45,000 civilians in Palestine, 78 years of dictatorship by the Zionist government, and the slow holocaust of a generation sufficed to prompt the prosecutor to act.[141] Even though he has since issued an arrest warrant for the Israeli criminal authorities, it is too late and he thus bears international criminal responsibility for his delinquency against over 45,000 civilians. When the conscience is sold, justice is killed. Although a prosecutor has a natural duty to uphold and promote further just institutions of humanity, such improvement of the notes of justice had no essential value in the heart of the prosecutor of the ICC. The requirements of international criminal justice do not work due to voluntary choices, but rather due to the original position of the conception of justice as fairness without any modification to its basic substance.

7. Blindness of the Prosecutor Regarding Utipolitianism

The problem of justice in the office of the prosecutor of the International Criminal Court is that all of the provisions of the Statute can be used to further illustrate the prioritisation of justice by the utipolitianist government. This represents the end of the freedom of prosecutors and, naturally, the subjectivity of the system of justice. One feature of the doctrine of utipolitianism in the system of the United Nations is that it restricts the extent to which the interests of certain governments of the Security Council are fulfilled. This reflects the welfare of the utipolitianist governments and the disregard of the fair value of equality, morality, and justice as a whole. This situation is not objected to, particularly when the utipolitianist government

---

[141] The report of Francesca Albanese indicates that "5. UN independent experts, scholars, and states, including South Africa before the International Court of Justice ("ICJ"), have warned that acts committed in this latest onslaught may amount to genocide. The ICJ found a plausible risk of "irreparable prejudice" to the rights of Palestinians in Gaza, a protected group under the Genocide Convention, and ordered Israel, inter alia, to "take all measures within its power" to prevent genocidal acts, prevent and punish incitement to genocide, and ensure urgent humanitarian aid. 6. In its defense, Israel has argued that its conduct complies with international humanitarian law ("IHL"). A key finding of this report is that Israel has strategically invoked the IHL framework as "humanitarian camouflage" to legitimize its genocidal violence in Gaza. 7. The context, facts and analysis presented in this report lead to the conclusion that there are reasonable grounds to believe that the threshold indicating Israel's commission of genocide is met. More broadly, they also indicate that Israel's actions have been driven by a genocidal logic integral to its settler-colonial project in Palestine, signalling a tragedy foretold." Anatomy of a Genocide: Report of the Special Rapporteur on the situation of human rights in the Palestinian territories occupied since 1967. https://www.ohchr.org/sites/default/files/documents/hrbodies/hrcouncil/sessions-regular/session55/advance-versions/a-hrc-55-73-auv.pdf (visited 03/11/2024). Footnotes omitted.

supports international crimes as humanitarian norms of equal justice and justice for the freedom of hostages.

This has been seen in the arguments of the United States, which is compliant in the severe international crimes being committed by the Zionist government with the hope of occupying the latter's sovereignty and resources in the process. Thus, the brutal American governments have ignored the British and Israeli crimes for several decades. This was explained clearly by the President of the United States government long ago: "If there was no Israel, we had to create one."[142] Furthermore, utipolitianist governments may also maintain that there are no inequalities in the system of international human rights nor its provisions. They may also assert the same reasoning in the concerning the Statute of the International Criminal Court. This means that the conduct and decisions of utipolitianists do not violate the principles of justice, and they may even be justified if the subsequent conduct in support of criminal governments, e.g., Israel, benefits them enough.

In order to further support their arguments, they may point to examples of acts of self-defence committed by Palestinian defenders and use such attacks as justification for continuing to kill Palestinians. Moreover, the ICC prosecutor supports the widespread attacks carried out by the Israeli government and ignores occupied nations' right to self-defence. If this conclusion is incorrect, then why has the prosecutor of the ICC failed to defend the right to the self-determination of an oppressed population over the course of the last year? The problem here is that the system of international criminal justice is attempting to prevent the unequal interpretation of the principles of justice, which are more competent and just methods of raising the level of security of the international population. The system of international criminal courts has only worked when African governments are on the stand, which is clear proof of the Court's vassal position within the system of international criminal law.

The self-indulgence of the aristocracy that has entered the system of the United Nations can be seen clearly by every wise man. This is particularly evident concerning how utipolitianist governments act and make decisions concerning certain significant international matters. The decision-making system is riddled with clear examples of injustices, which are not ostensible and cannot even be denied by dogs and cats. Additionally, several decades-

[142] Joe Biden clarifies ""If there was no Israel, we would have to create one" or "we would have had to create one." See also Salman Abu-Sitta, The Palestinian Nakba 1948: The Register of Depopulated Localities in Palestine (The Palestinian Return Centre, 2000); Cited in Uri Davis, "Palestine into Israel," Journal of Palestine Studies, vol. 3, no. 1 (Autumn, 1973).

worth of injustices and humiliation, imprisonment, mistreatment, torture, mass killings, and genocidal acts cannot be ignored by powertionist governments, judges of the ICJ, ICC, or its prosecutors. Otherwise we would have to believe that the prosecutor of the ICC is blind and mentally ill, which is not the case. Therefore, there must be other reasons why he stayed silent for so long. One must also say that he is being paid—which he would deny. The question then arises: What is wrong with him that he failed to act to prevent the commission of the most serious international crimes of the twenty-first century?

We need not consider whether these contentions are true or not. It is important to note that, contrary to what one might have asserted, victims are not permitted to suffer under the present system of international human rights law. Additionally, priority must be given to providing fair justice for all victims and rejecting utipolitianist theory from the very beginning. It is clear that the inequalities presented in the system of the United Nations are the essential reasons why the victims suffer, and any resolution of the Security Council of the United Nations that promotes their security and independence from the power of colonialism or occupation is violated by utipolitianist governments such as those of the United States, the United Kingdom, Canada, Australia, Germany, and France.

All this means that the notion of morality has been hidden by utipolitianism in favour of the self-indulgence of aristocracies. The victims or weak nations are cut off from their rights of somebodiness and placed in a position of nobodiness.[143] As a result, no real happiness exists for them. With happiness, I do not mean to exploit the balance of pleasure over pain. This is precisely what the Israeli Zionist government does in Gaza, and its governments and soldiers feel pleasure seeing the pain of the Palestinian population, including by writing messages to the victims on hospital walls or

[143] Read Farhad Malekian, International Criminal Law, the Law of Somebodiness, the Law of Nobodiness (New York: Nova Science Publishers, 2021); Farhad Malekian, International Criminal Law: The Legal and Critical Analysis of International Crimes (2 vols. 1991); Farhad Malekian, The Monopolization of International Criminal Law in the United Nations, A Jurisprudential Approach (Stockholm: Almqvist Wiksell International, 1st ed., 1993); Farhad Malekian, Jurisprudence of International Criminal Justice (Introduction by Professor Benjamin B. Ferencz, the former Prosecutor of the Nuremberg Tribunal (Cambridge: Cambridge Scholars Publishing, 2014); Farhad Malekian, The Monopolization of International Criminal Law in the United Nations, A Jurisprudential Approach (Stockholm: Almqvist Wiksell International, 2nd ed., 1995); Farhad Malekian, Paralysing International Criminal Justice (New York: Nova Science Publishers, 2021); Farhad Malekian, Orchestrating Diversity in International Criminal Justice (New York: Nova Science Publishers, 2021).

in their houses, or by destroying their schools and hospitals.[144] That is not morality, but rather a vice that must be overcome. All this reflects utipolitianism's savage theory of monopolisation and humiliation. Combining joy and sorrow into one entity is not the way to achieve moral excellence. Happiness is a way of living in harmony with virtue, not just a state of mind.

Speaking about morality and its existence in human rights instruments does not mean that we have achieved the stage of morality or that we are competent. It has to be proven in practice. Having a piano at home does not mean that we are able to play it. We have to actually play the piano in order to prove our competency. Faith in justice, the conscience of the prosecutor, and the oath to carry out his duties mean nothing if he is not capable of upholding them in practice; otherwise, he is the vassal of the utipolitianist governments. Even if he does play his piano of justice, it has lost its soft sound since his delay led to deaths of hundreds of civilians and the destruction of property and social systems. Any positive made by decision by Karim Khan from here on out does not remove him from the list of vassal subjects of the utipolitianist theory. A man who is hungry for a position and a job is not a man who can be trusted to end starvation and bring criminals under proper prosecution and punishment.

[144] Id.

Chapter 7

Utipolitianist Rejecting the Elements of Complementarity

1. Confirming Impunity by the Vassal Courts

The strain in the application of the system of international human rights law and morality should not be hindered by relying on the theory of utipolitianism—however it is. This is a very vital point in the proper application of the system of international criminal justice. The principle of fair and equal application of justice must be applied in all circumstances and should not be denied as a result of the immeasurable power of utipolitianist governments. We are led to consider what must be argued to excuse our shortcomings within international criminal justice, which in turn fails to function, even concerning the application of the principle of complementarity. This is one of the most significant complications for international criminal justice when the parties to a crime refuse to submit themselves to the jurisdiction of the ICC. Strictly speaking, the principle of complementarity is the fundamental basis of the juridical connection between the International Criminal Court in The Hague and the national courts of any states parties as it relates to the fulfilment of the principles or rules of international criminal law and justice as dictated by the Statute of the ICC.

The principle of complementarity indicates that the nature or character of the jurisdiction of the ICC is secondary to any national criminal jurisdiction. This means that the principle of complementarity of international criminal jurisdiction is saved for when the national criminal jurisdiction of a state that has access to the offenders of international crimes does not assert jurisdiction over international crimes that have been committed by its citizens. Thus, the ICC's jurisdiction has a secondary character concerning the prosecution of those who have committed international crimes such as crimes against humanity, war crimes, aggression, and genocide. In other words, the ICC can only act if the relevant states are unwilling or unable to initiate prosecution for the commission of the relevant international crimes. The infringement of this criterion and how to formulate the appropriate criminal jurisdiction by a state permits the prosecutor of the ICC to issue arrest warrants for criminals who have received impunity under their own national criminal law systems. This can occur in different ways and depends on the jurisdiction of the state of the offenders. For instance, a state may politically support the offenders.

A clear example of the complementarity principle of the ICC being an option is the case of Tony Blair, who was responsible for the deaths of millions of civilians. However, neither the British criminal courts nor the International Criminal Court could prosecute him for his serious violations of the system of international criminal justice. Both courts demonstrated their vassal positions, which means they are unable to prosecute certain leaders even if they have committed war crimes, crimes against humanity, apartheid, and genocide. In other words, both courts helped Blair receive impunity.[145]

This indicates that utipolitianist governments simply use the theory of utipolitianism to pursue their interests and escape from their international criminal responsibility. The whole theory of the moral approach to international rules should be abandoned. A similar case can be seen regarding a number of American politicians who escaped from their various international crimes by referring to and threatening the ICC. Thus, the theory of international criminal justice is chained to the daily needs of the utipolitianist governments and their plans, and the Court should never violate the systems controlling it.

Many writers hold that the fair application of the system of international criminal justice and the international criminal accountability of serious offenders of international crimes are necessary and vital to the health of the system of legal and political relations. The fact is that we have witnessed severe repercussions that suggest there is a system of criminal hierarchy as well as a centralized criminal pyramid, not only under the jurisdiction of national criminal courts, but also more seriously under the jurisdiction of the ICC. This is a pervasive hereditary feature of the system of criminal justice, which acts with several different versions of justice. Certain justice applies to ordinary criminals and may work if they are not corrupted, however other forms of justice apply to those who have killed millions through the direct contribution of their governments and have escaped criminal prosecution

[145] A clear example of this was proven in the case of British government crimes and the killing of millions. The Prime Minister, Tony Blair, simply asserted his regret by saying that he did not know George Bush's plans for murder. Later on, Queen Elisabeth II as a Knight Companion of the Garter knighted him in 2022. He became Sir Tony. Consult also Pauline Wakeham, "The Slow Violence of Settler Colonialism," Journal of Genocide Research, vol. 24, no. 3 (2022), pp. 340-346; Gregory H. Stanton, The Ten Stages of Genocide, Genocide Watch (1996).

under the system of international criminal courts. This means that the utipolitianist theory is much stronger than the Statute of the ICC, which was drafted, signed, and ratified by the majority of governments in the world.

This indicates that we are not looking to promote good to the general population nor for a positive contribution to the sorrows of the victims. Eventually, the theory of complementary principles will be more theoretical than practical. The theory was orchestrated by the Special Iraqi Tribunal against Saddam Husain by the utipolitianist governments, who artificially gave the gavel of justice to the Iraqi national criminal court, the masters and directors of which were the United States government, the CIA, and their two international jurists who were working with a CIA agent, including Professor Michael Scharf.[146] *The Iraqi Special Court was clearly a vassal Court that appeared to function independently, while in reality it was not independent and operated as a puppet vassal Court. This proves that the Court was a legislative vassal territory controlled by certain utipolitianist governments.*[147]

The Special Court was established by utipolitianists. Consequently, the vassal Court had, at the time of creation of its vassalisation, promised its masters to remain honest with them and to not take any decisions that could complicate matters for the Saddam Court or reveal the invisible vassal part of the Special Court. This is how we exercise national or international criminal traditions through the false and biased use of the complementarity principle of international criminal justice. The courts and men whose ambitions are moderated by the false propaganda, privileges, amenities of their assured criminal positions must escape from prosecution and punishment. This is how we punish others, excuse our own international crimes, and cover up crimes using the provisions of international human rights law.

2. Nullifications of International Criminal Justice

Nullification is the term used to describe utipolitianist governments' decisions and actions that hinder or try to prevent the imposition and enforcement of international human rights and international criminal justice. All arguments of justice include how to control the power of the system of international criminal

---

146 Michael Scharf, High Crimes, High Drama: An Insider's Account of the Saddam Hussein Trial, https://www.youtube.com/watch?v=QDlL9fegZHw. From Case Western Reserve University School of Law in the United States of America.

147 Farhad Malekian, 'Emasculating the Philosophy of International Criminal Justice in the Iraqi Special Tribunal,' Cornell International Law Journal, 58/5 (2005), pp.675-725.

justice and nullify any decisions made by an international criminal court. And all these descriptions are morally right for those who have the opportunity to work with the evil groups of injustice. Consequently, any belief that the system of international human rights is working properly and that politicians contribute to the general prosperity and happiness of the victims of international crimes through the wisdom of their political rules is not only the propaganda of utipolitianist governments, it is also how we ride the elephant of injustice into the jurisdiction of national and international criminal courts, even with lawyers who are guiding utipolitianist leaders. This means that there are firm and clear restrictions on the definitions of equality, justice, humanity, and criminality.

All these matters are under the control of the utipolitianist governments, who only accept money to recognise justice and only work for the satisfaction of the utipolitianist theories of the monopolisation of resources for all nations by various means and tactics. This is how their lawyers view the definitions of human rights law and continue to work to ensure the satisfaction and enforcement of political rules. A clear example of the double morality of utipolitianist governments and their corrupt policies can be seen with the case of Julian Assange and how he was accused of releasing and revealing the truth. However, this proviso is compatible with denying the principle of fair international criminal justice for victims who hope that the system of international criminal justice will one day work effectively under the principle of complementarity.

This means that our actions and decisions in the United Nations, international human rights institutions, and in the offices of international criminal courts are not consistent with the theories of justice, morality, and equality for all nations in the world. The existence of different treatments and the weak principles of justice are not enough to make an argument concerning the rights of victims. Players and victims are alike, and ultimately, they are left on the field for the next round of war. During wars and the commission of serious international crimes, the applauding audiences are Western governments who claim to have created, drafted, and ratified institutions such as European Human Rights law and the European Court. This proves that the notion of complementarity is just part of another form of utipolitianist impunity.[148]

---

[148] Farhad Malekian, 'Judging International Criminal Justice in the Occupied Territories,' 12 International Criminal Law Review (2012), pp.627-869.

Utipolitianist governments have the right to monopolise the rights of victims and continue to kill their children until they annihilate a population.[149] We are urged to limit the practical implementation of the international criminal justice system or ignore the standard of justice and accept the least favourable conditions and inequality. Thus, we empower the immoral and unjustified rights of utipolitianist governments. Therefore, any claim by the super-political powers of the Security Council concerning their attempts to eliminate these inequalities would interfere with their own utipolitianist rights, and thus, it will never happen.

As a result, there is a significant disadvantage between the rights of victims and the rights of those who have committed the worst international crimes. Therefore, speaking about the complementarity principle and its real function is truly painful. When we speak about the principle of complementarity, we are really limited in our fair presentation of criminal justice and disregard the rights of the victims. The chances given to those who commit crimes, in other words, are much better than the chances that speak up about the rights of the victims of international crimes.

Again, the practical modalities of the system of international complementarity principles are always handicapped and do not work due to the significant differences between the opportunities given to the victims and those given to utipolitianist governments. We must recognise that a wider range of more necessary replacements does not exist for the victims because of the unjustified divisions of power in the Security Council and the lies that are orchestrated by certain politicians of certain governments. As a result, we see utipolitianist governments being granted rights while the victims of international crimes are forgotten and are not granted any rights. This is known as nullification. A clear example of this is the Gaza War, which was started by the utipolitianist governments i.e., those who present truths as lies and lies as truths. Another example of the use of force and aggression by the utipolitianist governments is the case of Ukraine and the murder of half a million civilians as a result of the criminal plans of the United States government. This is a war that serves as a symphony to utipolitianist theory.

---

[149] Consult Karin Arts and Vesselin Popovski (eds.), International Criminal Accountability and the Rights of Children (Heidelberg: Springer, 2006), at 37–52 and 53–65; Farhad Malekian, 'Judging International Criminal Justice in the Occupied Territories,' 12 International Criminal Law Review (2012), pp.627-869. ; Sonja Grover, Prosecuting International Crimes and Human Rights Abuses Committed Against Children – Leading International Court Cases (2010), at 169– 279.

3. Immobile Role of Complementarity

When the power of the law is in the possession of the utipolitianist governments, the will for the imposition of the complementarity principle loses its value to a great extent, and the prosecutor of the ICC cannot initiate any prosecution against the offenders. As a result, the offenders gain impunity, and the number of victims of international crimes eventually increases. Thus, the claim that the complementarity principle encourages positive national action for prosecution and therefore promotes anti-impunity measures is not true in practice. Despite this, we do not reject the fact that international criminal ad hoc and permanent international criminal courts such as the International Criminal Tribunal for Yugoslavia, the International Criminal Tribunal for Rwanda, and the International Criminal Tribunal in The Hague have the main responsibility and right to prosecute international criminals according to the provisions.

The ICC can only impose its legal jurisdiction over the commission of international crimes if national legal systems fail to do so. In other words, in such cases, the relevant states where the crimes have been committed are given priority in taking action against the offenders, but fail to do so. Such courts may be unwilling or even genuinely unable to carry out proceedings against the offenders. The ICC is then responsible for exercising jurisdiction over the accused individuals due to the principle of complementarity. However, the reality is that the very immoral power of the theory of utipolitianist governments controls the exercise of all these arguments and gives a very strong position to this military power.[150] In other words, the offenders can go

[150] It is stated that "The controversial use of deferral and referral powers by the UNSC, exacerbated by the ASP's unnecessary political compromises, has generated allegations of lack of credibility, impartiality and independence towards a Court that many had hoped would transcend state politics. The driving force of politicizing the ICC, however, comes from states, albeit through various political fora such as the UNSC, the ASP or the AU. The ICC is a young institution trying to establish itself, and is far from enjoying universal participation and support. There is inevitable resistance from powerful non-States Parties, especially when both the United States and China, permanent members of the UNSC, share similar concerns regarding ICC jurisdiction and nationals from third states. While the outcome of this tension is still uncertain, it is essential that ICC States Parties defend the Court against claims of politicization or bias. More importantly, rather than standing up to political manipulation by the outside actors, ICC States Parties have to a certain extent become part of the problem of politicization. This cements doubts about the independence and, consequently, legitimacy of the ICC. While the legal basis of the Court has not changed since these states ratified the Statute, the political will to implement it has eroded. The way ICC States Parties handle political pressure will determine whether the Court will be perceived as a legitimate actor in its own right or just another political tool in the hands of

on vacation, even though the tears of justice continue because of the violations of its fundamental norms. This is regardless of the fact that the principle of complementarity promotes respect for the primary jurisdiction of states and promotes efficiency and effectiveness based on the fact that the states where crimes have been committed generally have the best access to evidence and witnesses.[151]

All these discussions and arguments concern the notions of mirage within the process of fair justice, the process of application, and the process of who-knows-who. For example, it would be very unrealistic to expect that Netanyahu will be arrested and prosecuted by the national criminal courts of the Israeli Zionist government for his crimes in Gaza. It is also very doubtful that he will be prosecuted under the complementarity principle. This will unfortunately remain a dream within international criminal justice. His potential arrest is subject to very hesitant jurisdiction, although we may refer to the complementary power of the ICC. This is because under the ICC terms of jurisdiction, prosecutions, and proceedings, are all influenced by alliances. Thus, even though the prosecutor of the ICC has issued an arrest warrant against Netanyahu, an arrest is highly unlikely to transpire because of the involvement of the British, French, and American governments. Therefore, the ICC is the workhorse of the utipolitianist governments and is responsible for carrying out what they want. As a result of this, Netanyahu will possibly stay on vacation for the great crimes that have been committed by the military bodies of the Zionist government under his supervision. However, as the report of Francesca Albanese clarifies:

> II. Contextualizing genocide
> A. Genocide as inherent to settler-colonialism
> 8. Genocide, as the denial of the right of a people to exist and the subsequent attempt or success in annihilating them, entails various modes of elimination. Raphael Lemkin, who coined the term "genocide," observed that genocide is "a composite of different acts of persecution or destruction," ranging from physical elimination to the "forced

---

the powerful. Civil society, on the other hand, should be the defendant of the independence of the ICC. But this depends on the integrity and professionalism of the main NGOs in this area. Have they sufficiently developed and articulated concrete recommendations on how to manage or contain the issue of politicization? Is their performance adequately professional given the seriousness of the challenge to an independent and impartial ICC?" By ZHU Dan, Who Politicizes the International Criminal Court? FICHL Policy Brief Series No. 28 (2014). file:///C:/Users/uub-b24-2014/Desktop/141012-PBS-28.pdf.

[151] Id.

disintegration" of a people's political and social institutions, culture, language, national sentiments and religion. Genocide is a process, not an act.

9. Genocidal intent and practices are integral to the ideology and processes of settlercolonialism, as the experience of Native Americans in the U.S., First Nations in Australia or Herero in Namibia illustrates. As settler-colonialism aims to acquire Indigenous land and resources, the mere existence of Indigenous peoples poses an existential threat to the settler society. Destruction and replacement of Indigenous people become therefore 'unavoidable' and take place through different methods depending on the perceived threat to the settler group. These include removal (forcible transfer, ethnic cleansing), movement restrictions (segregation, largescale carceralization), mass killings (murder, disease, starvation), assimilation (cultural erasure, child removal) and birth prevention.18 Settler-colonialism is a dynamic, structural process and a confluence of acts aimed at displacing and eliminating Indigenous groups, of which genocidal extermination/annihilation represents the peak.

B. Palestine and the context of genocide

10. Historical patterns of genocide demonstrate that persecution, discrimination and other preliminary stages prepare the ground for the annihilation stage of genocide. In Palestine, displacing and erasing the Indigenous Arab presence has been an inevitable part of the forming of Israel as a 'Jewish state.' In 1940, Joseph Weitz, head of the Jewish Colonization Department stated: "there is no room for both peoples, together in this country. The only solution is Palestine without Arabs. And there is no other way but to transfer all of them: not one village, not one tribe should be left."

11. Practices leading to the mass ethnic cleansing of Palestine's non-Jewish population occurred in 1947–1949, and again in 1967, when Israel occupied the West Bank, east Jerusalem and the Gaza Strip with mass displacement of hundreds of thousands, killings, destruction of villages and towns, looting and the denial of the right to return of expelled Palestinians.[152]

[152] Anatomy of a Genocide: Report of the Special Rapporteur on the situation of human rights in the Palestinian territories occupied since 1967, p.3, https://www.ohchr.org/sites/default/files/documents/hrbodies/hrcouncil/sessions-regular/session55/advance-versions/a-hrc-55-73-auv.pdf (visited 03/11/2024). Footnotes omitted.

However, the substance of international criminal justice doubts if there will be any resources to carry out proceedings concerning Netanyahu's Holocaust against the Palestinians. Moreover, there are many other limitations concerning the prosecution of the heads governments that are working in conjunction with utipolitianist governments and have no limits when it comes to the commission of international crimes. We are mixing the values of the fundamental elements of the system of international criminal justice with the evil intentions of the utipolitianist governments controlling the complementarity principle here. As a result, national institutions should respond effectively to international crimes, or international bodies such as the ICC should not obviate the need for trials of offenders of international crimes. In reality, many judges, lawyers, and prosecutors have submitted themselves to the needs and wishes of the utipolitianist theories of monopolisation of international crimes. Their decisions are solely based on maintaining their seats in the Court. As a result, the question of the need for major success for the national or international criminal courts becomes secondary in value.

Of course, it is expected that the principles of international criminal responsibility of the offenders of international crimes will be worked out in practice. However, this is very rare concerning offenders who are integral parts of the projects of utipolitianist governments. Thus, although the trials before the ICC are very important, the unfortunate reality is that national institutions, like the system of complementarity of the ICC, have frequently been proven powerless, incapable, or unwilling to address international crimes. This situation therefore demonstrates that the prosecutor of the ICC and the prosecutors of the national courts are under direct pressure from the utipolitianists. They are both chicken-hearted and sheepish. As a result, the most serious international crimes go unpunished, and there is no way to prevent this or put an end to impunity. Clear examples here include a number of US presidents who have been involved in the commission of international crimes under the provisions of international human rights—including Joe Biden. The principle of contemporary international crimes has been omitted, whether directly or indirectly, under his orders. It is not without reason that the current President of the United States of America has been called '*Butcher-Biden.*' Despite this, one may say that it is almost impossible to see that the Netanyahu and Gallant arrest warrants issued by the ICC prosecutor will be implemented.[153]

---

[153] See Clare Daly and her statements in the meetings of European Parliament. Consult also Rashid Khalidi, The Hundred Years' War on Palestine (New York, Metropolitan Books, 2020); Minorities at Risk Project, Chronology for Palestinians in Jordan, (2004); Patrick

4. Dismembering the Complementarity Principle

The complementarity regime of the system of international criminal justice should encourage and facilitate the compliance of the governments of different states parties concerning their primary responsibility to examine, investigate, and prosecute core international crimes such as crimes against humanity, war crimes, aggression, genocide, torture, or apartheid. It is a fact that utipolitianist governments fail to genuinely carry out proceedings or decisions that overlap with the complementarity principle. We shall not pursue these complications concerning how the system of international criminal justice has been legally, politically, and socially influenced. However, we should note that the influence of the utipolitianist governments is inconsistent with fair criminal justice and interferes with the rights of victims. In other words, although the principle of complementarity is welcomed, the barrier to promoting equal opportunities between nations and individuals has increased and there is no desire to minimise the distance between criminals and victims. Therefore, the situation raises the question as to how far the notion of equality of treatment of criminals and criminals and victims and victims is in focus.

All these matters are integral parts of the theory of international criminal justice, and we should use its ability to enforce its intentions. The relevant point is that while such claims may be made concerning the values of the principle of complementarity, the self-serving and hypocritical system of international criminal justice has become a norm itself as well as a very leading policy in the theory of utipolitianism. This means that any possible opportunity to favour the rights of victims comes down to who-knows-who. Inequalities between different subjects of international criminal justice are established in advance, such that it is least advantageous for the imposition or establishment of a fair system of international criminal justice and punishment of brutal criminals. Although we believe that the tale that the principles of complementarity fight against impunity is just from the law books and not the current established norms, I make this statement based on the fact that in the case of the most serious international crimes committed by the utipolitianist governments, criminals have been rewarded and protected by their national powers. As a result, even though we presume that the principle of complementarity is strong enough to appropriately prosecute and punish the perpetrators of international crimes, their needs and requests are rejected by

---

Wolfe, "Settler colonialism and the elimination of the native," Journal of Genocide Research, vol. 8, no. 4 (2006).

politically-strong governments. This indicates that utipolitianist governments avoid submitting accused individuals to the jurisdiction of the International Criminal Court, and, as a result, the principle of impunity is strong and motivates the offenders.[154]

Although it is a high priority of the Office of the Prosecutor to actively remind violators of their international responsibility under the Statute of the ICC to adopt and implement effective legislation corresponding to the wills and intentions of the Statute, such actions have not been seen in the office of utipolitianism.[155] On the contrary, the legislation of the utipolitianist governments has been acting contrary to the needs of the principle of complementarity, and as a result, the principle of non-punishment has been strongly influenced by the utipolitianist theory.[156] Therefore, effective investigations into, and prosecutions of, the leaders of the utipolitianist governments have not been seen, and criminals have been encouraged through public statements. This means that even though fact-finding missions and inquiries are necessary for the administration of international criminal justice, they have not been exercised. The exertion of a powerful reminder of the existence of the provisions of international criminal justice for accountability under the provisions of the Court and the interest of the international community in the punishment of the violators of international criminal justice has not been enforced. How can this situation be interpreted without emphasising that the underlying cause is the poisonous vassal position of the Court?

At no point can there be any doubt that the system of international criminal justice is working contrary to its own intentions. The primary and most elementary reason for this is the existence of utipolitianist theory, which prevents truthful relations and communication between members of the United Nations. Thus, one of the most essential reasons for the ineffectiveness of the principle of complementarity is the existence of fundamental inequality within the system of the United Nations and, most importantly, the monopolisation of the entire system by certain permanent members. If the cornerstone of a

---

[154] Benjamin B. Ferencz, 'Ending Impunity for the Crime of Aggression,' 41 Case W. Res. J (2009), pp.281-290, at 288; Matthew Parish, 'International criminal law – justice or mirage?' (2013), http:// www.transconflict.com/2013/05/international-criminal-law-justice-or-mirage-025/ (visited on 2 November 2017); William A. Schabas, Justice, 'Democracy and Impunity in Post Genocide Rwanda: Searching for Solutions to Impossible Problems,' 7 Criminal Law Forum (1996).

[155] Id.

[156] Examine also Georg Schwarzenberger, 'The Problem of an International Criminal Law,' 5 Current Legal Problems (1950).

building is placed incorrectly, then the entire building will be crooked. In other words, it does not matter how provisions of international criminal justice fulfil their mandate—whether on the basis of objective criteria or utipolitianism. Whatever happens and whatever agreement is ratified, the outcome is the same. Thus, it does not really matter if the prosecutor has an appropriate role to play in relevant international cases based on the fact that the final result is controlled, and the extent to which it is controlled depends on whose case is brought before the principle of complementarity. In other words, who knows who? This is regardless of the fact that intergovernmental organisations are also responsible for taking consistent and decisive action in preventing the commission of international crimes and punishing the perpetrators.

Which international human rights organisation, national or international, challenges bringing certain criminals under its jurisdiction when the platforms of the jurisdiction are built, directed, and applied by the utipolitianist governments? Article 17 in the ICC Statute defers to investigations and prosecutions that are carried out genuinely by a state party. Has such prosecution occurred concerning Blair, Obama, Bush, Biden, Hillary Clinton, or others? This indicates that as long as the basic foundation of international criminal justice is monopolised in the Security Council, the principle of complementarity will also be monopolised. That is why the functions of hybrid courts such as the Sierra Leone Special Court, the ICTY, and the ICTR have been more decorative rather than preventive. A clear example of this is the commission of genocide in Gaza by the brutal Israeli Zionist government without any regard for, or fear of, the practice of other *ad hoc* or permanent international criminal courts.[157] We should not ignore the fact that the intention of punishment and criminal jurisdiction is not only to hold the offenders of international crimes accountable, but also to prevent the future commission of such crimes in other parts of the globe. However, the ICC, and particularly its prosecutors, have varying degrees of independence concerning their implementation of the provisions. They essentially play a game with the Statute and hide under the desk of the prosecutor. This in turn gives the Prosecutor of the ICC the illusion that he is the one making the decisions. The fact remains that the provisions of the statute are ineffective and inapplicable

---

[157] Consult Anatomy of a Genocide - Report of the Special Rapporteur on the situation of human rights in the Palestinian territories occupied since 1967, Francesca Albanese (A/HRC/55/73) (Advance unedited version). https://www.ohchr.org/sites/default/files/documents/hrbodies/hrcouncil/sessions-regular/session55/advance-versions/a-hrc-55-73-auv.pdf (visited 03/11/2024). Footnotes omitted.

when the provisions of the internal office do not prioritise the wishes of the utipolitianist governments.

5. Utipolitianism and the Complementarity Principle

One of the significant principles of international criminal justice is the principle of efficiency. This principle is vital and significant to the entire structure of the system of justice and the imposition of the principle of complementarity. This principle of justice requires zero tolerance concerning violations of the legislation of international criminal justice. However, there is no doubt that my statement about the value of the principles of international criminal justice is incomplete and invalid because the efficiency of these principles is not practical and demands a strong policy of force behind the intentions of the principles. I shall not further complicate the essence of the principles in law and what their effects are in practice. It is sufficient to observe that suggesting that the principles of international criminal justice have priority over all other arguments and principles would be redundant. This is because whatever we suggest, it seems reasonable enough that the complementarity principles would have already been stated. In many cases, we speak about the reality of the function of the principle instead of the decorated and orchestrated norms of international criminal justice.

Millions of children have been killed and murdered by the immoral and aggressive acts of utipolitianist governments, and the function of the system of the principles of justice has been violated in the office of the ICC because of its non-preventive policy. Thus, the ranking of the principles of international criminal justice is indeed a superlative philosophy that reflects the needs of the international legal community as a whole. It identifies which measures are necessary to be dealt with in conjunction with the commission of international crimes and permanently opens the doors of justice to the professional criminals while also blocking the same door for the weaker criminals. This in turn indicates that utipolitianist powers get stronger and gain impunity. In more extreme and complex instances of crimes against humanity, war crimes, aggression, and genocide, the court and its prosecutor fail to punish criminals. As a result of this, the most obvious and visible genocide of the century is still occurring in Gaza, and the ICC has failed to act for months. Even if we suppose that the ICC has initiated investigations into Israel's international crimes, it is too late, even if they were to ultimately punish Israel.

The fact is that the ICC has committed all these crimes because of its failure to punish the crimes, and, as a result, the massacre of over 40,000 civilians has occurred. *Indeed, we are unable to find satisfactory answers to all of the crimes that have been ignored by the prosecutor of the ICC. All we know is that the hands of Karim Khan are covered with the blood from the holocaust of Palestinians, despite the fact that he has started to issue arrest warrants. He has repeatedly postponed all matters.*[158] *Exchanging information and evidence to facilitate international or national investigations for the prosecution of criminals is his duty. Regrettably, he has been colluding with his British political-legal masters and other governments.*[159] Any action he is now taking is only to save face. This means that although it is the duty of the office of the prosecutor to declare arrest warrants, the office has worked slowly and done the opposite.[160]

At the same time, the credibility of the Court is dismissed and its vassal position is exposed, and any requirement for its credibility is without any particular clear standards. Thus, the prosecutor has not acted in time and no good faith can be seen in the conduct of the whole office. In other words, utipolitianist ideology has firmly monopolised the UN as well as both the present and future conduct of the International Criminal Court in The Hague. Consequently, the system of institutions of criminal justice, whether under national legal systems or regional ones, is looking at and following the same policy of the ICC in order to obey the utipolitianist orders. This is not only dangerous for the future development of the system of international criminal justice, but it will also cause there to be more victims of international crimes. This demonstrates that international criminals will not be punished under national criminal jurisdiction.

One of the most intriguing aspects of utipolitianism is its allowance for unlimited wills and interests, specifically the use of force and threats made against prosecutors or judges of the ICC regarding the enforcement of the complementarity principle. The United States government has made threats against the Court under the political directives of certain presidents on multiple occasions. The threats have been extended to the prosecutor of the ICC and judges by some of the members of the United States government as well. While the prosecutor of the ICC has been evaluating issuing arrest

---

[158] Consult Farhad Malekian, *Hypocrisy in International Criminal Justice* (New York: Nova Science Publishers, 2025); Farhad Malekian, *International Crime of Blackboard-Barbarism* ((New York: Nova Science Publishers, 2025).

[159] Id.

[160] Id.

warrants against the Zionist government, the present threats being made by certain members of the United States government are clearly scaring him into being cautious regarding issue of arrest warrants against the leaders of one of the most brutal governments in the history of civilisation. It is not without reason that the brutal and savage criminal conduct of the occupier is similar to the conduct of the Nazi government and many other brutal governments in the world. A few more examples thereof include the British, French, American, and German governments, all of which have committed serious international crimes throughout different points in history.

When the basic structures of the systems of international human rights law and international criminal justice come under the authority of the utipolitianist governments, humanitarian protection becomes impossible, and, consequently, violations become the normal practice of the utipolitianist governments and their allies. This is how we devalue the systems of jurisdictions and empower the wills and interests of the masters of the commission of international crimes. Concerning Gaza, the Israeli government consistently defends its actions by claiming that those who speak the truth and support the principle of complementarity pose a threat to their existence. This has been a consistent practice of the Israeli government since its establishment. The practice of the Zionist government of Israel, therefore, goes against the elements of pure procedural justice. No attempt has been made by the United Nations Security Council, nor by the ICC since its establishment, to prevent those savage crimes of a government that have imprisoned a nation and occupied its sovereignty for several decades. This means that the strongest utipolitianist governments support and protect the Israeli government. This is where brutality of conduct such as the crimes committed against Jews in the Second World War and the genocide committed against Palestinians become law and utipolitianist theory trumps the moral notion of the complementarity principle.[161]

---

[161] Benjamin B. Ferencz, New Legal Foundations for Global Survival: Security Through the Security Council (Oceana Publications,1994). See also Farhad Malekian, 'Judging International Criminal Justice in the Occupied Territories,' 12 International Criminal Law Review (2012), 827–869; Farhad Malekian, Trading Virginity of International Criminal Justice (Nova Sciences Publishers, 2020); Mark J Osiel, Obeying orders: Atrocity, Military Discipline, and the Law of War (Transaction Publishers, 1999); Timothy L. H McCormack, The Law of War Crimes: National and International Approaches (Brill, 1997); Rene Provost, International Human Rights and Humanitarian Law (2002); see also Farhad Malekian, 'Judging International Criminal Justice in the Occupied Territories,' 12 International Criminal Law Review (2012), 827–869.

6. Reasons for the Failure of the Complementarity Principle

The reality is that, through the threat of the use of force, the majority of governments have been silenced and are now the slaves and subjects of utipolitianist theory. The just implementation of the systems of international human rights and international criminal justice is just a dream. Although this sort of international human rights or international criminal justice is regarded as unlawful and immoral from various points of view, it is still enforced and empowered by the power of utipolitianist governments. Therefore, regardless of the subject of the complementarity principle of the International Criminal Court, its orders to establish its jurisdiction over accused persons to pursue accountability become impossible to enforce. This introduces complexities that cannot be handled by the principles of international human rights law and criminal justice because the notion of pure procedural justice does not exist under the authority of the ICC. Simply put, when the Court is in a vassal position, the theory of complementary loses all meaning. This also indicates the fact that utipolitianists have a very strong influence over presenting the lies as truths and vice versa. Thus, establishing impartiality in a just system of international criminal justice that is based on the rules of law is practically impossible.

The reliance on pure procedural justice presuppositions that constitute the most essential need for the basic structure of international criminal jurisdiction is no longer compatible with the rights of victims, and the promotion of the rights of victims has simply become impossible to achieve through the implementation of the complementarity principle. The result is that justice, along with the outcome of a fair jurisdiction under the power of the ICC, does not work. It is crucial to ensure that those responsible for genocide are held accountable and face justice. This must be done with consideration for the rights of the victims and the need to implement international criminal justice through national courts in accordance with the principle of complementarity. The problem may be viewed in different ways and be argued by different parties involved in the commission of the crimes. However, we must not forget the fact that we cannot bargain with the principles of international criminal justice under any condition.[162]

---

[162] Farhad Malekian, Trading Virginity of International Criminal Justice (Nova Sciences Publishers, 2020); William A. Schabas, War Crimes and Human Rights: Essays on the Death Penalty, Justice and Accountability (Cameron May, 2008); Steven R. Ratner, Jason S. Abrams, and James L. Bischoff, Accountability for Human Rights Atrocities in International Law: Beyond the Nuremberg Legacy, (3rd ed., Oxford Press, 2009); Eric

The principle of complementarity has its own independent function, which the Court ought to carry out. There is no way to be released from the imperative order of the provisions of the Statute except by imposing the immoral and illegal vassal theory on the Court by utipolitianist leaders. This means employing the use of force, the threat of force, corruption methods, and, in the end, direct wars are against any notion of morality. That is why certain members of the United States government have threatened the ICC and even their family members with entering certain countries. This is the complete terrorist use of force under the theory of utipolitianism, all with the purpose of achieving certain objectives. As a result of this situation, we also encounter an individualist-to-utipolitianist theory implying that a member of a parliament illegally, immorally, and irrationally threatens the members of the ICC. Moreover, such a threat constitutes a serious violation of the provisions of international human rights and aiding, assisting, cooperating, helping, and contributing to the hiding of international crimes under parliamentary power in its nature.

It is even possible to consider whether the common sense precepts of international criminal justice are not harmed and reduced to another level of invalidity under the individualist utipolitianist approach. However, we should not forget the fact that a sufficient number of the provisions of the system of international criminal justice will not permit dependency and instead promote its full independence. The balance of legal rules is the key component of the justice system—not the orders issued by utipolitianist governments. It is thus easy to see how the various precepts of justice are significant and vital for maintaining the balance and stability of a global system. The purpose of this policy is to promote the principles of justice to serve the interests of all men and reduce the commission of crimes. The objective is to minimise the impact of the utipolitianist power within the system of justice and the hearts of the victims, who are looking forward to seeing the application of the complementarity principle.

Stover, My Neighbour, My Enemy: Justice and Community in the Aftermath of Mass Atrocity (Cambridge University Press, 2004); Benjamin B. Ferencz, New Legal Foundations for Global Survival: Security Through the Security Council (Oceana Publications,1994).

7. Obstacles to the Empowerment of Complementarity Issues

If the theory of international criminal justice wishes to reduce the commission of international crimes and bring the perpetrators of those crimes under its jurisdiction, it has to work more radically and effectively to mitigate the complementarity principle and increase the value of international criminal law within national and international criminal courts. This entails working for evidence to facilitate a national investigation as much as possible. It is crucial for states to cooperate with the ICC system in order to strengthen the international criminal justice system and uphold the credibility of the Court and its legal principles. Clear standards for international criminal justice must be upheld to prevent the imposition of utipolitianist interpretations of criminal justice. Upholding the principle of complementarity will allow the ICC to enforce its values through its norms. Otherwise, we will continue to see ineffective, visible norms that cannot be enforced.

The ICC is obligated to encourage States parties to prevent and punish the commission of international crimes. In accordance with their international peremptory *jus cogens* obligations, the ICC should direct all states parties, as well as non-parties, to comply with international legal obligations.[163] This in turn prevents impunity for the worst international crimes. However, this very essential and reasonable function of international criminal justice is to make all governments aware that punishment for international crimes is non-existent due to the actions of utipolitianist governments and only impunity remains. This implies that the victims of horrible international crimes not only suffer

[163] International law prohibits not only the killing of children but also their use as soldiers. Farhad Malekian and Kerstin Nordlöf, Confessing the International Rights of Children: The Basic documents with Analysis (Cambridge: Cambridge Scholars Publishing, 2012); Farhad Malekian and Kerstin Nordlöf,'International Legal Status of Children' in Jay S. Albanese (ed.), The Encyclopaedia of Criminology & Criminal Justice (United States: Wiley-Blackwell (5 volumes, 2013), vol. III, pp. 1173-1178; Farhad Malekian, Kerstin Nordlöf, Prohibition of Sexual Exploitation of Children Constituting Obligation Erga Omnes (Cambridge: Cambridge Scholars Publishing, 2013); Farhad Malekian, Kerstin Nordlöf, The Sovereignty of Children in Law (Cambridge: Cambridge Scholars Publishing, 2012). Examine also Farhad Malekian, Prohibition Governing Child Soldiers Constituting an Integral Part of *Jus cogens* and Obligatio Erga Omnes, XVII World Congress of the International Association of Youth and Family Judges and Magistrates, Belfast, Northern Ireland, 27 August – 2 September (2006); Farhad Malekian, 'Conundrums of *Jus cogens*: In Case Law' (Part II), No. 13 Вісник Південного регіонального центру Національної академії правових наук України, [No. 13 Journal of the South regional Center of National Academy of Legal Sciences of Ukraine] (2017), pp. 12-21; Farhad Malekian, 'Conundrums of *Jus cogens*: in International Criminal Law' (Part I), Вісник Південного регіонального центру Національної академії правових наук України [No.12 Journal of the South regional Center of National Academy of Legal Sciences of Ukraine] (2017), pp. 8-16.

due to the crimes themselves at the hands of governments, but also from the complications resulting from the interests of the powertionist governments. Given the aims of international criminal responsibility and accountability for criminals, those who commit crimes under superior orders are considered to be innocent. These criminals, such as Israeli leaders, escape the consequences of the commission of the crime of holocaust against the Palestinian nation.

The jurisprudence of millions of cases in various national and international criminal courts around the world tends to recognise such crimes as violations of all norms of international criminal law. For the purposes of our definition, those who commit international crimes call them acts of self-defence. However all these actions and interpretations are supposed to be reasonably right and in accordance with the provisions of international human rights. However, justice in the name of the complementarity principle fails and again becomes the tool of the utipolitianist theory. More importantly, the different conceptions of justice eventually die since the definition of justice is chained and the common sense precepts of justice are ignored. In a system of international law taken from the Statute of the United Nations to the systems of the International Court of Justice or International Criminal Court, the principle of utility of the interests of those relevant Western governments invalidates the real definition of criminal justice and gives priority to utipolitianist theory. The court becoming a vassal is a sign that the Western powers want the ICC to comply with their decisions internationally. Consequently, the vassal prosecutors, judges, and lawyers are the preferred children of Western aristocracies.

As long as the aims of utipolitianist governments are similar, the imposition of the principle of complementarity of jurisdiction of international criminal courts in order to fulfil what has not been fulfilled by the prosecutors or judges of national criminal courts does not function and we are left with figurative principles because of the vassal position of the courts. Thus, the duty of the ICC, which is to give different advice for the punishment of criminals under the jurisdiction of national courts, would generally be unnecessary. Accordingly, prosecuting mass crimes committed under the supervision of criminal governments reflects no movement towards the unique and unparalleled international criminal procedures under the judgments of which criminals have to be punished. The extent to which contemplated priorities should be given to national or international courts also become irrelevant.

8. Figurative Complementarity Principle

The primary requirement governing questions of international criminal justice concerns the fact that the International Criminal Court needs to systematically increase its capacity to deal with its obligations and mandate, as underlined in the Statute, due to the context of its provisions. However, the utipolitianist governments' theories and interests do not allow this significant mandate to come to fruition in the Court. As a result, any notion of training or the like becomes unnecessary and invalid. Thus, the court will not be able to carry out any effective prosecution. It seems that it may be advisable to proceed gradually and evaluate the opinions of the Assembly of States Parties. However, this also does not work. This is based on the fact that the system of international criminal courts sits in a speedy carousel which constantly fires grenades at the behest of the utipolitianist governments.

Similarly, international crimes were committed by the United States in Afghanistan for decades and many Afghans died as a result. The ICC was ultimately threatened and announced that taking on *the case was not in the interest of justice*. The threat was a serious humiliation of the system of international human rights and the rights of the victims. Again, the ICC was not capable of imposing the principle of complementarity on the criminals because they were all protected under national constitutions in some way. This is a very clear example of corruption within the system of international criminal justice under the monopolised provisions of the United Nations Charter. Due to this, states may assist each other in carrying out national proceedings concerning the commission of international crimes, which is an obstacle to the system of justice, and, therefore, the system of justice is already jeopardised by the system of the United Nations Charter.

Eventually, under the present monopolisation of the system of international criminal justice, any experience and training for the better enforcement of the legal capacity and ability of the Court have no practical effect in addressing the dilemma that has been created by the aggressive paternalist governments under the theory of utipolitianism.[164] These particular characteristics of the system of international criminal justice, the powerless position of the ICC, and the nervousness and anxiety in the heart of the present prosecutor after not being killed by criminals or condemned by his masters,

---

[164] Examine Mary Margaret Penrose, 'Lest We Fail: The Importance of Enforcement in International Criminal Law An Essay on the Nature and Immutability of Truth,' 15 (2) American University International Law Review (1999), pp. 321-394, at 349-50.

all hinder the productivity of the court. *The utipolitianist governments commit international crimes, run around with full impunity, and applaud vacations. This explains why the basic principles of human rights are continuously and seriously violated and why we are unable to demand the enforcement of the system of justice.* Additionally, the majority of Western governments are on their knees and follow the orders of powertionist governments in order to avoid being condemned. This means that there are categories of vassal subjects under the system of international criminal justice, all of which depend on the intentions of the controlling power. Even so, one can say that the European Union or certain Western governments are the vassal governments.

As a result, we generally have a number of legal systems, whether national, regional, or international, under the control of the United States or the UK. Eventually, governments that do not follow the orders of the utipolitianist governments are sanctioned, and they are always on the lookout for guns. Examples thereof include certain Latin American governments. All these events represent dangerous and unpleasantly vigorous conditions within the system of international criminal justice. As a result of this, the conditions under which the victims of grievous international crimes are permanently at risk arise. Even when the victims are forcibly displaced because of the decisions of criminals, they are still massacred because of the desire of the criminals to gradually entirely destroy their traditional sovereignty and annihilate them, as we have seen in Palestine.

This is how the system of morality works under the system of international law and how international criminal justice is ignored in order to serve the economic interests of the utipolitianist brutal governments.[165] In the end, the complementarity principle is dismembered and bargained with by one means or another without any consideration being given to the rights of the victims of the massive Holocaust. We then discuss cases and provisions to convince the international community that the criminal government of the United States of America is a strong supporter of international human rights law. This is the

[165] More or less similar questions concerning justice "may also be drafted about Cambodia, Egypt, Palestine, Syria, Yemen, Vietnam, and many other countries. Certainly, a large number of people have been killed and became homeless, because it is obviously impossible to provide a precise statistic of the killings based on the Security Council resolutions. A rapid glance at the books by Richard Falk, particularly the four volumes in The Vietnam War and International Law, implies the miserable facts of bad maxims in the practice of the permanent members of the United Nations. His books say precisely what Kant says, and he tries to prevent the universalisation of these horrible maxims." Farhad Malekian, The Mirage of International Criminal Law: Kant Metaphysics of Mens Rea (Cambridge: Cambridge Scholars Publishing, 2018), p.44.

situation facing International Criminal Justice and the ethical morality of those who are supposed to uphold peace, justice, equality and humanity as per the provisions of the United Nations Charter.[166]

[166] Examine Joseph Raz, Ethics in the Public Domain: Essays in the Morality of Law and Politics (Oxford: Oxford University Press, 1994); Joseph Raz, The Morality of Freedom (1986); P. M. S. Hacker and J. Raz, (eds.), Law, Morality and Society: Essays in Honour of H. L. A. Hart (1977); Farhad Malekian, Classical Morality in International Peremptory Criminal Law (Newcastle: Cambridge Scholars Publishing, 1st ed. 2018, 2nd ed. 2021).

Chapter 8

Utipolitianism Defeating the International Legal Personality of the ICC

1. Utipolitianism as an *Ad Hoc* Tribunal

Utipolitianism is the theory of the monopolisation of the entire power of the law, particularly international criminal law. Its aims are to conquer any decision and action of the system of the United Nations Charter, the body of international human rights treaties, and monopolize the entire international legal personality of the International Criminal Court in The Hague. However, the utipolitianist theory is not satisfied with the monopolisation of the ICC. Rather, it seeks to hold complete power over all international criminal courts that are established as *ad hoc* or temporary international criminal tribunals established by the monopolised body of the Charter of the United Nations. This indicates that all investigations carried out by international criminal tribunals have been under the complete control of certain resolutions of the Security Council which were drafted under the very strong power of utipolitianist governments. Such governments thus have influence and control over the system of international criminal justice and the judgments of the temporary tribunals.

The proper weights of justice that are assigned to these precepts of the temporary tribunals are controlled and evaluated in conjunction with a number of matters which are relevant to the interests of the utipolitianist governments. The result of such judgments therefore cannot be the same, and the judgments of the tribunals are fully under the control of the powertionist governments. This indicates that the conceptions of appropriate authentic justice depend largely on the wills of utipolitianist governments, and since they are the masters of decision-making, the notion of justice is always connected to the policies of governments that have been strong enough to monopolise the theories of peace, equality, justice, and judgments. As a result, the notion of accountability is evaluated on a case-to-case basis. This is why the Iraqi Special Tribunal was created, prosecuted, and issued judgments based on the desires of the CIA and the will and interests of the utipolitianist United States government.

The first offender prosecuted by the Tribunal, Saddam Hussein, received capital punishment and was quickly executed. The judges of the Special Tribunal for Saddam were hastily chosen from a pool of lawyers, judges, and even laymen, in order to punish the accused without delay. There were many intentions behind the establishment of this political-criminal jurisdiction. One of the most significant intentions was to monopolise oil resources controlled by the Iraqi government. All these policies were adopted using utipolitianist theory and through the occupation of the territories of Iraq.[167] This had all long been planned by the CIA. Prior to this, Saddam had been working side-by-side with CIA agents. These reasons prompted utipolitianism to plan how to conquer possession of Iraq's oil, even before the occupation of Iraq and the start of the Gulf Wars. It is also why the report of the special official rapporteur of the United Nations, Hans Blix, was rejected. The report concerned whether the Iraqi government had weapons of mass destruction in its possession, and the report showed they did not. The true result of the report of the rapporteur of the United Nations resulted in the rejection of all his statements, and consequently, the American government removed him from official duties.

The aforementioned situation indicates that utipolitianist governments do not have any limitations on their political actions, and the only thing that matters to them is achieving their final goals, even if it results in the deaths of millions, including over half a million children. This is why the utipolitianist

---

[167] The notion of morality may be at risk due to the motives of certain Security Council members. "The fact is that many resolutions of the Security Council have caused thousands and thousands of people to be killed and, similarly, millions and millions of people have become refugees. The reality, however, is that we ignore these events and do not pay particular attention to them, because we are used to believing that the Security Council is doing good and the right things. In addition, we never answer the following simple questions: Are the permanent members in the territories of Iraq or the contrary? Has the Iraqi military power destroyed the homes and installations of the United States/the United Kingdom or the contrary? Have the estimated number of 550,000 children died in the United States and the United Kingdom or Iraq because of the Security Council sanctions during the first Gulf War? Does the Iraqi government have the intention to occupy the territories of the permanent members or the contrary? Has ISIS really been created by the Iraqi government or the contrary? Were the Abu Ghraib events perpetrated against the United States Army or the contrary? Have the provisions of international criminal law been seriously violated by the government of the permanent members or by the government of Iraq? Were the questionable events of September 11 against the Muslim World or the contrary? Was the intention to occupy Iraq, Libya, Afghanistan, and Iran or was it to occupy Israel, the United Kingdom, and the United States?" Farhad Malekian, The Mirage of International Criminal Law: Kant Metaphysics of Mens Rea (Cambridge: Cambridge Scholars Publishing, 2018), p.44.

government of the United States of America has created the collective defence ideology under the North Atlantic Treaty Organisation (NATO). NATO was founded in 1949 and originally consisted of a group of three countries from Europe and North America. Its sole intention is to protect and implement the ideology of the utipolitianist governments such that they can achieve their economic, military, and political goals.

Consequently, it can be said that the foundation of international criminal justice is not free from monopolisation and is constantly under control by the masters of war, i.e., utipolitianist governments. It was for this reason that the utipolitianist American government had full control over the judgments of the Iraqi Special Court, and capital punishment was applied even though the imposition of capital punishment had long since been abolished within the system of international criminal courts.[168] One of the essential motivations for the utipolitianist governments of the United States has been to bring the entire international society and all governments of the world, including Russia and China, under their control. This is also why the ICC has never been able to bring the leaders of the United States under its jurisdiction and prosecute them for the crimes that they have committed all around the world. Although we do not reject the very established fact that one of the closest allies of the United States government has been the British criminal governments, the French governments and others have also played large parts in those crimes. The concept of utipolitianist justice is also backed by the new or vassal governments, such as those of Sweden, Denmark, Norway, Finland, and other Western countries. For example, the Norwegian government strongly supported the notorious utipolitianist leader Barack Obama and awarded him a Nobel Prize.[169] Obama is known to have committed massacres in Iraq and also ordered the destruction of several hundreds of thousands of documents detailing his crimes in the Abu Ghraib prison. Consequently, the application of capital punishment in the case of the Iraqi dictator was not done for the sake

---

168 See the preceding sections.

169 Examine also Proof Obama Lied!! The Terrifying Truth Behind Obama Chef's Disappearance, https://www.youtube.com/watch?v=0j1botxJnXw; Read the United States National Security Advisor John Bolton statements about the victims https://www.timesofisrael.com/bolton-warns-icc-not-to-go-after-israel-confirms-close-of-plos-dc-office/. Barack Obama Is A War Criminal, Harvard Political Review https://harvardpolitics.com (29 September 2021); Takudzwa Hillary Chiwanza, Barack Obama is a War Criminal Whose Crimes Against Humanity Must Be Punished, Barack Obama is a War Criminal Whose Crimes Against Humanity Must Be Punished – Janata Weekly (June 11, 2023).

of justice, but rather to conceal the injustices of utipolitianist governments by not permitting him to tell the truth in ICC proceedings.

2. Utipolitianist Seats in the ICC

The problem of international criminal justice is not really a question of who is right and who is wrong, but rather of who is closely allied with the utipolitianist government of the United States of America? When the systems of international law and international human rights institutions are governed by distinct conceptions of justice, or justice for the powerful governments and injustice for those who do not follow the order of those governments, then justice has failed. Consequently, the entire philosophy of justice has become complicated and fallen into the hands of authoritarian powertionist governments such as those of the United States, the United Kingdom, France, and Israel, among others. As a result, a different balance of power politics and different notions of international criminal justice generate various ideas concerning a balance of justice that lacks any moral legal balance at all and instead represents the philosophy of monopolisation of weaker nations with the military power of the state.

This explains why the International Criminal Court in The Hague is currently incapable of bringing utipolitianist governments under its jurisdiction, particularly the Zionist criminal government. This is also why we have repeatedly emphasized that the prosecutor of the ICC, namely Karim Khan, has several heads and several masters and plays the game of utipolitianism in the office of the ICC. This is despite the prosecutor's recent application to the judges to issue arrest warrants against the Israeli Zionist government. As a result, victims are presented as criminals, and criminals as victims. We have seen that offenders have the right to self-defence, even if they have placed the entire population of a nation under arrest or occupied a country for 78 years and counting. Under the theory of utipolitianist governments, resorting to self-defence is permitted when it targets victims of 78-years-long occupations, but resorting to the right of self-defence is not permitted for the population of occupied state. This shows the double standard of morality of the utipolitianist governments and how they utilise the established rights of victims. The fact is that the utipolitianists kill the rights of *somebodiness* of a nation and place it in the position of *nobodiness*. Above all, any military manoeuvres or acts of defence by the occupied nations are viewed as war crimes or crimes against civilisation, while the Israeli government has the right to full defence. Additionally, any resistance towards the people of the occupied land constitutes a crime, but any criminal conduct towards the offenders is viewed as exercising the right to defend their criminal conducts. That is to say violating even the system of natural law. Spooner Lysander correctly says:

> If justice be not a natural principle, it is no principle at all. If it be not a natural principle, there is no such thing as justice. If it be not a natural principle, all that men have ever said or written about it, from time immemorial, has been said and written about that which had no existence. If it be not a natural principle, all the appeals for justice that have ever been heard, and all the struggles for justice that have ever been witnessed, have been appeals and struggles for a mere fantasy, a vagary of the imagination, and not for a reality. If justice be not a natural principle, then there is no such thing as injustice; and all the crimes of which the world has been the scene, have been no crimes at all; but only simple events, like the falling of the rain, or the setting of the sun; events of which the victims had no more reason to complain than they had to complain of the running of the streams, or the growth of vegetation. If justice be not a natural principle, governments (so-called) have no more right or reason to take cognizance of it, or to pretend or profess to take cognizance of it, than they have to take cognizance, or to pretend or profess to take cognizance, of any other nonentity; and all their professions of establishing justice, or of maintaining justice, or of regarding justice, are simply the mere gibberish of fools, or the frauds of imposters. But if justice be a natural principle, then it is necessarily an immutable one; and can no more be changed—by any power inferior to that which established it—than can the law of gravitation, the laws of light, the principles of mathematics, or any other natural law or principle whatever; and all attempts or assumptions, on the part of any man or body of men—whether calling themselves governments, or by any other name—to set up their own commands, wills, pleasure, or discretion, in the place of justice, as a rule of conduct for any human being, are as much an absurdity, an usurpation, and a tyranny, as would be their attempts to set up their own commands, wills, pleasure, or discretion in the place of any and all the physical, mental, and moral laws of the universe.[170]

[170] Spooner Lysander, Natural Law; or the Science of Justice: A Treatise on Natural Law, Natural Justice, Natural Rights, Natural Liberty, and Natural Society; showing that all Legislation whatsoever is an Absurdity, a Usurpation, and a Crime. Part First. [1882], available at http://oll.libertyfund.org/titles/spooner-natural-law-or-the-science-of-justice-1882 (Accessed 2023).

The contrast between conceptions of international criminal justice and international human rights justice is no longer equivalent to the common sense norms that benefit the entire population of the world, including both Jews and Muslims. Therefore, our challenge is not determining who is first and who is last, but rather to highlight the fact that all nations are comprised of humans and not animals, and that all groups, regardless of their cultural, language, ethnical, or religious differences, are equal under universal natural law.[171] This is pure human morality. Utipolitianism should not dominate the international criminal justice system or make the Court a vassal subject of Western theocracy. That is why we insist that all states should be respected, and all governments should have the same voting rights within the United Nations. Furthermore, this is why we speak about the equal international legal personality of all states and also call for the full respect of the international legal personality of the International Criminal Court in The Hague.

However, there is unfortunately a large gap between the international legal personalities of states because of the unjust rules and norms promoted by the utipolitianist theory, and this is particularly evident concerning the quality of the international legal personality of the ICC. The deciding governments have taken the legal personality of the ICC under their control, whether by the choice of their judges, the choice of the prosecutors, or with their assistance. As a result, utipolitianist theory controls the judgments, actions, and cases in the ICC. This means that the ICC sits on a platform that is controlled by the utipolitianist governments of the United States and the United Kingdom. The ICC has been functioning in this way since its establishment. It is handicapped in its decisions regarding the crimes of the British or American governments, but it is very active in other cases, such as

[171] "The philosophy of both theoretical and religious disciplines, i.e., Christian and Islamic law, intends to reduce human mistreatment while not mistreating their own subjects. This is one of the most significant aspects of these theories that have misled or created confusion, whether intentionally or otherwise. A fact to be remembered is that both religious authorities have been mostly active when their subjects have been mistreated. Christians, for example, were demanding restitution when ISIS committed crimes against Christians, even though the entire concept of ISIS was created by westerners in order to strengthen their counter-terrorist ideologies. At the same time, they had not shown any particular sympathy to the genocide of Palestinians nor that of the Yemeni population. No Christian authority condemns the occupation of the Palestinian capital, Jerusalem. The city, without any historical doubt, belongs to both Muslims and Jews. Jerusalem's occupation using guns means the occupation of the peaceful theories of Christ through the power of military force, which Christ was predominantly against. The result of this criminal situation is that the political Zionism government is committing barbarous crimes against the population of occupied territories." Farhad Malekian, Exploitation of Christian Islamic International Criminal Justice (New York, Nova Sciences Publishers, 2024), p.31.

those involving African states. As a result, when African leaders come under the procedures of international criminal courts, they are controlled by the utipolitianist governments such as the British and Americans.

3. Corrupting the Principle of *Erga Omnes*

Without any hesitation, the international legal personality of the ICC is completely under the control of utipolitianist governments. Accordingly, the courts do not have freedom when it comes to their decisions or actions. Although we understand that the International Criminal Court is a subject of international law and has all three fundamental duties under the system of international law, they are not being carried out. The Court has the legal right to write treaties to aid in the execution of its duties. The Court also has the right to entertain diplomatic relations with any state for the promotion of justice—not to ignore justice as it does today, under the threat of use of force by the United States and its allies. Thirdly, it has both active and passive international responsibility to promote international peace and defending the rights of victims. Thus, the international legal personality of the International Criminal Court is treated under the very established principle of *erga omnes*.

Erga omnes is a Latin term and is a principle the states that rights and obligations have an international nature, apply to all subjects, and must be upheld and respected. Due to this, the legal duties of the ICC should not be derogated by the theory of utipolitianism that paralyzes the international legal capacity of the ICC. However, it does, and it prevents the ICC from functioning properly and achieving its goals. Utipolitianist theory is therefore a theory of the destruction of the value of any legal system that goes against the orders of the utipolitianist theories. The theory of utipolitianism affects and ignores the very established element of *erga omnes*, which is enforceable against any state or international organisation. This is why we speak about the ICC as an independent international legal organisation.

Based on its nature as an international legal entity, the ICC has specific mutual duties towards all states, especially concerning the Assembly of States Parties. Although this situation is between the ICC and its Assembly, it becomes even more complex when it comes to the visible and invisible aggressive theory of utipolitianism. With this, the executive and inclusive power of the ICC is extremely limited and does not even function for the victims of unjustified wars by the occupying force or its brutal criminal conduct. Even if we make a comparison between the ICC, which is an organ comprised of state representatives, with that of the ICTY and ICTR, the international legal personality of the ICC should reflect the principle of the separation of powers of utipolitianist governments concerning the accountability of criminals, but unfortunately, it does not. The utipolitianist ideology controls the Assembly of States Parties, which in turn strongly violates the principle of complementarity.

Therefore, the very valuable elements of the ICC Statute are disregarded in the orders given by certain members of the United Nations Security Council. This is one of the reasons why the prosecutor of the ICC, Karim Khan, was recommended by the British criminal utipolitianist government so he could be used to control the power of law and any prosecution and accountability under the jurisdiction of the International Criminal Court. In addition, summoning suspects and the issuance of arrest warrants are controlled by the utipolitianist governments, and the question of international criminal responsibility changes and accuses the victims, as we have seen in the case of serious, brutal international crimes committed by the Israeli Zionist government. Consequently, the question of justifying all orders issued directly by the ICC concerning aggressive criminals will never arise, and utipolitianist governments will label any course of criminal proceedings of the ICC as supranational.

Such a situation arose with *Luis Moreno Ocampo*, one of the richest men in the history of the ICC. His huge bank accounts were filled due to corruption while he was asserting that his salary at the ICC "was not enough." According to the Statute of the International Criminal Court, the Prosecutor ought to be a person of "high moral character."[172] Additionally, the Statute plainly states that "Neither the Prosecutor nor a Deputy Prosecutor shall engage in any activity which is likely to interfere with his or her prosecutorial functions or to affect confidence in his or her independence. They shall not engage in any other occupation of a professional nature." Additionally, *Fatou Bensouda*, who was the second prosecutor of the ICC, could not bring leaders of powertionist governments under the jurisdiction of the ICC, and the ICC asserted that prosecuting the killing of Afghans was not in the interest of justice. This demonstrates that both prosecutors violated the merit of the principle of *erga omnes* with reference to their oath before the Court.

This is how the utipolitianist theory controls the international legal personality of the ICC, and consequently, the Court does nothing more than

[172] See also How the Chief Prosecutor at the International Criminal Court Owns Companies in Tax Havens at https://www.legal-tools.org/doc/56cfa8/pdf/.

accept the situation based on its vassal conditions. Our moral substance is expressed practically in this way. Speaking about international legal personality is thus neither useful, nor practical when we have given the power of law to those who control the entire system of the United Nations. This reflects monopolisation beyond monopolisation. In other words, each stone of the UN is based on an array of provisions, and each provision is shifted to the theory of monopolisation by the utipolitianism powertionist governments. This is the end of the story of international human rights and international criminal justice. This has led to the destruction of the principle of *erga omnes* and the strengthening of the positions of utipolitianist governments.

4. Hallucinatory Nature of the ICC's Personality

Although the ICC should function independently because of its established international legal personality and the rights that it enjoys directly under international law as a result of its great capacity to act within the international arena, it still faces the contradiction between its validity as a subject of international law and the serious monopolisation of the power of criminal law in the Security Council. The power of monopolisation in the Charter creates another serious conflict when it comes to the question of *international peremptory criminal law*. This is a law that should not be modified by any political or ideological power. The Statute of the ICC falls under this system of peremptory international law, which means it enjoys immunity from certain conducts by international organisations or states. However, the utipolitianist theory entirely ignores the legal notion of international peremptory criminal law and promotes its own peremptory interests. As a result, the idea of the ICC as an entity possessing an objective international personality and not merely a personality recognised by the member states becomes altogether invalid.

The International Criminal Court complements the UN's functions concerning the maintenance of justice, equality, peace, and the rights of victims.[173] It establishes a collective system of criminal justice, which also concerns the collective security system of the UN Charter.[174] Moreover, it is the key component of an international legal order devoted to the rights of victims and the maintenance of impartial judgments.[175] However, despite all

---

[173] Examine T. Markus Funk, Victims' Rights and Advocacy at the International Criminal Court (2015).

[174] Id.

[175] Id.

this, the ICC's key purpose is to deal with crimes—not the desires of the utipolitianist governments. According to the Statute of the ICC and its Preamble, the Court is specifically supposed to deal with crimes that concern the international community as a whole. This means that utipolitianist theory should not have any control over the independence of the decisions or jurisdiction of the ICC. It is thus an arguable nature of international legal personality, which is *rational materiae*. Although there are a considerable number of criteria that can be used to categorise international organisation and their real functions, the ICC must be a completely independent body. The character of the ICC is different from all other organisations due to its fully independent jurisdiction that is used to prosecute those accused of committing international crimes.

Moreover, the traditional system of international law differentiates between international organisations that are working for peace and other international organisations that generally pursue economic goals. Thus, the international legal personality does not exist for commercial purposes, and, above all, its duties include preventing the commission of international crimes and prosecuting those who violate the framework of international criminal law and justice. This again emphasizes that any intervention by the utipolitianist governments, whether directly or indirectly, represents the monopolisation of the law through new forms of colonialism. Without any hesitation, the International Criminal Court's main intention is to prevent the commission of international crimes, implying that it is against any person or institution that violates its criminal provisions. That is why the Statute of the ICC, as far as it is understood, is linked to upholding international justice and, consequently, the maintenance of international peace.

The Court complements the collective security system of the United Nations with a mechanism of collective criminal justice. This also indicates that the Statute of the ICC prevents violations and that it should be a significant component of the notion of an international order established on the rule of law. The Court also empowers the accountability of individuals and strengthens individual criminal responsibility. These are some of the significant functions of the ICC that are implemented to prevent utipolitianist ideology and the monopolisation of international criminal justice. This is why one of the primary functions of the ICC is to bring superiors under its jurisdiction for prosecution and punishment. The Court also extends international criminal responsibility to heads of state or governments that have ordered the commission of certain acts with the sole intention of achieving their malicious goals. These are all indications of the power and influence of utipolitianist ideology on the legal and impartial function of international criminal justice and, in the end, monopolisation of its decisions and, if necessary, its judgments.

Despite a considerable number of provisions existing within the structure of international human rights and the United Nations Charter concerning the equal treatment of all individuals and their rights to self-defence or the struggle for self-defence, ICC policy is still hindered by many different factors, and all these factors have some visible or invisible connection with powertionist governments. That is why I have, in a separate volume, evaluated the idea of powertionism in international criminal justice and how powertionist governments use the whole mechanism of international criminal law for their own goals. With these interpretations and reinterpretations, we seek to demonstrate that, although the ICC is independent international legal body and is free to conclude international treaties for the promotion of its intentions, it is controlled by the unjust theories of powertionist governments.

Therefore, respecting treaty obligations, which is essential for the Court's integrity and its international legal personality, does not happen. The notion of a fair or just balance, which are fundamental in the relations of ICC with subjects of international criminal jurisdictions, is disregarded because of the greed of utipolitianist governments and naturally, its interests. A utipolitianist government wishes all states or entities to respect its criminal decisions and act as vassals of its authoritarian power. In other words, there are no benefits to accepting and training judges or prosecutors where the positions of both categories are under the monopolised influence of the utipolitianist theories. That is why the notion of morality is normally more a question of conscience rather than a question of legal norms. In such a situation, all the notions of righteousness lose their true character and are rendered incompetent because of the roles and rules of the utipolitianist governments. The international legal personality of the ICC thus becomes *fata morgana*.[176]

---

[176] "The heterogeneity divides those born in Europe or other parts of the world and those born in non-Western countries, particularly Africa, Iran, Iraq, Yemen, Libya, and Afghanistan. It has also created a division between rules and reality, between the United Nations Charter and the practice of the Security Council members, and between international human rights law and the rights of the politically weak nations. Entire populations of the world, especially in the Middle East, including Palestine, Iraq, and Saudi Arabia, are facing and observing a mirage of justice that can never be achieved. In other words, justice exists, but in the form of a superior fata morgana." Farhad Malekian, The Mirage of International Criminal Law: Kant Metaphysics of Mens Rea (Cambridge: Cambridge Scholars Publishing, 2018), p.173. On July 7th, 2016, Tony Blair, who was once Prime Minister of Britain, expressed regret over his failings. With "more sorrow, regret and apology and in greater measure than you can know." Stephen Castle, Iraq Report Prompts More Defensiveness Than Regret From

5. Restrictions on Freedoms of Personality

In the first stage of the requirement of justice for all, we face the fact that the idea of fair justice is under the control of those states for which authentic justice has no crucial character. However, evil and criminal conduct against the moral capacity of the rules of law and practice is the main entry into the platforms of justice. This is likely to remain true, even if we presume that the system of international criminal justice suggests that appropriate justice should actually include the identification of the violated rights of victims. However, we have seen that the international legal personality of the ICC cannot function properly in practice because the rights of victims cannot be recovered and receiving true justice is impossible due to the utipolitianist governments' limitless greed to consume the rights of victims.

If there are no restrictions on the power of the monopolisation of the rules of law, and if the principles of the United Nations permit such monopolisation without any limit, speaking about the international legal personality of the International Criminal Court is like a garden without any particular practical benefit. Thus, the precept for each interpretation of the concept of the international legal personality of the ICC and its benefit for the administration of international criminal jurisdiction according to the rules of justice and the principles of international human rights remain unclear. Of course, a conception of fair international criminal justice requires an appropriate balance of international human rights principles and their proper application. If a proper application is not fulfilled, speaking about the rights of victims is equivalent to lying about the natural rights of men and victims.

Over time, the consistent notion of the international legal personality of the International Criminal Court has been interwoven with the power of the utipolitianist governments and their demands for the maintenance or disregard of the truth. This is absolutely true. A vassal court becoming free is thus very unlikely, and if there is any freedom, it violates the system of international criminal justice. All this means that there is nothing sacred about the existing balance between the principles of international criminal justice and the nature of the request of utipolitianist interests. The only matter that is actually imperative is the wills of the utipolitianist government triumphing over the impartial intentions of the international criminal court. As a result,

---

Tony Blair (New York Times), available at http://www.nytimes.com/ 2016/07/08/world/ europe/tony-blair-chilcot-report-iraq.html?_r=0 (accessed on 18 May 2017).

utipolitianist rules become justice and then influence the judgments of the Court, thereby creating a justice of injustice.

Moreover, it is essential to keep in mind the subordinate position of the provisions of the Statute of the ICC in relation to the provisions of the United Nations. Although the ICC is a separate and independent legal entity, it is still under the control of the members of the powertionist or utipolitianist governments. As a result, victims are generally denied their international human rights, even under the legal authority of the ICC. This has been seen in the statements of the United States government addressed both to the ICC as well as to the international legal and political community as a whole. Making these threats and requiring us to follow the orders of the utipolitianist governments is a contemporary situation, as seen in the case of Palestinians' victims and the denial of their rights.

It is therefore important to identify the right direction for the system of international criminal justice and to not justify the mistreatment of the principles of justice with the immoral and unjustified rules of utipolitianist norms.[177] In particular, a distinction is usually made between the true norms of international criminal justice and the effect of the unjustified decisions of the utipolitianist governments. If this distinction were correctly recognized, then we would realise that there is a large gap between the intentions of the Rome Statute of the International Criminal Court in The Hague and those of the controlling monopolised principles of utipolitianist governments, as we have seen in the case of Gaza.

The ugly fact of a feature of the utipolitianist theory is that it conceals illegal methods as being moral and employs them to defeat and control the international legal personality of the ICC. This is the policy that the utipolitianist governments also use concerning the international legal personalities of all states that do not accept that their international legal personalities are either dependent on, or not equal to, the international legal personalities of the utipolitianist governments. Consequently, utipolitianist governments believe that the decision-making power of the ICC should be fully

---

[177] Consult Martti Koskenniemi, The Gentle Civilizer of Nations: the Rise and Fall of International Law, 1870-1960 (Cambridge University Press 2002); Martti Koskenniemi, Mónica García-Salmones Rovira, and Paolo Amorosa, *International Law and Religion*: *Historical and Contemporary Perspectives* (2017); Martti Koskenniem, The Politics of International Law (Hart, 2011); Read also views of Friedrich Nietzsche, Beyond Good and Evil (2014); Friedrich Nietzsche, On the Genealogy of Morality: A Polemic (19998); Clark, Maudemarie Nietzsche on Truth and Philosophy (1991); Farhad Malekian, Classical Morality in International Peremptory Criminal Law (Newcastle upon Tyne: Cambridge Scholars Publishing, 2018, republished 2021).

under their control, even though, per the ICC Statute, the Court should be independent concerning the prosecution and punishment of those accused of violations of the provisions of its Statute.

6. Violating the Basic Norms of Personality

The organisational construction of the ICC establishes a fully-independent international legal personality for the Court, such that it can ensure international criminal justice for the victims of international crimes. This is even evident in the preamble of the Statute.[178] Article 40 of the International Criminal Court, which again clarifies that the internal organs of the ICC—the so-called integrated organs—should be independent of all forms of utipolitianism.[179] The article states that the bodies will not be subject to instructions from governments. Although this matter is clear even in the case of the internal organs of the ICC which witness the existence of the international legal personality of the ICC, the utipolitianist theory ignores all these facts, despite the fact that the bodies are an integral part of the ICC's existence.

Moreover, even the Assembly of States Parties has no right to interfere with the decisions of the ICC. Therefore, when utipolitianist governments interfere and hinder the ICC in some way, the ICC or even the Assembly do not act concerning in cases, such as with the massacres in Afghanistan. As a result, the prosecution of serious international crimes is prevented and American criminals go on vacation. Utipolitianist governments even violate rules that cannot even be violated by the Assembly of States Parties. We should not forget the fact that the Assembly is not an integrated organ of the ICC. One of the most important duties of the Assembly's power is to adopt the recommendations of the Preparatory Commission. This means that when the utipolitianist governments impose their own political and legal sanctions

---

[178] "Determined to these ends and for the sake of present and future generations, to establish an independent permanent International Criminal Court in relationship with the United Nations system, with jurisdiction over the most serious crimes of concern to the international community as a whole."

[179] "Independence of the judges 1. The judges shall be independent in the performance of their functions. 2. Judges shall not engage in any activity which is likely to interfere with their judicial functions or to affect confidence in their independence. 3. Judges required to serve on a full-time basis at the seat of the Court shall not engage in any other occupation of a professional nature. 4. Any question regarding the application of paragraphs 2 and 3 shall be decided by an absolute majority of the judges. Where any such question concerns an individual judge, that judge shall not take part in the decision."

on ICC members and do not act against the United States, the United Kingdom, and the Israeli governments, they have directly threatened the international legal personality of the ICC and invalidated it. This is how the highest international organisation in the world deals with justice for the victims and how it swallows up the imposed aggressive force of utipolitianist theory.

The Assembly of States Parties is not included among the organs listed in Article 34 of the Statute in order to maintain the integrity of the independent decisions of the ICC. If this is the case, then how can certain members of the United States government threaten the ICC or even members of the South African government? This is one of the very serious questions relating to the criminality of those involved in the commission of various international crimes against the Palestinian population, for example. Thus, with all these actions, we are further complicating the institutional structure of the ICC. This is a particularly significant point with regard to the principle of the separation of powers, not only in the international arena, but also within the structure of international organisations. This indicates that no political power or military strength should be used to interfere in the decisions of the ICC and its judgments. Any interference is equal to violating the natural rights of man and ignoring the existence of the moral principle within the law.

Our point is utipolitianist theory has not only monopolised the system of the United Nations Charter, it has also monopolised all future events and decisions concerning violations of international criminal justice and the value of the Court. This means that committing international criminal violations of any form never constitutes a violation of international criminal justice for certain powertionist governments. As a corollary to this supranational authoritarian military and political strength, we have no way for victims to get their rights back legally, other than to fight with their own hands against the strongest weapons in the world from the criminal states of the world. With all these actions and decisions, we are failing to recognise and respect to the notion of the international legal personality of the ICC.

Certainly, adopting the principles of the utipolitianist system into the system of international criminal law and particularly into the judgments of the ICC will lead to the neglect of other matters that are very essential in the system of justice and concerning international human rights. This means that rules that should be taken into account instead lose their power and become discriminatory. We thus officially discriminate not only between criminals and between criminals, but also between states and states, which also leads to discrimination when comparing the international legal personality of one state with that of another. And if all these significant questions of international criminal law and justice are treated differently, then there is no gain in the systematic clarity of the rules of law and the function of international criminal justice as a whole. This indicates that exhibiting natural, good judgment concerning the international human rights of victims is not the correct form of application.

In order to enforce the appropriate provisions of international criminal justice and guide them in the right direction, one must step behind them and strengthen not only the requirements of the notion of morality, but also the full intention of the enforcement of the principle of complementarity. This principle calls for the establishment of an independent international criminal court with full respect for its international legal personality, thereby implying its independence. The principle of complementarity builds the foundation of the relationship between the International Criminal Court and national courts concerning the authentic application of the system of international criminal law. The International Criminal Court in The Hague has secondary jurisdiction if national courts do not prosecute the offenders for whatever reason. This indicates that the ICC can only act if the relevant states in which crimes have been committed are unwilling or unable to prosecute the crimes within their jurisdiction. Admittedly, some precepts of the system of international criminal justice appear quite necessary, and thus it is impossible to deny them. These are such things as the freedom of prosecutors or judges of the ICC concerning how they handle a case and the very important principle of establishing the rights of victims. This is particularly significant when we talk about the victims of core international crimes.

7. Utipolitianist Sanctioning Legal Personality

When the utipolitianist theory rejects the international legal personality of the International Criminal Court in some way, the victims of international crimes that have suffered massive brutal conduct carried out by the offensive acts of perpetrators have no power and, as a result, no personal values.[180] We have

---

[180] Fiona. McKay, Victim participation in proceedings before the International Criminal Court (2008), https://digitalcommons.wcl.american.edu/cgi/viewcontent.cgi?article=1027&context=hrbrief. A significant source of discord that has generated profound political, legal, and moral tensions within the Durban process relates to the atrocities committed during periods of colonial domination, including slavery and the slave trade. Western nations, which have a questionable historical record in this context, have exhibited strong opposition to addressing this issue. They have demonstrated considerable reluctance, if not outright

seen this with the Vietnam War, the Iraqi War, and the Afghan War all waged by the United States and its allies. The victims of brutal Israeli crimes are called animals.[181] This means that with the imposition of the utipolitianist theory, we not only deny the international legal personality of the ICC, but also the rights of victims of crimes against humanity, war crimes, genocide, apartheid, and aggression, among others. The fact is that the imposition of the utipolitianist theory or the theory of one-eyed justice diminishes respect for the integrity of victims and may directly put their social and international *somebodiness* into the position of *nobodiness*. However, it is significant to note that under the temporary international legal personality of the International Criminal Tribunals for the Former Yugoslavia and for Rwanda, the punishment of accused persons was not objected to by the utipolitianist governments. The reason for this was simply that the utipolitianist theory was in favour of the establishment of such tribunals, and therefore, such a condition for the rejection of their international legal personalities did not emerge. The Court belonged to them and was created thanks to the power of their resolutions in the Security Council.

Consequently, the system of international criminal justice has seen the establishment of temporary international criminal tribunals that have not opposed the interests of the utipolitianist governments—and some have even directly served the interests of such governments. For example, the powertionist government of the United States had a particular interest in the creation of the Special Tribunal for Lebanon (STL). Due to this, it supported its creation per Security Council Resolution 1757 in 2007 in response to the assassination of Rafi Hariri, who was the Prime Minister of Lebanon between 2004 and 2005. The establishment of the Tribunal and prosecution of those accused of the commission of crimes against corrupt multi-billionaires were not rejected by the utipolitianist government of the United States. This was because the minister had very good relations with the leaders of the United States criminal government, such as President George W. Bush i.e., the president who killed millions during the war in Iraq in the name of establishing international human rights. However, in reality, he used the war to seize control of oil production.

---

unpreparedness, to confront the potential legal and financial repercussions for injustices committed in the past that would now be classified as crimes against humanity under contemporary international law.

[181] See previous sub-sections. Farhad Malekian, 'Emasculating the Philosophy of International Criminal Justice in the Iraqi Special Tribunal' 38 issue 38 Cornell International Law Journal (2005).

When reporters asked Bush if the actions of the American government conformed with human rights principles he simply responded, "What is that?" The Lebanese minister also had a close relationship with Donald Henry Rumsfeld, a notorious American politician who encouraged war between Iran and Iraq. We are trying to demonstrate here that the utipolitianist government is not really against the international legal personality of any international court, if and only if the tribunal or the court is carrying out utipolitianist, military, and economic interests. This how the system of morality in criminal justice, the work of criminal justice, and the judgments of monopolised courts function. Therefore, the Special Tribunal for Lebanon, like the Iraqi Special Tribunal, served the interests of the powertionist government in a utipolitianist system of criminal courts. The intentions of both tribunals were for the full satisfaction of the utipolitianist government of the United States of America.

This position should be re-examined in the context of United Nations resolutions that apply immediately when they serve the interests of the utipolitianist government. However, similar issues are not taken into consideration when an international court, such as the International Criminal Court in The Hague, wishes to operate autonomously. The powers and wills of a utipolitianist international criminal tribunal are therefore different from those of the ICC. Thus, both characteristic courts must be under the control of the utipolitianist governments if they want to survive and be respected by governments that promote evil justice or have the gavel of injustice under their control.[182] That is why there is a difference between the process of justice for weak states and strong criminal states. This in turn means that no such courts can be established. As a result, the international legal personality of the Court in The Hague comes under question and becomes a puppet court. The situation is more serious when the judges or prosecutors of the ICC are close friends with the utipolitianist governments, as seen with the British Prosecutor and the British governments, both of whom have participated in the commission of international crimes against the Palestine population over several decades but have not been condemned by any means at any level. It would be crazy to believe that Karim Khan's nomination as prosecutor had no connection with underground British political policies.

It is interesting to note that, in the view of the Chamber of International Tribunals, it is critical for the efficiency of international investigations that the

---

[182] In certain cases, certain judges even clearly demonstrate their vassal position. This is like the South African case against Israel, in which judge Julia Sebutinde from Uganda revealed her evil personality. She has been re-elected in 2020 for her second term in the ICJ based on her sold position to the utipolitianist governments.

courts and tribunals enjoy full independence and do not depend on the orders of the aforementioned powers. This means that the notion of an independent international legal personality of the ICC is under serious question. Therefore, the crucial difference between the ICC and other international tribunals is the nature of their international legal personalities and to what extent the principle of complementarity of the ICC functions. The ongoing Gaza war indicates that the ICC does not function and is the private office of the utipolitianist governments. We are also aware of the fact that the statute empowers the prosecutor of the ICC with a very wide-ranging investigative power. In particular, issuing an arrest warrant for Netanyahu is completely within the prosccutor's legal power, but he acted very late because justice for Karin Khan comes second to keeping his position, even when thousands are being killed and a country is being destroyed.

8. Collapse of the Judgements of the Court

According to the evidence presented in the Office of the Prosecutor concerning the barbarity of the ongoing genocide in Gaza, the Prosecutor of the ICC may also be found guilty of violating the basic principles of the Statute due to his delinquency in fulfilling his legal responsibility.[183] This is because he acted very late and only acted after 50,000 civilians had been murdered. He not only helped in the commission of crimes, he also rejected the existence of the International Criminal Court and its independent international legal personality. Although the international legal community has witnessed the commission of various crimes in Gaza, they have also seen the conspiracy of all utipolitianist governments, including the prosecutor of the ICC. This situation is very unfair. It appeals to the historical and traditional idea that colonialist governments still have significant power and have not left colonialism behind and have instead changed the direction of monopolisation

[183] Consult William A. Schabas, Genocide in International Law, the Crime of Crimes (2000); William L. Hurlock, 'The International Court of Justice: Effectively Providing a Long Overdue Remedy for Ending State-Sponsored Genocide (Bosnia-Herzegovina v. Yugoslavia),' 12 American University Journal of International Law and Policy (1997); George J. Andreopoulos, (ed.), Genocide: Conceptual and Historical Dimensions (Philadelphia, 1994); Machteld Boot, Genocide, Crimes against Humanity, War Crimes: Nullum Crimen Sine Lege and the Subjective Matter of Jurisdiction of the International Criminal Court, (2002); Christopher Browning, The Path to Genocide: Essays on Launching the Final Solution, (2002); Christian P., Scherrer, Iraq: Genocide by Sanctions (2011); Richard Falk, Slouching Toward a Palestinian Holocaust, www.transnational.org/Area.../Falk Palestine Genocide.html, 20 October 2010.

of law and politics. This in turn has led to the monopolisation of countries across the globe.

Therefore, to some writers, the precept of the systems of international law in the United Nations, in the body of international human rights, and under construction of the International Criminal Court in The Hague, are not only satisfactory, but also support correct and acceptable human rights norms. It is a tragedy that a considerable number of international lawyers are slaves to the interests of the utipolitianist theory and consequently pursue their own personal interests. The marginal theory of natural morality and the notion of legality and justice as a whole depend upon the quality of the provisions and not the quantity of provisions. What an international writer contributes to the system of international law is indeed a significant question as it concerns the international legal capacity of the ICC. This is because, with the confirmation of the utipolitianist theory, we encourage many more violations under the power of monopolisation by the authoritarian powers, and we object to, and prevent any development, including the promotion of the theories of equality, justice, peace, and morality in international relations.

Our notion of achievement in the system of international legal personality, in particular in the international legal personality of the ICC, comes out of the legal and customary notion of the juridical necessity of pure, authentic, and unbiased recognition. This in turn creates many more victims of international crimes and, as a result, life-long suffering for the victims of unlawful and immoral diplomacy by the utipolitianist governments. There is no presumption that following the precepts of utipolitianist governments leads to a very unjust outcome unless the underlying political philosophy of monopolisation is changed. It is clear that without the establishment of a truly free and united international body, the international legal personality of the ICC is basically running without proper shoes. How can the international human rights system function effectively when it lacks the practical power to enforce its principles? There is no way to give appropriate weight to the precepts of international criminal justice and of the Court except by instituting and introducing the power of honesty for morality and justice—which are required by the fundamental principles of humanity, if any exist. As a corollary of the system of utipolitianism in the system of international criminal justice, utipolitianist governments have the right to challenge any legal investigation by the office of the prosecutor concerning the arrest warrant directly at the international level. However, they do not see any right for the victims of 78 years of international crimes committed by the British, American, and Israeli Zionist governments to challenge those decades of barbarity. Because of this, there never be any judgments against the most brutal criminals in the world and the extreme effect of a decision by an international court of the character of the ICC will always be in the interests of the utipolitianist governments.

There is no doubt that some institutions, in connection with the system of international legal personality of the International Criminal Court, whether restrained or unrestrained by the utipolitianist theory or solely under the control of the United Nations Security Council, may express different sentiments concerning any judgment. It is important to recognize the special significance of certain principles within the framework of international legal personality and their pivotal role in the administration of justice. However, it is crucial to emphasize that the international legal personality of any state or legal entity should not be determined by power dynamics. Rather, it should be based on established facts, highlighting that international legal personality is a reflection of our values, rather than a subject of philosophical, political, or legal debates. In this sense, the recognition of a legal entity is indicative of its worth. We do not reject the fact that colonial utipolitianist governments traditionally and historically enforce the recognition of an international legal personality in order to control the existence or non-existence of the values of a nation.

This indicates that the precept of international legal personality was drafted, created, and enforced in order to indicate which group, body, or nation can be legitimized and have some sort of legal voice, albeit with certain limitations. *In other words, the idea was to interface with the ideas of justice, freedom, equality, peace, and morality as a whole.* The overall evaluation of the many precepts of international human rights law is done through respecting all notions of legal personality, and these legal personalities are in danger when they do not coincide with the characteristic international legal personality of the ICC. Assessing the justice of the ICC promised by its statute is therefore almost impossible if its practical legal theories concerning the accountabilities of international criminals fall under the control of the utipolitianist governments. Therefore, we must note that the idea of international human rights and ethical respect for individuals has no legal value when the subject of criminal justice is chosen under the authority of the utipolitianist governments.

The primary goal of international criminal justice is to prevent the subjugation of justice to political powers, akin to the practice of vassalage. This concept highlights the subordination of legislative authority to the control of more powerful governments, ultimately securing the balance of international criminal jurisdiction in their favour. This is particularly significant when one realizes that these Western powers are organised and supported by the power of NATO's new alliances in Europe in order to control the economy, morality, justice, and the Court. Thus, the vassal position of the ICC and its prosecutor demonstrates Western countries' hegemony. It particularly indicates that the legal position of the Court collapses to the sole benefit of the utipolitianist governments. Thus, any concept of peace and decriminalisation of the conduct of utipolitianist governments and arresting and bringing the offenders before the jurisdiction of the Court becomes a dream of international criminal justice in practice.

9. Latent Characters of Utipolitianism

When a utipolitianist government succeeds in relying on its military and political impulses without losing any soldiers, it is still responsible for what has been carried out as a result of its political lies. As previously stated, the value of our international human rights and international criminal justice does not depend on the ample number of provisions, but rather on their respect and implementation when they are violated by the aggressive policies of a utipolitianist government such as the Israeli Zionist government. The efforts that the international legal and political community should make concerning the seriousness of international criminal accountability of the leaders of the utipolitianist governments depend, like so much else, on the circumstances of the political power of the majority of states because the ICC is more politicized than legalized.

Although the principles of coherent decisions in the Court rely on concepts of substantial complexity, this does not mean that the ICC prosecutors or judges should ignore the brutal criminal conduct of the superiors of criminal governments, such as those of Israel, the United States, Britain, France, Canada, Germany, and Australia. It is therefore necessary to take note of certain general facts that have contributed to the ongoing genocide in Palestine. The basic structure of the system of international criminal justice is bound to encourage and support certain kinds of motivations within the ICC that seek to uphold the rights of victims.[184]

---

[184] However, the ICC acts contrary to this principle. Generally consult Alexander Laban Hinton, "The Dark Side of Modernity: Toward an Anthropology of Genocide," in Annihilating Difference: The Anthropology of Genocide, ed. Alexander Laban Hinton (University of California Press, 2002), pp. 1-40; Lorenzo Veracini, "Settler Collective, Founding Violence and Disavowal: The Settler Colonial Situation," Journal of Intercultural Studies, vol. 29,

Recognising these positive decisions of the ICC not only becomes necessary for the establishment of the rights of the victims but also for the prevention of the creation of future victims.[185] Given the definition of appropriate principles of justice, we are often unfortunately tempted to act unjustly, whether under the purview the United Nations Charter or the ICC. Although we believe that international criminal justice will eventually prevail by one means or another, no progress has been seen concerning the punishment of serious criminals. Such offenders include Josef Stalin, Franklin Roosevelt, Winston Churchill, Ronald Reagan, George H. W. Bush, George W. Bush, Barack Obama, Hillary Clinton, Joe Biden, Antony Blinken, John F. Kirby, Lloyd Austin, Tony Blair, Boris Johnson, Rishi Sunak, and Benjamin Netanyahu, to name but a few examples.

Even though international human rights and international criminal justice are supposed to love justice, the victims have had their rights infringed upon and justified with arguments that, as H. Clinton asserted, "The others do not understand." This is how the philosophy of international criminal justice has been qualified by criminal politicians around the world. This indicates that speaking about dependency on the values of international criminal justice and the Court is actually a threat and even an insult to the definition of faith in the truth. A vassal court is not an independent court, and a considerable number of cases have demonstrated their true nature concerning certain serious international crimes and the impunity of the leaders of the utipolitianist governments. Our arguments and explanations highlight the interdependency of the judgments of the ICC and the monopolisation of the power of dependency by the theory of utipolitianism, including the recognised values in the framework of international human rights law.

The intuitive philosophy here is to prove that the utility of the system of international legal personalities of the ICC and all states of the world is considered to be the main enriching intention of criminal governments, with the reasoning that others are criminals while utipolitianists are innocent and do not steal wealth from other nations. This is a humiliating statement concerning all nations and the principles of human rights law because

---

no. 4 (2008); Mohamed Adhikari, ed., Civilian-Driven Violence and the Genocide of Indigenous Peoples in Settler Societies (London: Routledge, 2019); see also Penny Green et al., Countdown to Annhilation: Genocide in Myanmar, (London: 2015); Raphael Lemkin, Axis Rule in Occupied Europe, (The Lawbook Exchange: 2008).

[185] Id. Examine also Anatomy of a Genocide: Report of the Special Rapporteur on the situation of human rights in the Palestinian territories occupied since 1967. https://www.ohchr.org/sites/default/files/documents/hrbodies/hrcouncil/sessions-regular/session55/advance-versions/a-hrc-55-73-auv.pdf (visited 03/11/2024). Footnotes omitted.

utipolitianist theory not only controls the bodies of international law, it also acts as if other nations are unaware of the facts and the games of the utipolitianist governments.

Since utipolitianists do not state such intentions implicitly or explicitly, they continue their political and legal behaviour and act as if they were the best promoters of human rights and criminal advocates. Therefore, statements of utipolitianism do not mean we are in a healthy or normal state of legal and political understanding. Rather, many of their arguments and presentations include the notion of faculties of monopolisation and brainwashing of the norms of human rights with the exercise and influence of their powers through the very leading view that they are directing all nations to cultivate good and workable humanity. This means that they exercise a more complex diplomacy of discrimination, so that talking about any conception of good, natural order, and human rights usually decreases.

In the end, the judgments of the values of the essence of man become the only valid arguments, and the truthful arguments fail. This is because the propaganda mechanism of the arguments is derived from the utipolitianist governments. This indicates that the will of justice is being implemented under the international legal personality of the ICC. In this context, it is difficult to present true evidence, and justice remains a vessel of injustice, indicating that the victims will never be helped. Once again, justice may or may not be granted to a few victims who are not necessarily targeted by utipolitianism for political reasons.[186] These are the nature and political tactics of propaganda used by powertionist governments, such as the propaganda mechanism of the Saddam Hussein Tribunal.[187] I shall not, however, discuss this puppet tribunal here, which was also protected and supported by an American professor and a Swedish lawyer.[188]

As we have seen, the imposition of international criminal jurisdiction upon the perpetrators of international crimes is selective and does not prevent crimes nor support the victims of crimes against humanity, war crimes, aggression, and genocide. The situations in Gaza and Ukraine demonstrate that the ICC acts selectively and is controlled by the utipolitianist governments. In the latter case, the prosecutor of the ICC, Karim Khan, received clear orders

---

[186] Examine also Statement of ICC Prosecutor, Fatou Bensouda, respecting an investigation of the Situation in Palestine (3 March 2021), https://www.icc-cpi.int/news/statement-icc-prosecutor-fatou-bensouda-respecting-investigation-situation-palestine (visited 03/11/2024).

[187] Farhad Malekian, 'Emasculating the Philosophy of International Criminal Justice in the Iraqi Special Tribunal,' Cornell International Law Journal, 58/5 (2005).

[188] Hans Corell and Michael Scharf.

from his British and American masters. He soon issued arrest warrants for the Russian leaders. Nonetheless, the fact is that the utipolitianist government of the United States is clearly the main instigator behind the killing of the innocent Ukrainian population due to the continuation of an American policy drafted in 1952 that seeks to keep Nazism alive and destroy Russia.

However, over seven decades of genocide, and now over nine months of genocide against two million people in Gaza, have not been enough to prompt arrest warrants to be issued against Israeli leaders since the Zionist government is protected by utipolitianist governments. Thus, the nature of utipolitianism is responsible for all crimes against the Gaza population. *That means that no equilibrium is reached concerning international criminal justice for all parties. In other words, when justice is sold and chained, the rights of victims are banished. Accepting that the utipolitianist theory is correct and necessary concerning the control of international legal personalities of the United Nations and International Criminal Court means that no United Nations or Court exist. A rational international criminal justice system should be constrained by the basic philosophy of respecting the rights of all nations without any influence of the utipolitianist theory in order for justice to flourish, to establish the rights of victims, and victims of any action nation should return to their traditional sovereignty. This must be the key element of rational justice.*

10. Authentic Challenges Against Utipolitianists

The precepts of international criminal justice may be objected to by the preceding account of case-by-case decisions made separately and the influence of utipolitianist governments on the idea of what constitutes international criminal violations. Any reply to the views of utipolitianism is therefore met with strong objections from utipolitianist governments as well as the rejection of any views that contradict their privatisation of values. When utipolitianists object to any view concerning the punishment of violators of international criminal law, they respond with the language of guns rather than the wisdom of punishment. The Gaza case is a clear example of this. The concept of international legal personality encourages regulated rules of international criminal law imbued with norms, regulations, principles, elements, and the rule of law. These reflect the ideal scheme for how the system of international law should function in order to examine international crimes under a microscope. This indicates that the system of international criminal law should be free from all ties and be organised to realise justice independently of any said ties.

The international legal personality of the International Criminal Court serves to illustrate the content of those significant principles and demonstrates the authentic imposition of justice at the international level. The intention is to satisfy the conceptions of justice promised in the Charter of the United Nations or the Statute of the ICC itself. If the existing conditions imposed by utipolitianism are not short of the ideal assumptions of the notion of independent international criminal justice, then any idea of appropriate criminal jurisdiction can be rejected. We must then ask: What is unjust, and what is actually just? Moreover, the systems of international human rights and international criminal justice are in a better position with the notion of the international legal personality of the ICC once it is respected. This is the most vital part of the system of international legal personality, and without respect, no law in force remains in force except for symbolic law.

Therefore, assessing how serious the existing imperfections of the system of international criminal justice and human rights are is essential to understanding the shortcomings of the essence of justice and its threat to the vanished rights of the victims. Moreover, the way in which the rights of victims are exploited and demonised by the utipolitianist governments reflects the imperfect legacy of international criminal justice under the power of the ICC. A clear example of this, as previously mentioned, is the situation in Gaza, where the civilian population continues to be targeted by the weapons of powertionist governments. Thus, any precepts of good and justice are violated because the utipolitianist governments are the masters of controlling justice and, therefore, the key elements of international criminal justice are no longer efficient. Nevertheless, as we have just seen in the Statute of the ICC, justice exists solely within the framework of the Statute and not in practice. This reflects the full monopolisation of the element of international legal personality and of the International Criminal Court.

The entire system of international criminal jurisdiction is therefore composed of controlling orders, and it remains to be seen in the future contribution of the lexicon of international criminal courts and its procedures if its shortcomings will be addressed. We must not forget the fact that it is the principle of the efficiency of the terms in the framework of the statute that has not been nullified. Otherwise, all forms of the evil notion of justice would be fulfilled. The fact is that the exploitation of the principle of international legal personality will continue for as long as justice is the monopolised power of the utipolitianist governments. It implies a deep injustice in the background systems of international human rights and international criminal justice as a whole. This means that justice has little to do with the inefficiencies of international criminal courts, based on the obvious fact that the ineffectiveness of criminal justice is essentially cultivated from the incompetence and unlawful position of the Security Council of the United Nations in the international legal and political community.[189]

This mainly concerns the permanent members of the Council, including the old colonial powers such as the British and French governments, as well as governments that were supported by the same colonial terrorists and brutal colonial powers such as the United States government. The US has essentially represented a continuation of British barbarism and authoritarianism. Consequently, the American government has become the first criminal terrorist government in the world, surpassing the immoral attitudes of barbaric states such as the British, which they believe to be civilised, while also believing that most other states are underdeveloped, uncivilised or barbaric. These states comprise the so-called "third world." It is therefore not surprising how the system of international criminal justice is interpreted and hindered by the same old colonial states. This is how the notion of inappropriate justice as fairness is interpreted as fair justice and how its inevitable deviations from other principles of justice are seen. Indeed, one cannot see any legal weight in the arguments presented by utipolitianism, only immoral precision. This is particularly worrisome when it comes to the field of interests of the utipolitianist governments.

It is more imperative that the system of monopolisation in the Security Council ends and gives way to the principle of equality of voting and the disappearance of the occupation of the United Nations against a background of fair equality of voice, proper equal international legal personality, and an

---

[189] Generally see Orakhelashvili Alexander, 'The Impact of Peremptory Norms on the Interpretation and Application of United Nations Security Council Resolutions' 16 (1), The European Journal of International Law (2005), pp. 59-88; In all situations, certain permanent members of the Security Council are always protected. According to one view, "The risk of political abuse would nonetheless exist in the sense that proceedings of this nature will most likely only be instituted against less powerful states. For example, it is not very likely that a permanent member of the Security Council would face civil claims in foreign courts for damages resulting from the violation of *jus cogens* norms." Erika de Wet, 'The Prohibition of Torture as an International Norm of *jus cogens* and Its Implications for National and Customary Law,' 15 (1) European Journal of International Law (2004), pp.97-121, at 110. Consult also report of Francesca Albanese: Anatomy of a Genocide: Report of the Special Rapporteur on the situation of human rights in the Palestinian territories occupied since 1967. https://www.ohchr.org/sites/default/files/documents/hrbodies/hrcouncil/sessions-regular/session55/advance-versions/a-hrc-55-73-auv.pdf (visited 03/11/2024).

end to private purposes of utipolitianism. A basic prerequisite for this is the complete abolition of unequal justice in the Council. Thus, if the rules of the United Nations are reasonably authentic and promote equality for all states, i.e., their international legal personalities, the notion of pure procedural international criminal justice will emerge in the basic structure of the International Criminal Court in The Hague, indicating that all states, strong or weak, should follow. This seems more reasonable and logical than any other traditional morals that are imposed by paternalistic governments. It is explicitly framed to coordinate the will and interests of all nations in the world, as well as to prevent brutality against weaker nations through the imposition of sanctions and the use of guns. This is what we call a multitude of possible criteria within one coherent system of international human rights law and international criminal justice with an effective, functioning concept of equality and a sincere interest in promoting, recognising, and protecting justice from violations. No further philosophical or ethical explanation is needed if we organise humanity on the basis of proper authentic wisdom.

Chapter 9

Conclusion

Utipolitianism is the notion of using politics as a tool of justice in the system of international criminal law, particularly under the jurisdiction of the International Criminal Court in The Hague. Utipolitianism simply implies the character of monopolisation. It shows how the states parties to the United Nations should respect the will and interests of certain big powertionist governments with regard to their decisions. Utipolitianists therefore conceal their intention to impose justice with one-eyed justice on any state that does not obey their military, political, or economic demands. I shall not attempt to enumerate here all the ways in which the process of the imposition of utipolitianism is perpetuated in the system of international law, since I have already explained it earlier to some extent. One can list a number of methods that utipolitianist governments employ in order to impose their will and interests. In short, a number of intentional and deliberate lies and mistakes are presented in the content and lexicon of international politics, and then they are slowly and gradually incorporated and introduced as normal provisions of international law, human rights, and international criminal justice.

When this evil intention of monopolisation, i.e., the system of legislation of humanity, is achieved, then the utipolitianist governments adopt new theories of leadership. Due to various political intrigues, their humanitarian legislative claims may be developed, modified, and imposed again. In the end, if human rights claims are not effective or if resorting to the threat and use of armed forces against an object does not have the desired outcomes, then the requirements of the utipolitianist government are enforced by resorting to intensive military attacks in the name of self-defence. Utipolitianist governments speak about the imposition of international human rights, and it is interesting to see how international human rights are imposed under the superior orders of these governments. As a result, the term "human rights" is used as a tool of justice in utipolitianist theory, and thereby imposes its malicious interests on the suffering victims.

Utipolitianist theory may therefore be defined as a theory that is presented in the context of the implementation of international human rights and international criminal justice with the full intention of convincing the majority of governments that the provisions of international human rights are being violated by particular nations or states. Consequently, utipolitianist governments use this as a justification to compel the relevant violators to comply with their policies and interpretations.[190] This indicates that the system of international criminal justice faces a new power that is above the law and all regulations and provisions of international law-making treaties. As a result of the actions and deductions made by utipolitianist governments, the objects under their control are constrained by various means and forced to adhere to interpretations that contradict the entire system of international human rights law. These actions violate the fundamental principles for recognising and identifying international crimes.

Moreover, the subjects of enforcement measures by the utipolitianist governments are unable to adopt an alternative method for establishing their rights. Such a situation ultimately forces the subjects under economic, military, or political attacks by the utipolitianist governments to resort to self-defence. However, this is not welcomed by the powertionist governments that are willing to control the relevant subject through the use of force. As a result, the relevant subject can only free themselves from the consequences of the use of force or occupation by taking up arms themselves. A clear example of this is the situation faced by the Palestinians who have been living under occupation for over seven decades and have been the target of international crimes such as crimes against humanity, war crimes, aggression, torture, apartheid, and genocide.

I have examined these aspects in my other works and have expressed that utipolitianist theory is the theory of rejecting all other human civilisations and their *somebodiness*, thereby putting them in the position of *nobodiness*, and ultimately monopolising the authority of the International Criminal Courts. Keeping in mind that our overall aim is to reach some sort of solution for the implementation of human rights and international criminal justice in order to prevent human suffering and reduce the number of victims of international crimes, it would therefore be pointless to try to prove that the lies within the utipolitianist theories are equivalent to the implementation of the provisions of international human rights. Although it is unreasonable and unjustified to use force against other equal members of the United Nations and other international organisations, utipolitianists do not care and continue to use military and political force against any party that does not comply with their

[190] Malekian Farhad, *Barrels of Justifications Violating International Criminal Responsibility* (New York: Nova Science Publishers, 2025).

policies. The power of utipolitianist governments can be enforced upon any state or nation through the adoption of sanctions or by blocking and freezing their economic movements around the world. In other words, utipolitianist governments have no limitations or restrictions on its lies. Such governments might thus massacre millions of people and reject the existence of the value of the system of the International Criminal Court in The Hague by various means, including in official statements and letters to the ICC.

The power of a utipolitianist government is wielded to reject the international legal authority of the ICC and render its actions meaningless. The most concerning aspect of this situation is that the concept of justice promoted by utipolitianist governments against the ICC creates anarchy within the system of the Court and could potentially lead to a global conflict that threatens human civilisation. Therefore, the significant reflection of the system of international criminal courts is unfortunately situated under the political power of the utipolitianist governments, especially the United States government. For these basic reasons, the international criminal system and the complementarity principle are facing catastrophic scenarios that have been orchestrated by governments that are recognized as masters of lies and wars. As a result, neither the complementarity principles nor the frame of peremptory international criminal law function, and when one examines the value of the *jus cogens* norms, one realizes that all of the values throughout the international legal system are unable to be enforced. As a result, the notion of justice disappears, and any attempt to improve this unbalanced situation of international law faces brutal sanctions from the utipolitianist governments.

Additionally, insofar as states do not act against the injustices carried out by utipolitianists, the monopolisation of international criminal justice reaches the maximum number of violations and priorities in decisions. The Security Council has seen this in relation to the adoption of resolutions. Consequently, we observe the poor treatment of the concept of justice under the power of utipolitianist theory, and injustices prevail because we believe the lies of utipolitianist governments. This is especially common when utipolitianists wage wars against a dictatorial government and confuse the international legal and political community into thinking that they stand for peace, equality, freedom, justice, and human rights—all while they are actually planning to destroy the relevant government, as we have seen in the Middle East. This indicates that the dark reality of the situation of international criminal justice comes into focus when we speak the language of equality and peace exclusively with the terms of warfare. Awareness of the wills and interests of utipolitianist power can often make it clear to the international legal and political community that utipolitianist governments make certain judgments in order to establish more rights for themselves.

This in turn produces more victims of utipolitianist governments, and the virtue of international human rights law disappears entirely and is replaced with the terrors of war. Thus, the fear of being massacred by the guns provided by the utipolitianist governments to their political allies continues to grow among certain populations and simultaneously destroys civilians' lives. There is not a separate utipolitianist power in every part of the world. Nonetheless, there exist certain strong utipolitianist governments that have the veto power in the Security Council, and all those old colonial powers or their new friends are controlled by and benefit from the authoritarian power of the United States governments. This indicates that there is, in fact, one strong and very aggressive, warlike government in the world that leads and orders all other states to follow its legal order.

Not only does the United States have the key element of monopolisation under their political, economic, and military control, they also have control over the territory of many nations, whether through the threat of the use of force or through the diplomacy of lies and the installation of military bases. As a result, the political and territorial sovereignties of a considerable number of states are strongly under the control of the authoritarian or paternalistic United States government. We may therefore define the theory of utipolitianism as the theory of the circulation of injustice in the name of justice. This reflects the picture of utipolitianist human rights depending on how well it fits its plans of the monopolisation of nations with deliberate irrationality.

Let's say that a rational government does not force other governments to be under the Security Council's rules of slavery and does not monopolize the world's first international organisation by force through the imposition of various brutal sanctions and wars for decades. Moreover, the absence of the use of force is not sufficient to ensure that the utipolitianist governments' plans of monopolisation of the rights and resources of other nations are rational. There may be other plans behind the degrading, humiliating power of the utipolitianist government of the United States that are much more catastrophic than they appear because of the adopted resolutions of the Security Council, which may lead to in the complete destruction of certain countries such as Vietnam, Iraq, Afghanistan, Libya, and others. The best example of this is the Palestinian State, which has been broken into pieces under the immoral and unjust plans of utipolitianist theory.

Utipolitianist governments such as the British, American, France, and Israeli Zionist governments, have committed the most invisible genocide in the history of human civilisation, with the help of Germany and many other states. Despite this, they consider their actions to reflect a lawful and logical imposition of international human rights and international law. *Nevertheless, if our statements are not accurate and our sympathetic interpretation of the real philosophy of human rights is insufficient, then we should bind the theory of the international legal personalities of states to the theory of the international legal personality of utipolitianism. This form of utipolitianism has always received the power of the international legal personality of all states. Thus, the notion of an international legal personality of the utipolitianist theory is much stranger than the notion of an international legal personality of any state, even including that of the United States government itself. This means that the systems of international human rights and international criminal courts are facing a new theory of power, politics, and economy that is directed, guided, interpreted, and imposed using the international legal personality of utipolitianist theory. As a result, the philosophy of law, nation, states, governments, peace, justice, judgment, are created along with a new invisible international criminal court that ignores all forms of international legislation.*

The consequences of our actions are usually not seen in the logic of the theories, but rather in the result of what remains for us without being cut off from our own interests. Thus, everyone in the world can see the genocide in Gaza, including the blind, cats, and dogs. However, those who cannot see the brutal, aggressive power of the utipolitianist governments also cannot see that their actions or inactions violate the system of international criminal law and that they are contributing to the dismantlement of the international legal personality of the ICC. We, or our governments, may regret certain actions and decisions that have led to the massacre of other nations, but the fact is that something else is missing in our judgments at all times. We have taken decisions that have generated impossible and unavoidable consequences. Our governments may wish that they had never made such decisions. I am referring here to the principles of the wisdom of actions, wisdom of decisions, and wisdom of judgments—all of which are missing in the standard of a rational government pursuing subjectively rational political, economic, and military actions.

When children are seen as the enemies of utipolitianist governments and Western governments are silent, this indicates that they have lost their moral compasses. When hospitals, patients, doctors, and nurses are bombed in the name of fighting against resistance, the stage of brutality embodies all international crimes from which our governments turn their faces. I may be wrong in all my interpretations, and my views may be outright rejected by authoritarian governments, however this does not affect the principles of wisdom and humanity. Such governments take decisions without deeply considering the consequences of their decisions in the process of international criminal justice or human rights. Additionally, even though they may understand that their decisions were not wise and later prove to be mistaken with the untoward results of killing millions of members of the population of the victim or the target nation, such governments do not see the flaws and shortcomings of their decisions. This phenomenon can be called self-pardon and self-respect, and it is also the cause of self-reproach concerning certain matters of political interest. This is how the system of international criminal justice or the international legal personality of the International Criminal Court is evaluated, voted on, and then ignored by utipolitianist governments in practice.

In sum, we have the leading guiding principle of complementarity, which has to be respected by all governments in the world if the balance of reasons required for the systems of international human rights and international criminal justice is going to be respected. This principle will certainly not prevent the system of international law from prosecuting international criminals—but the contrary. The intention is to put an end to the international criminal vacations of the leaders of the utipolitianist governments and call for them to be held accountable or take international criminal responsibility before an official international criminal court. Otherwise, our shortcomings encourage us to take steps that lead to calamity in the system of international criminal justice, and the international legal personality of the ICC is removed from the geopolitical map of morality, as we have already seen with the numerous serious crimes committed by the powertionist governments. Natural law and natural rights go hand-in-hand with the inhumanity of the leaders of utipolitianist governments. Nothing can protect us from the uncertainties and limitations of our wisdom or the assurance that we can prevent the commission of the next genocide or holocaust.[191]

Naturally, the systems of international human rights and international criminal justice are both in great danger due to inhumanity, which in turn has been created by the utipolitianist governments with the hope of occupying the

[191] The powertionist government supported the holocaust of several millions in Germany during the Second World War and in Palestine now.

international legal personalities of all states of the world, including China and Russia. This can be seen through the continuous sanctions imposed by American governments. These sanctions include not only economic, military, and political sanctions, but also sanctions concerning the accusation of other nations or governments of various international crimes, such as terrorism. Why and from where utipolitianists have received such authority is indeed a very important question that concerns morality, legality, and the basic philosophy of international criminal jurisdiction. *As a result, there actually exists a utipolitianist government whose existence cannot be objected to by a realistic, unrealistic, or idealistic government. Such an utipolitianist government is above all other utipolitianist governments acting under its power of decisions and military abilities.* As we have indicated elsewhere, the primary utipolitianist power is the United States of America, and the second and third are the United Kingdom and France, respectively. Israel is also among such powers. It is not without reason that all serious, barbaric international crimes have been committed by the aforementioned governments, which have justified these crimes as the promotion of the principles of international human rights and attempts to achieve authentic jurisprudential international criminal justice. These governments label those fighting for the right to self-determination as perpetrators of international crimes and allow the leaders of the utipolitianist governments to escape from accountability.

Acting with deliberative false rationality can only ensure that our international criminal conduct is above all rules of criminal justice and that the leaders of utipolitianist governments have no responsibility for their criminal conduct. However, the system of international criminal justice is not surprised when a utipolitianist government asserts that it is not at all responsible for the conduct of others because they have ignored its orders concerning certain ongoing questions of justice. This is the main principle of utipolitianists and the chief reason why the international criminal justice system is not successful in its duty of bringing the real perpetrators of international crimes under prosecution and punishing them. This principle does not, of course, care about any matter concerning the rights of others or the killing of other nations' populations, occupying their territories, and then taking the entire international legal personality of the International Criminal Court under their control. From the standpoint of the original position on the creation of the notion of international criminal responsibility, it reveals that governments cannot agree on the concept of justice. They cannot comprehend justice that is free from the commission of international crimes. They prevent the reestablishment of violated human rights through the procedures of an international criminal court.

My interpretation does not rest upon any misunderstanding of the system of human rights and criminal justice, rather the contrary. As time goes by and more tomorrows come, more notions of morality die in the systems of international criminal justice. This is because the criteria for the value of the provisions of international criminal law and the identification of various crimes rest on the independent power of international criminal courts and the implementation of the principle of complementarity and international criminal responsibility—however neither is successful. If finding international criminals is not the duty of the ICC, and if the ICC is not responsible for arresting serious criminals, then who is, and what is the ICC's true function? These criteria are primarily defined with reference to the already-established international legal personality of the ICC, which was selected by the states parties to give value to the structural legal body of international criminal law. The hypothetical nature of the definition of the concept of an international criminal court is therefore inconceivable without the concept of international criminal responsibility for states, leaders, superiors, or any other individuals who have committed crimes in any context.

Bibliography*

Adhikari Mohamed, ed., *Civilian-Driven Violence and the Genocide of Indigenous Peoples in Settler Societies* (London: Routledge, 2019).

Adil Ahmad Haque, Law and Morality at War (2017).

Alexy Robert, '*Effects of Defects—Action or Argument? Thoughts about Deryck Beyleveld and Roger Brownsword's Law as a Moral Judgment'* (Ratio Juris, 2006), pp. 169–79.

Alexy Robert, '*The Dual Nature of Law, Ratio Juris'* (2010), pp. 167–82.

Alexy Robert, 'The Reasonableness of Law' in *Reasonableness and Law Ed. Giorgio Bongiovanni, Giovanni Sartor, and Chiara Valentini* (Dordrecht: Springer, 2009), pp. 5–15.

Alexy Robert, Discourse Theory and Fundamental Rights' in *Arguing Fundamental Rights Ed. Agustín José Menéndez and Erik Oddvar Eriksen* (Dordrecht: Springer, 2006), pp. 15–29.

Alexy, Robert, *On the Concept and the Nature of Law* (Ratio Juris, 2008), pp. 21: 281–99.

Allison Henry, *Kant's Theory of Freedom* (Cambridge University Press, 1990).

Amato A. D., 'It's a Bird, It's a Plane, It's *Jus cogens*' 6 *Connecticut Journal of International Law*, (1990).

Ambion Bienvenido C., Organization of a Court of International Criminal Jurisdiction, 29 *Philippine Law Journal* 345 (1954).

Andreopoulos George J., (ed.), *Genocide: Conceptual and Historical Dimensions* (Philadelphia, 1994).

Annacker, C., 'The Legal Régime of erga omnes Obligations in International Law' 46 *Austrian Journal of Public International Law*, (1994), pp. 131–66.

Anthony D'Amato, 'The Moral Dilemma of Positivism,' 20 *Valparaiso University Law Review*, (1985-86), 43-53.

Antonio Cassese and Paola Gaeta, *Cassese's International Criminal Law* (3rd, 2013).

Aquila Richard E., *Matter in Mind: A Study of Kant's Transcendental Deduction* (Indiana University Press, 1989).

Arthur Naiman. '9/11: *The Simple Facts — Why the Official Story can't Possibly be True*,' (US: Soft Skull Press, 2011).

Arts Karin, Vesselin Popovski. (eds.), *International Criminal Accountability and the Rights of Children* (Heidelberg: Springer, 2006), pp. 37–52 and 53–65.

Austin John, *The Province of Jurisprudence Determined and the Uses of the Study of Jurisprudence* (1954).

---

* Mention here neither includes nor excludes in the text. It neither confirms nor rejects the work.

Baderin Mashood A., *International Human Rights and Islamic Law* (New York, NY: Oxford University Press, 2005).

Baderin Mashood, A., 'A Comparative Analysis of the Right to a Fair Trial and due Process under International Human Rights Law and Saudi Arabian Domestic Law,' 10 (3) The *International Journal of Human Rights*, (2006).

Bantekas Ilias, Susan Nash, *International Criminal Law*, (2007).

Barron Anne, (Legal) Reason and its "Others": Recent DevelopmentinLegal Theory, in *Introduction to Jurisprudence and Legal Theory: Commentary and Materials* (Schiff Penner, and Nobles, eds., 2002), 1038-63.

Bartlett Eva, *'What's Happening in Syria? The Media 'Kills the Truth,' 'Terrorism' is Described as 'Moderate Opposition.'* (Global Research, February 05, 2017).

Bartlett Eva, *How We Were Mislead about Syria.*

Bartlett Eva, *Is Eva Bartlett Credible?* https://www.quora.com/Is-Eva-Bartlett-credible (Accessed: 14th 2016).

Bassiouni C., 'International Crimes: *Jus cogens* and Obligatio Erga Omnes' 59 *Law and Contemporary Problems*, (1996).

Bassiouni M. Cherif and Benjamin B. Ferencz, The Crime Against Peace and Aggression: From Its Origins to the ICC, in *International Criminal Law,* vol. I, (M. Cherif Bassiouni, ed. 2008), pp. 207-242.

Bassiouni M. Cherif, (ed.), *International Criminal Law* (US: Ocean Publication, 3 vols., 1999).

Bassiouni M. Cherif, (ed.), *International Terrorism and Political Crimes* (1975).

Bassiouni M. Cherif, 'A Comprehensive Strategic Approach on International Cooperation for the Prevention, Control and Suppression of International and Transnational Criminality, Including the Establishment of an International Criminal Cour,' 15 *Nova Law Review*, 353, (1991).

Bassiouni M. Cherif, 'The Discipline of International Criminal Law,' in M. cherif Bassiouni (ed.), *International Criminal Law*, Vol. 1, (2008), pp. 5-40.

Bassiouni M. Cherif, 'The Subjects of International Criminal Law: Ratione Personae' in M. Bassiouni Cherif (ed.), *International Criminal Law*, Vol. 1, (2008), pp. 41-70.

Bassiouni M. Cherif, Benjamin B. Ferencz, *The Crime Against Peace and Aggression: From Its Origins to the ICC, in International Criminal Law*, vol. I, (M. Cherif Bassiouni, ed. 2008).

Bassiouni M. Cherif, *Crimes Against Humanity in International law*, (1999).

Bassiouni M. Cherif, *Criminal Justice in the Time of War and Peace* (Cambridge University Press, Cambridge, 2014).

Bassiouni M. Cherif, *Introduction to International Criminal Law*, (2005).

Bassiouni M. Cherif, The Discipline of International Criminal Law, in *International Criminal Law,* Vol. I (M. Cherif Bassiouni, ed., 2008).

Bassiouni M. Cherif, *The Shariah and Islamic Criminal Justice in the Time of War and Peace* (Cambridge University Press, Cambridge, 2014).

Baum L. M., 'Pursuing Justice in a Climate of Moral Outrage: An Evaluation of the Rights of the Accused in the Rome Statute of the International Criminal Court,' 19 *Wisconsin International Law Journal* (2001).

Beccaria Cesare, *On Crimes and Punishments*, (1764).

Bellamy, A., *Responsibility to Protect: the Global Effort to End Mass Atrocities* (Polity Press, Cambridge, 2009).

Bellamy, R. (ed.), *C Beccaria, On Crimes and Punishments*. (1995).

Benneh E. Y., 'Sovereignty Immunity and International Crimes,' 22 *Ghana Law Journal*, (2002–2004), 112.

Bennett Jonathan, *Kant's Analytic* (Cambridge University Press, 1966).

Bennett Jonathan, *Kant's Dialectic* (Cambridge University Press, 1974).

Bennoune Karima, 'As-Salamu 'Alykum? Humanitarian Law in Islamic Jurisprudence,' 15 *Michigan Journal of International Law*, (1994), pp. 605-643.

Berman Schiff (ed.), *The Oxford Handbook of Legal Pluralism* (Oxford University Press, 2019).

Berman Schiff, *Global Legal Pluralism: A Jurisprudence of Law Beyond Borders Global* (2012).

Bermann George A. et al., *Cases and Materials on European Community Law* (1993).

Bernstein Richard J. *Radical Evil: A Philosophical Interrogation* (New York: Blackwell Publisher, 2002).

Beth van Schaack, "The Crime of Political Genocide: Repairing the Genocide Convention's Blind Spot," 106 *Yale Law Journal* (1997).

Bianchi A, 'Human Rights and the Magic of *Jus cogens*,' 19 *European Journal of International Law*, (2008), pp. 491-508.

Bigi Giulia, 'Joint Criminal Enterprise in the Jurisprudence of the International Criminal Tribunal for the former Yugoslavia and the Prosecution of Senior Political and Military Leaders: The Krajišnik Case' 14 Guyer Paul, *The Cambridge Companion to Kant,* (1992).

Bigi Giulia. 'Joint Criminal Enterprise in the Jurisprudence of the International Criminal Tribunal for the former Yugoslavia and the Prosecution of Senior Political and Military Leaders: The Krajišnik Case' 14 *Max Planck United Nations Yearbook*, (2010), pp. 51-83.

Bird Graham, *Kant's Theory of Knowledge*, (Humanities Press, 1962).

Bix Brian, 'Natural Law: The Modern Tradition' in Jules Coleman and Schott Shapiro (eds.), *The Oxford Handbook of Jurisprudence and Philosophy of Law*, (2002).

Bloxham Donald, *Genocide on Trial: War Crimes Trials and the Formation of Holocaust History and Memory* (2001).

Boas Gideon, International Criminal Justice: Legitimacy and Coherence, (2012).

Boerefijn Ineke. 'Towards a Strong System of Supervision: The Human Rights Committee's Role in Reforming the Reporting Procedure under Article 40 of the Covenant on Civil and Political Rights,' *Human Rights Quarterly*, 17.4, (1995), pp. 766-793.

Boot Machteld, *Genocide, Crimes against Humanity, War Crimes*: *Nullum Crimen Sine Lege and the Subjective Matter of Jurisdiction of the International Criminal Cour*t, (2002).

Brilmayer Lea, *American Hegemony: Political Morality in a One Superpower World* (1994).

Broomhall Bruce, *International Justice and the International Criminal Court: Between Sovereignty and the Rule of Law* (2003).

Browning Christopher, *The Path to Genocide: Essays on Launching the Final Solution*, (2002).

Browning Don (eds.), *Universalism vs. Relativism: Making Moral Judgements in a Changing, Pluralistic, and Threatening World* (Rowman and Littlefield Publishers, United Kingdom, 2006).

Brownlie Ian, *International Law and the Use of Force by States* (Oxford: Oxford University Press, 1996).

Brownlie Ian, *Principles of Public International Law* (Oxford: Clarendon Press, 5th ed., 1998).

Brunnée J., 'The Prohibition on Torture: Driving *Jus cogens* Home?' 104 *Proceedings of the Annual Meeting of the American Society of International Law*, (2010).

Buchanan Allen, 'Toward a Drone Accountability Regime,' 29 (1) *Ethics and International Affairs*, (2015), pp. 15–70.

Burke-White William W, 'Implementing a Policy of Positive Complementarity in the Rome System of Justice,' 19 *Criminal Law Forum*, (2008), 59-89.

Burns Peter. 'An International Criminal Tribunal: The Difficult Union of Principle and Politics,' 5 *Criminal Law Forum*, (1994).

Byers M. 'Conceptualising the Relationship Between *Jus cogens* and *Erga Omnes Rules*' 66 *Nordic Journal of International Law*, (1997).

Caenegem R. C., Van, *European Law in the Past and the Future: Unity and Diversity over Two Millennia* (Cambridge: Cambridge University Press, 2001).

Cançado Trindade, A. '*Jus cogens* in Contemporary International Law,' *UN Audiovisual Library*, (http://www.un.org/law/avl).

Carvin Stephanie, 'Getting Drones Wrong,' 19 (2) *International Journal of Human Rights*, (2015), pp. 127–141.

Cassese Antonio and Albin Eser (eds.), *The Rome Statute of the International Criminal Court: A Commentary* (2002).

Cassese Antonio, (ed.), *The New Humanitarian Law of Armed Conflict* (Naples: Editoriale Scientifica, 1979).

Cassese Antonio, 'First Annual Report of the ICTY,' *Yearbook of International Law Commission*, (1994).

Cassese Antonio, 'For an Enhanced Role of *Jus cogens*' in Cassese, A (ed.), *Realizing Utopia*, (2012).

Cassese Antonio, Albin Eser, Giorgio Gaja and Robert E. Conor, *Justice at Nuremberg* (1980).

Cassese Antonio, *International Criminal Law* (Oxford: Oxford University Press, 2nd, ed., 2008).

Cassese Antonio, On the Current Trends Towards Criminal Prosecution and Punishment of Breaches of International Humanitarian Law, 9 *European Journal of Internaitonal Law* 2 (1998).

Chinkin C, '*Jus Cogens*, Article 103 of the UN Charter and Other Hierarchical Techniques of Conflict Solution,' 17 *Finnish Yearbook of International Law* (2008), pp. 63-90.

Chomksy N. and Barsamian D., *Keeping the Rabble in Line.* Boston: Common Courage Press (1994).

Chomsky, N., *Media Control: The Spectacular Achievements of Propaganda.* New York: Seven Stories Press (2004).

Chossudovsky Michel, *War and Globalisation: The Truth Behind September 11* (Global Outlook, 2002).

Christian P., Scherrer, *Iraq: Genocide by Sanctions* (2011).

Clark Maudemarie, *Nietzsche on Truth and Philosophy* (1991).

Clark Ramsey, *War Crimes – A Report on United States War Crimes against Iraq* (Maisonneuve Press, 1992).

Clark Roger S., 'The Crime of Apartheid,' in M. Cherif Bassiouni (ed.), *International Criminal Law*, vol. I (1986), pp. 299-323.

Claus Kress, 'Aggression and the Use of Force in International Law,' *Proceedings of the 108th Annual Meeting of the American Society of International Law,* No. 108, 2014, pp. 325–346.

Cohen Morris, 'Moral Aspects of the Criminal Law,' 49 *Yale Law Journal* (1949), pp. 987-1026.

Crawford J., Olleson S., 'The Continuing Debate on a UN Convention on State Responsibility,' 54 *ICLQ*, (2005), 959–71.

Cryer Robert, 'The Doctrinal Foundations of International Criminalization,' in M. cherif Bassiouni, ed., *International Criminal Law*, Vol. 1, (2008), pp. 107-128.

Cryer Robert, *Prosecuting International Crimes, Selectivity and the International Criminal Law Regime* (Cambridge University Press, Cambridge, 2005).

D'Amato A., 'It's a Bird, It's a Plane, It's *Jus cogens'* (1990) 6 *Connecticut Journal of International Law*.

D'Amato A., 'The Moral Dilemma of Positivism,' 20 *Valparaiso University Law Review* (1985-86), 43-53.

Danilenko G., 'International *Jus cogens*: Issues of Law-Making,' 2 *European Journal of International Law* (1991).

Dautricourt Jean, The Concept of International Criminal Court Jurisdiction-Definition and Limitations of the Subject, in *A Treatise on International Criminal Law* 636 (M. C. Bassiouni & V. P. Nanda eds., 1973).

David Lyons, 'Moral Aspects of Legal Theory,' in Kenneth Himma and Brian Bix (eds) *Law and Morality* (2005).

David MacGregor, 'September 11 as 'Machiavellian State Terrorism,' in Paul Zarembka, *The Hidden History of 9-11-2001* (New York: Seven Stories Press, 2008).

David Sugarman, (ed.), *Legality, Ideology and the State* (1983).

Davis Michael C., Dietrich Wolfgang, Bettina Schoolman and Sepp Dieter, *International Intervention in the Post-Cold War World: Moral Responsibility and Power Politics* (M. E. Sharpe, Inc., 2003).

de Hoog A. J. J., 'The Relationship between *Jus cogens*, *Obligations Erga Omnes* and International Crimes: Peremptory Norms in Perspective,' 42 *Österreichische Zeitschrift für öffentliches Recht und Völkerrecht* (1991).

de Hoogh A., *Obligations Erga Omnes and International Crimes: A Theoretical Inquiry into the Implementation and Enforcement of the International Responsibility of States* (Kluwer The Hague, 1996).

de Wet Erika, 'The Prohibition of Torture as an International Norm of *Jus cogens* and its Implementation for National and Customary Law,' 15 (1) *European Journal of International Law* (2014), Vol. 15, No. 1, 97-121.

de Wet, E., '*Jus Cogens* and Obligations Erga Omnes' in de Wet, E and Vidmar (eds.), *J Hierarchy in International Law: The Place of Human Rights*, (2012).

Delmas-Marty Mireille, 'The Contribution of Comparative Law to a Pluralist Conception of International Criminal Law,' 1 *Journal of International Criminal Justice*, (2003), pp. 13-25.

DeSon Jason S., 'Automating the Right Stuff? The Hidden Ramifications of Ensuring Autonomous Aerial Weapon Systems Comply with International Humanitarian Law,' *72 Air Force Law Review*, (2015), pp. 85–122.

Detmold M. J., *The Unity of Law and Morality: A Refutation of Legal Positivism* (Canada: Law Book Co. of Australasia, 1984).

Dhanapala Jayantha, *Under-Secretary-General for Disarmament Affairs United Nations, International Law, Security, and Weapons of Mass Destruction*, (New York, 9 May 2002).

Dhokalia. 'Problems Relating to *Jus Cogens*,' in S. Agrawala (ed.), *Essays on the Law of Treaties*, (1972).

Dickson Julie, *Evaluation and Legal Theory*, (2001).

Don Paul, Jim Hoffman, *Waking Up from Our Nightmare, the 9/11/01 Crimes in New York* City (New York: I/R Press, 2004).

Douzinas Costas, *Peter Goodrich and Yifat Hachamovitch, Politics, Post modernity and Critical Legal Studies* (1994).

Drost Pieter Nicolaas, *The Crime of State: Genocide* (Original from Indiana University, 1959).

Dryer Douglas P, *Kant's Solution for Verification in Metaphysics* (Allen and Unwin, 1966).

Duffett J., *Against the Crime of Silence* (New York, London, 1968).

Dugard John, 'Lifting the Guise of Occupation and Recourse to Action before the ICJ and ICC,' *Palestine Yearbook of International Law*, Vol. 17, 2013–14, pp. 9–27.

Duncan A. R. C., *Practical Reason and Morality* (Nelson, 1957).

Dupuy P., 'Some Reflections on Contemporary International Law and the Appeal to Universal Values: a Response to Marti Koskenniemi' 16 *European Journal of International Law*, (2005).

Duțu Mircea, *Vespasian V. Pella*. (1897-1952) Founder of International Criminal law, Promoter of the Unification of the Criminal Law, *Architect of the International Criminal Justice* (Universul Juridic, Bucharest, 2012).

Eric David, *Principes de Droit des Conflits Armés*, (2nd, ed. 1999).

Ewald F., 'Unger's Philosophy: A Critical Legal Study,' 5 *Yale Law Journal* 665(1988).

Ewing A. C., *A Short Commentary on Kant's 'Critique of Pure Reason'* (Methuen, 1978).

Falk Richard, 'The Accountability of Leaders: A Challenge to Civil Government and Society' in Jeremy Brecher, Jill Cutler, Smith Brendan, *In the Name of Democracy: American War Crimes in Iraq and Beyond* (American Empire Project), (New York: Metropolitan Books, Henry Holt and Company, 2005).

Falk Richard, *Slouching Toward a Palestinian Holocaust*, www.transnational.org/ Area.../Falk Palestine Genocide.html, 20 October 2010.

Falk Richard, *The Vietnam War and International Law (*Princeton University Press, 1968).
Farmer John, *The Ground Truth: The Story Behind America's Defense on 9/11* (New York: Riverhead Books, 2009).
Feimpong J. K. & S. Azadon Tiewel, 'Can Apartheid Successfully Defy the International Legal System?' 5 *The Black Law Journal* (1977), pp. 287-311.
Fein Bruce, *'Hillary Clinton's 5 lies about Syria, Terror Threat,'* The Washington Times (25 October, 2016).
Feld Werner, *The Court of the European Communities: New Dimension in International Adjudication* (1964).
Ferencz Benjamin B. 'Ending Impunity for the Crime of Aggression,' 41 *Case W. Res. J*, (2009), pp. 281-290.
Ferencz Benjamin, 'An International Criminal Code and Court: Why They Stand and Where They're Going,' 30 *Columbia Journal of Transnational Law*, (1992), 375.
Ferencz Benjamin, International Criminal Court (2 vols. 1980).
Findlay Escrito por Mark J, *International and Comparative Criminal Justice: A Critical Introduction* (Routledge, London, 2013).
Finnis John (ed.), *Natural Law*, (1991).
Finnis John, *Aquinas: Moral, Political and Legal Theory* (1998).
Fischer-Lescano A., Teubner G., 'Regime Collision: The Vain Search for Legal Unity in the Fragmentation of Global Law,' 25 *Michigan Journal of International Law*, (2004), pp. 999-104.
Fitzpatrick P. (ed.), *Dangerous Supplements: Resistance and Renewal in Jurisprudence* (1991).
Focarelli, C., 'Promotional *Jus cogens*: A Critical Appraisal of *Jus Cogens*' Legal Effects' 77 *Nordic Journal of International Law*, (2008), 429.
Fouladvand, S., Complementarity and Cultural Sensitivity: Decision-making by the International Criminal Court (ICC) *Prosecutor in Relation to the Situations in the Darfur Region of the Sudan and the Democratic Republic of Congo* (DRC), (2012).
Franck Thomas M., *Fairness in International Law and Institutions* (1997).
Fuller Lon Luvios, *The Morality of Law* (Virginia: Yale Law University, 2nd, ed., 1969).
Fuller S., "Playing Without a Full Deck: Scientific Realism and the Cognitive Limits of Legal Theory," 97 *Yale Law Journal* 549 (1988).
Funk T. Markus, *Victims' Rights and Advocacy at the International Criminal Court* (2015).
Gebrehana Teklewold, *Duty to negotiate: An Element of International law* (1978).
Gebrehana Teklewold, T Arbitration - *An Element of International Law* (1984).
George J. Andreopoulos, (ed.), *Genocide: Conceptual and Historical Dimensions* (Philadelphia, 1994).
George Robert P, *Natural Law Theory: Contemporary Essays*, (1994).
George Robert P. (ed.), *The Autonomy of Law: Essays on Legal Positivism*, (1995).
Gerhard O. W. Mueller & Edward M. Wise (eds), *International Criminal Law* (1965).
Gideon Boas, William A. Schabas (eds.), *International Criminal Law Developments in the Case Law of the ICTY* (2005).
Glennon, MJ., 'De l'Absurdité du Droit Impératif (*Jus cogens*)'/*On the Absurdity of Imperative Law (Jus cogens)* 110 *Revue Générale de Droit International Public*, (2006), 529.

Goldstone Richard J., For Humanity: Reflections of a War Crimes Investigator (2000).
Gómez Robledo, *A., El Ius Cogens Internacional* (Estudio Histórico Crítico), (1982).
Goodrich Peter, *Languages of Law* (1990).
Gracia-Amador, 'The Crime of Apartheid: Responsibility and Reparations,' *Review of Contemporary Law* (1981), pp. 31-38.
Gray C., *International Law and the Use of Force*, (2000).
Grayeff Felix, *Kant's Theoretical Philosophy* (Barnes & Noble, 1970).
Green Penny et al., Countdown to Annhilation: Genocide in Myanmar, (London: 2015).
Green, P. J. and Ward, T., State crime, Human rights, and the Limits of Criminology, 27 *Social Justice* (2000), pp. 101–120.
Greenawalt Alexander KA., 'The Pluralism of International Criminal Law,' 86 *Indiana Law Journal*, (2011), 1063-1130.
Grover Sonja, *Prosecuting International Crimes and Human Rights Abuses Committed Against Children – Leading International Court Cases*, (2010), pp. 169–279.
Haas Jacob De, *History of Palestine - The Last Two Thousand Years* (USA: Macmillan, 1934).
Hacker P. M. S. and J. Raz, (eds.), *Law, Morality and Society: Essays in Honour* of H. L. A. Hart (1977).
Hannikainen L., *Peremptory Norms (jus cogens) in International Law: Historical Development*, Criteria, Present Status (1988).
Harees Lukman, *The Mirage of Dignity on the Highways of Human 'Progress': the Bystanders Perspective*, (2012).
Harle Vilho, *Ideas of Social Order in the Ancient* World (1998).
Harris J. W., *Legal Philosophies*, 2 edition (1997).
Harris W., *Tyranny on Trial* (Dallas: Southern Methodist University Press, 1999).
Hart H. L. A., *The Concept of Law, 2nd ed.*, (P. A. Bulloch and J. Raz, eds., 1994).
Hartnack Justus, *Kant's Theory of Knowledge* (Harcourt, Brace and World, 1967).
Heller Kevin Jon, 'The Shadow Side of Complementarity: The Effect of Article 17 of the Rome Statute on National Due Process,' 17 *Criminal Law Forum* (2006), available at file:///C:/Users/admin/AppData/Local/Temp/SSRN-id907404.pdf.
Heller Kevin Jon, *The Nuremberg Military Tribunals and the Origins of International Criminal Law* (2010).
Heller Kevin Jon, *The Nuremberg Military Tribunals and the Origins of International Criminal Law*, (2010).
Hinton Alexander Laban, "The Dark Side of Modernity: Toward an Anthropology of Genocide," in *Annihilating Difference: The Anthropology of Genocide, ed. Alexander Laban Hinton* (University of California Press, 2002), pp. 1-40.
Hitchens C., *The Trial of Henry Kissinger* (London: Verso Books, 2001).
Hoffe Otfried, *Immanuel Kant* (State University of New York Press, 1994).
Hoover Joseph, *Moral Practices: Assigning Responsibility in the International Criminal Court*, 76 *Law and Contemporary Problems* (2014), pp. 263-86.
Hughes G., Validity and the Basic Norm, 59 *California Law Review* 695 (1971).
Huntington Cairns, 'Plato's Theory of Law,' 56 *Harvard Law Review*, (1942), pp. 559-587.

Hurd Heidi, Challenging Authority, 100 *Yale Law Journal* 1611 (1991). https://www.gordogan.com.hr/gordogan/wp-content/uploads/2011/10/2001-Hitchens-The-Trial-of-Henry-Kissinger.pdf

Hurlock William L., "The International Court of Justice: Effectively Providing a Long Overdue Remedy for Ending State-Sponsored Genocide (Bosnia-Herzegovina v. Yugoslavia)," 12 *American University Journal of International Law and Policy* (1997).

Husabø Erling Johannes, Ingvild Bruce, *Fighting Terrorism through Multilevel Criminal Legislation: Security Council Resolution 1373, the EU Framework Decision on Combating Terrorism and their Implementation in Nordic, Dutch and German Criminal Law* (Martinus Nijhoff Publishers, 2009).

Jacovides A., *Treaties Conflicting with Peremptory Norms of International Law and the Zurich-London 'Agreements,'* (1966).

James Paul, Jonathan Friedman, Globalization and Violence, Vol. 3: *Globalizing War and Intervention* (London: Sage Publications, 2006).

Janis, M. W., 'The Nature of *Jus* Cogens' 3 *Connecticut Journal of International Law*, (1988), 59.

Jevons W. S., *The Theory of Political Economy* (London: Macmillan and Co., 1871).

John Carey and John R. Pritchard (eds.), *International Humanitarian Law: Origins, Challenges and Prospects* (2000).

Jørgensen, *The Responsibility of States for International Crimes* (OUP Oxford 2000).

Jori Mario. (ed.), *Legal Positivism,* (1992).

Kairys David (ed.), *The Politics of Law: A Progressive Critique* (1982).

Kant Immanuel, *Answering the Question: What is Enlightenment?* (1784).

Kant Immanuel, *Critique of Judgment* (1790).

Kant Immanuel, *Critique of Pure Reason* (1781).

Kant Immanuel, *Groundwork of the Metaphysic of Morals* (1785).

Kant Immanuel, *Metaphysical Foundations of Natural Science* (1786).

Kant Immanuel, *Opus Postumum* (1995).

Kant Immanuel, *Perpetual Peace, and Other Essays on Politics, History, and Morals* (1784).

Kant Immanuel, *Perpetual Peace: A Philosophical Sketch* (1795).

Kant Immanuel, *Practical Philosophy* (editor: Mary J. Gregor, 1999).

Kant Immanuel, *Prolegomena to Any Future Metaphysics* (1783).

Kant Immanuel, *Religion within the Bounds of Bare Reason* (1793).

Kant Immanuel, *The Critique of Practical Reason* (1788).

Kant Immanuel, *The Metaphysics of Morals* (1797).

Kant Immanuel, *The Only Possible Argument in Support of a Demonstration of the Existence of God* (1763).

Kant Immanuel, *The Science of Right* (1790).

Kawasaki Kyoji, 'A brief Note on the Legal Effects of *Jus Cogens* in International Law,' 34 *Hitotsubashi Journal of Law and Politics* (2006), pp. 27-43.

Kelman Mark, *A Guide to Critical Legal Studies* (1987).

Kelsen Han, *What is Justice? Justice, Law and Politics in the Mirror of Science* (1957).

Kelsen Hans, 'Will the Judgement of the Nürenberg Trial Constitute a Precedent in International Law,' 1 *International Law Quarterly* (1947), 153.
Kelsen Hans, 'Will the Judgement of the Nürenberg Trial Constitute a Precedent in International Law,' 1 *International Law Quarterly* (1947), 153.
Kelsen Hans, *What is Justice? Justice, Law and Politics in the Mirror of Science* (1957);

Kemal Salim, *Kant's Aesthetic Theory: An Introduction* (St. Martin's Press, 1992).

Khadduri Majid, *Major Middle Eastern Problems in International Law*, (1972).

Khalidi Rashid, *The Hundred Years' War on Palestine* (New York, Metropolitan Books, 2020).

Kitcher Patricia, *Kant's Transcendental Psychology* (Oxford University Press, 1990).

Klein David, F., 'A Theory for the Application of the Customary International Law of Human Rights by Domestic Courts,' 13 (2) *Yale Journal of International Law* (1988), pp. 332-365.

Kolb Robert. '*Jus cogens*, Intangibilité, Intransgressibilité, Dérogation 'Positive' et 'Négative' 109 *Revue Générale de Droit International Public* (2005), 305.

Koskenniemi Martti, "The Politics of International Law," *European Journal of International Law* (2011).

Koskenniemi, Martti, 'Solidarity Measures: State Responsibility as a New International Order?' 72 *BYIL*, (2001), pp. 337–56.

Kos-Rabcewicz-Zubrowski Louis, The Creation of an International Criminal Court, in *International Terrorism and Political Crimes* 519 (M. Cherif Bassiouni ed., 1975).

Kramer, R. C., Michalowski, R. and Kauzlarich, D., 'The origins and development of the concept and theory of state-corporate crime,' 48 *Crime and Delinquency* (2002), pp. 263–282.

Kress Claus, 'Aggression and the Use of Force in International Law,' *Proceedings of the 108th Annual Meeting of the American Society of International Law* (2014), pp. 325–346.

Kuper Leo, *International Action against Genocide* (Minority Rights Group Report No. 53, London, 1982).

Kuper Leo, *The Prevention of Genocide* (New Haven and London, 1985).

Lefenya Kesolofetse, 'Use of Explosive Weapons in Densely Populated Areas: Implications for International Humanitarian Law,' *African Yearbook on International Humanitarian Law* (2014), pp. 68–86.

Leonetti. 'Interprétation des traités et rêgles impératives du droit international général (*jus cogens*),' 24 *ÖZÖR*, (1973).

Lemkin Raphael, Axis Rule in Occupied Europe, (The Lawbook Exchange: 2008).

Linderfalk Ulf, 'The Creation of *Jus cogens* – Making Sense of Article 53 of the Vienna Convention,' *Max-Planck-Institut für ausländisches öffentliches Recht und Völkerrecht* (2011), pp. 259-278.

Luper-Foy, Steven, 'Introduction: Global Distributive Justice' in Steven Luper-Foy (ed.), *Problems of International Justice* (London: Westview Press, 1988), pp. 1-24.

MacGregor, 'State Immunity and *Jus cogens,*' 55 *International & Comparative Law Quarterly* (2006), 437.

MacIntyre Alasdair, *A Short History of Ethics: a History of Moral Philosophy from the Homeric Age to the Twentieth Century* (1965).

MacIntyre Alasdair, *After Virtue: A Study in Moral Theory* (University of Notre Dame Press, 1982).

Madsen Wayne, Jean-Charles, Guillaume Dasquie. *Forbidden Truth: U.S.-Taliban Secret Oil Diplomacy,* Saudi Arabia and the Failed Search for bin Laden, (2002).

Malekian Farhad and Kerstin Nordlöf, 'International Legal Status of Children' in Jay S. Albanese (ed.), *The Encyclopaedia of Criminology & Criminal Justice* (United States: Wiley-Blackwell (5 volumes, 2013), vol. III, pp. 1173-1178.

Malekian Farhad and Kerstin Nordlöf, *Confessing the International Rights of Children: The Basic documents with Analysis (*Cambridge: Cambridge Scholars Publishing, 2012).

Malekian Farhad, 'Armenian Genocide and the Questions of Responsibility of the Turkish Government,' *House of Commons Conference on the Armenian Genocide, Armenian Solidarity, British-Armenian All-Party Parliamentary Group, No Security Publication* (2007), pp.31-9.

Malekian Farhad, 'Comparative Substantive International Criminal Justice,' in Ronald Slye (ed.), *The Nuremberg Principles in Non-western Societies: A Reflection on their Universality, Legitimacy and Application* (2017), pp. 10-44.

Malekian Farhad, 'Conundrums of *Jus Cogens:* In Case Law' (Part II), No. 13 *Вісник Південного регіонального центру Національної академії правових наук України,* [No. 13 *Journal of the South regional Center of National Academy of Legal Sciences of Ukraine*] (2017), pp. 12-21.

Malekian Farhad, 'Conundrums of *Jus Cogens*: in International Criminal Law' (Part I), *Вісник Південного регіонального центру Національної академії правових наук України* [*No.12 Journal of the South regional Center of National Academy of Legal Sciences of Ukraine*] (2017), pp. 8-16.

Malekian Farhad, 'Emasculating the Philosophy of International Criminal Justice in the Iraqi Special Tribunal,' *Cornell International Law Journal*, 58/5 (2005), pp.675-725.

Malekian Farhad, *Hypocrisy in International Criminal Justice* (New York: Nova Science Publishers, 2025).

Malekian Farhad, *International Crime of Blackboard-Barbarism* ((New York: Nova Science Publishers, 2025).

Malekian Farhad, 'International Criminal Responsibility: International Criminal Responsibility of Individuals' in M. Cherif Bassiouni, *International Criminal Law,* Vol. *Crimes* (2[ed], ed., New York: Transnational Publishers, 1999).

Malekian Farhad, '*International Criminal Responsibility,*' in International Criminal Law (M. Cherif Bassiouni, 2[ed], ed., 1999).

Malekian Farhad, *'Islamic Law Justice Systems' in* Jay S. Albanese, *The Encyclopaedia of Criminology and Criminal Justice* (United States: Wiley-Blackwell (5 volumes, 2013), vol. III, pp.1220-1225.

Malekian Farhad, 'Judging International Criminal Justice in the Occupied Territories,' 12 *International Criminal Law Review* (2012), pp. 627-869.

Malekian Farhad, 'Mutilating the Philosophy of Justice in the Time of Armed Conflicts,' *Contemporary Journal of International Criminal Law* (2007).

Malekian Farhad, 'The Canon of Love against the Use of Force in Islamic and Public International Law: Part II: The Anatomy of Love Against Violations,' 15 *International Criminal Law Review*, 2015), pp. 861-895.

Malekian Farhad, 'The Canon of Love against the Use of Force in Islamic and Public International Law: Part I: The Chamber of Love within Legal Discipline,' 15 *International Criminal Law Review*, 2015), pp. 591-628.

Malekian Farhad, 'The Child as an Autonomous Subject of Justice' in Farhad Malekian, Kerstin Nordlöf, *Sovereignty of Children in Law* (Cambridge: Cambridge Scholars Publishing, 2012), pp. 2-55.

Malekian Farhad, 'The Functions of International Criminal Law and the Problem of Positivism and Neutralism Philosophy,' *Contemporary Journal of International Criminal Law* (2007).

Malekian Farhad, 'The Heaven of Justice with Love,' *The Journal of the Henry Martyn Institute* (2017), pp. 5-29.

Malekian Farhad, 'The Homogeneity of International Criminal Court with Islamic Jurisprudence,' 9 (4) *International Criminal Law Review* (2009), pp.595-621.

Malekian Farhad, 'The Laws Governing Crimes against Women Constituting *Obligatio Erga Omnes*' in David Wingeate Pike, *Crimes Against Women* (2011).

Malekian Farhad, 'The Miserable Wedding of Naturalism into Positivism,' 2 *ID EST Journal* (2009).

Malekian Farhad, *Allegations by Political Laundering* (Cambridge Scholars Publishing, 2019).

Malekian Farhad, *Classical Morality in International Peremptory Criminal Law* (Newcastle: Cambridge Scholars Publishing, 2018).

Malekian Farhad, *Classical Morality in International Peremptory Criminal Law* (Newcastle: Cambridge Scholars Publishing, 2021).

Malekian Farhad, *Concreting Righteousness in International Criminal Justice* (New York: Nova publishers, 2024).

Malekian Farhad, *Condemning the Use of Force in the Gulf Crisis* (Almqvist & Wiksell International, 1st ed., 1992).

Malekian Farhad, *Conscience of Judges in International Criminal Law, the Heart of Judgements* (New York: Nova Science Publishers, 2021).

Malekian Farhad, *Conscience of Lawyers in International Criminal Law, the Burden of Doppelgängers* (New York: Nova Science Publishers, 2021).

Malekian Farhad, *Conscience of Prosecutors in International Criminal Law, the Heart of the Matter* (New York: Nova Science Publishers, 2021).

Malekian Farhad, *Conundrums of Paternalism in International Criminal Justice* (New York: Nova Science Publishers, 2024).

Malekian Farhad, *Corpus Juris of Islamic International Criminal Justice* (Newcastle: Cambridge Scholars Publishing, 2017).

Malekian Farhad, *Documents on the Principles of International Human Rights* (Stockholm: Norstedts Juridik AB, 2007).

Malekian Farhad, *Exploitation of Christian Islamic International Criminal Justice* (New York: Nova Science Publishers, 2024).

Malekian Farhad, *Gravity of Wisdom in International Criminal Law* (New York: Nova Science Publishers, 2021).

Malekian Farhad, *Imperative Philosophy of International Criminal Justice: Visible Power – Invisible Essence* (Nova Sciences Publishers, 2022).

Malekian Farhad, *International Criminal Law of Children* (New York: Nova Science Publishers, 2021).

Malekian Farhad, *International Criminal Law, the Law of Somebodiness, the Law of Nobodiness* (New York: Nova Science Publishers, 2021).

Malekian Farhad, *International Criminal Law: The Legal and Critical Analysis of International Crimes* (2 vols. 1991).

Malekian Farhad, *International Criminal Responsibility of States: A Study on the Evolution of International Responsibility of States with particular Emphasis on the Concept of Crime and Criminal Responsibility* (Stockholm, 1985).

Malekian Farhad, *International Criminal Vacations: Tears of Justice* (New York: Nova Science Publishers, 2024).

Malekian Farhad, *Judgments of Love in Criminal Justice* (Switzerland: Springer: 2017, 2018).

Malekian Farhad, *Jurisprudence of International Criminal Justice* (Introduction by Professor Benjamin B. Ferencz, the former Prosecutor of the Nuremberg Tribunal (Cambridge: Cambridge Scholars Publishing, 2014).

Malekian Farhad, *Kerstin Nordlöf, Prohibition of Sexual Exploitation of Children Constituting Obligation Erga Omnes* (Cambridge: Cambridge Scholars Publishing, 2013).

Malekian Farhad, *Kerstin Nordlöf, The Sovereignty of Children in Law* (Cambridge: Cambridge Scholars Publishing, 2012).

Malekian Farhad, *Orchestrating Diversity in International Criminal Justice* (New York: Nova Science Publishers, 2021).

Malekian Farhad, *Paralysing International Criminal Justice* (New York: Nova Science Publishers, 2021).

Malekian Farhad, *Powertionism in International Criminal Justice* (Nova Sciences Publishers, 2022).

Malekian Farhad, *Principles of Islamic International Criminal Law: A Comparative Search* (Netherlands: Brill & Nijhoff, 2011).

Malekian Farhad, *Prohibition Governing Child Soldiers Constituting an Integral Part of Jus Cogens and Obligatio Erga Omnes*, XVII *World Congress of the International Association of Youth and Family Judges and Magistrates*, Belfast, Northern Ireland, 27 August – 2 September (2006).

Malekian Farhad, *System of International Law: Formation, Treaties, Responsibility* (Uppsala, 1987).

Malekian Farhad, *The Concept of Islamic International Criminal Law, A Comparative Study* (Netherlands: Brill, 1994).

Malekian Farhad, *The Mirage of International Criminal Law*: Kant Metaphysics of *Mens Rea* (Cambridge: Cambridge Scholars Publishing, 2018).

Malekian Farhad, *The Monopolization of International Criminal Law in the United Nations, A Jurisprudential Approach* (Stockholm: Almqvist Wiksell International, 1st ed., 1993).

Malekian Farhad, *The Monopolization of International Criminal Law in the United Nations, A Jurisprudential Approach* (Stockholm: Almqvist Wiksell International, 2nd ed., 1995).

Malekian Farhad, *Tour de force of Moral Virtue in International Criminal Justice* (Nova, Science Publishers, 2022).
Malekian Farhad, *Trading Virginity of International Criminal Justice* (New York: Nova Science Publishers, 2020).
Malekian Farhad, *Barrels of Justifications Violating International Criminal Responsibility* (New York: Nova Science Publishers, 2025).
Malekian Farhad, *Utipolitianist International Crimiminal Court* ((New York: Nova Science Publishers, 2025).
Manacorda Stefano, '*Cesare Beccaria e la pena dell'ergastolo'* Jus (2015), pp. 165–182.
Marc Weller, *Iraq and the Use of Force in International Law* (Oxford: Oxford University Press, 2010).
Mario Jori (ed.), *Legal Positivism* (1992).
Mark J. Osiel, Why Prosecute? Critics of Punishment for Mass Atrocity, 22 *Human Rights Quarterly* 118 (2000).
Matthew Lippman, 'Genocide,' in *International Criminal Law*, Vol. I (M. Cherif Bassiouni, ed., 2008) pp. 405-455.
May Larry, *Aggression and Crimes Against Peace* (New York: Cambridge University Press, 2008).
May Larry, *Crimes against Humanity: A Normative Account* (New York: Cambridge University Press 2004).
May Larry, *War Crimes and Just War* (New York: Cambridge University Press, 2007).
May Lary, 'Habeas Corpus as *Jus cogens* in International Law' 4 (3) *Criminal Law and Philosophy* (2010), 249–265.
Mearsheimer John J and Stephen Walt, The Israel Lobby and U.S. Foreign Policy (New York: Farrar, Straus and Giroux. 2007).
Mendus Susan, 'The Importance of Love in Rawls's Theory of Justice' 29 (1) *British Journal of Political Science* (1999), pp. 57-75.
Meron T., 'On Hierarchy of International Human Rights' 80 *American Journal of International Law*, (1986), 1.
Meron Theodor, *The Humanization of International Law* (Netherlands: The Hague Academy, 2006).
Meyssan Thierry, *11 September 2001: L'effroyable Imposture*, (2002).
Mokhtar Ali, '*Nullum Crimen, Nulla Poena, Sine Lege*: Aspects and Prospects,' 26 *Statute Law Review*, pp. 41-55.
Morten Bergsmo, Emiliano J Buis, *Philosophical Foundations of International Criminal Law* (2018).
Mosaddeq Ahmed, N. (2006), "Terrorism and Statecraft: Al-Qaeda and Western Covert Operations after the Cold War," Zarembka, Paul. (Ed.) *The Hidden History of 9-11-2001*. (*Research in Political Economy, Vol. 23*), Emerald Group Publishing Limited, Bingley, pp. 149-188. https://doi.org/10.1016/S0161-7230(06)23005-0.
Moyn Samuel, *Not Enough: Human Rights in an Unequal World*, (2018).
Muchnik Pablo, *Kant's Theory of Evil: An Essay on the Dangers of Self-love and the Aperiodicity of History* (Lexington Books, 2010).
Mueller Gerhard O. W., 'International Criminal Law: Civitas Maxima,' 15 *Case Western Reserve Journal of International Law* (1985).

Mullins Christopher W., Kauzlaric David, Rothe Dawn, "The International Criminal Court and the Control of State Crime: Prospects and Problems," 12(3) *Critical Criminology* (2004), pp. 285-308.

Naomi Roht-Arriaza, State Responsibility to Investigate and Prosecute Grave Human Rights Violations in International Law, 78 *California Law Review* 451 (1990).

Nietzsche Frederick, *The Genealogy of Morals: A Polemic* (translated J. M. Kennedy, Vol. 8th, 1913).

Nietzsche Friedrich Wilhelm, *The Will to Power,* https://en.wikisource.org/wiki/The_Will_to_Power.

Nozary Fariborz, *Unequal Treaties in International Law* (Stockholm, 1971).

O'Connor Susan, 'Up in Arms: A Humanitarian Analysis of the Arms Trade Treaty and Its New Zealand Application,' 11 *New Zealand Yearbook of International Law* (2013), pp. 73–105.

O'Neill Onora, *Constructions of Reason: Explorations of Kant's Practical Philosophy* (Cambridge University Press, 1989).

Ogunfolu Adedokun, Oludayo Fagbemi, 'I Have a Drone: The Implications of American Drone Policy for Africa and International Humanitarian Law,' 23 (1) *Revue Africaine de Droit International et Comparé* (2015), pp. 106–128.

Olivecrona K. 'The Imperative Element in Law,' *Rutgers Law Review* (1964).

Olson Peter M., 'The Lawfulness of Russian Use of Force in Crimea,' 53 (1) *Revue de Droit Militaire et de Droit de la Guerre* (2014), pp. 17–40.

Orakhelashvili Alexander, 'The Impact of Peremptory Norms on the Interpretation and Application of United Nations Security Council Resolutions' 16 (1), *The European Journal of International Law* (2005), pp. 59-88.

Orakhelashvili, A., *Peremptory Norms in International Law* (2006).

Osiel Mark, *The End of Reciprocity* (Cambridge University Press, 2009).

Otterman Michael, *American Torture: From the Cold War to Abu Ghraib and Beyond* (Pluto Press, 2007).

Pardo Pilar Villanueva Sainz, 'Is International Criminal Law a living discipline?,' 3:4 *The International Journal of Human Rights* (1999), pp. 92-100.

Paris Declaration, International Conference on Sanctions Against South Africa (And Special Declaration on Namibia), 27 May1981, Published by the United Nations Center Against Apartheid.

Parish Matthew, *International criminal law – Justice or Mirage? Transonflict* (2013).

Paton Herbert James, Kant's Metaphysic of Experience (Humanities Press, 1961).

Patrides, CA, Joseph Anthony Wittreich. *The Apocalypse in English Renaissance Thought and Literature: Patterns, Antecedents, and Repercussions* (Manchester University Press, 1984).

Patterson Dennis (ed.), *Postmodernism and Law* (1994).

Paulus A., '*Jus cogens* in a Time of Hegemony and Fragmentation,' 74 *Nordic Journal of International Law* (2005), pp. 297-334.

Paust J. 'The Reality of *Jus cogens*,' 7 *Connecticut Journal of International Law* (1991), 83.

Pella V. Vespasian., *La criminalité collective des états et le droit pénal de l'avenir, Bucarest : Imprimerie de l'état* (1925).

Pella Vespasian V., 'Plan for World Criminal Code,' 17 *Revue Internationale de Droit Penal* (1946).

Pella Vespasian V., Plan d'un Code Répressif Mondial, 6 *Rewe International de Droit Pénal* 1948, (1955).

Pella Vespasian, *Revue Internationale de Droit Penal* (1928).

Pella Vespasian, V. *La Guerre-Crime et les Criminels de Guerre/War-Crime and War Criminals* (Paris, 1946).

Pella Vespesian V., 'Towards an International Criminal Court,' 44 *American Journal of International Law* (1950), 57.

Pellet A., 'Comments in Response to Christine Chinking and in Defense of *Jus cogens* as the Best Bastion against the Excesses of Fragmentation,' 83 *Finnish Yearbook of International Law* (2006).

Pellet A., 'Vive le crime! Remarques sur les degrés de l'illicité en droit international' in United Nations/International Law Commission (ed.), I*nternational Law on the Eve of the Twenty-first Century: Views from the International Law Commission* (United Nations New York 1997), pp. 287–315.

Penrose Mary Margaret., 'Lest We Fail: The Importance of Enforcement in International Criminal Law An Essay on the Nature and Immutability of Truth,' 15 (2) *American University International Law Review* (1999), pp. 321-394.

Perelman C., *The Idea of Justice and the Problem of Argument* (1963).

Peterson Jeremy, 'Unpacking Show Trials: Situating the Trial of Saddam Hussein,' 48 *Harvard International Law Journal* (2007).

Postema Gerald J, *Bentham and the Common Law Tradition* (1986)Dickson Julie, Evaluation and Legal Theory (2001).

Potter R. B., *War and Moral Discourse* (Richmond, Va., John Knox Press, 1969).

Power Jonathan, *Conundrums of Humanity*: *The Quest for Global Justice* (2007).

Protector J. Harris., *Islam and International Relations* (New York, 1965).

Ragazzi, M., *The Concept of International Obligations erga omnes* (Clarendon Press Oxford 1997).

Rahmdel Mansour, 'Money Laundering in Iranian Law: Present and Future,' *Journal of Money Laundering Control* (2002).

Rahmdel Mansour, 'The *Ne Bis In Idem* Rule in Iranian Criminal Law,' *Journal of Financial Crime* (2004).

Rahmdel Mansour, The Role of the Courts in the Reform of Iranian Criminal Law Policy,' *Criminal Law Forum*, (2006).

Rawls John, *A Theory of Justice* (1999).

Raz J., 'Why the State?' in N. Roughan and A. Halpin (eds) In *Pursuit of a Pluralist Jurisprudence* (CUP 2017).

Raz Joseph, *Ethics in the Public Domain: Essays in the Morality of Law and Politics* (Oxford: Oxford University Press, 1994).

Raz Joseph, *The Morality of Freedom* (1986).

Reddy Enuga S., 'India and the Struggle Against Apartheid,' 26 *Indian Journal of International Law* (1986), pp. 551-567.

Reddy Enuga S., *Apartheid: The United Nations and the International Community* (1986).

Rehman Javaid. *International Human Rights Law* (London and New York: Longman Pub Group, 2nd ed., 2010).

Reisman W. Michael, 'Legal Responses to Genocide and Other Massive Violations of Human Rights,' 59 *Law and Contemporary Problems* (1996), 75.

Reiss Hans Siegbert, *Kant: Political Writings*, (2003).

Report of the Independent Inquiry into the actions of the United Nations during the 1994 genocide in Rwanda, UN Doc S/1999/1257, (1999) [Rwanda Report].

Rinceanu Johanna, 'Criminal Liability of Legal Persons in Romania' in Riccardo Borsari, *Responsabilita` da reato deli enti* (Padova: Padova University Press, 2016). pp. 407–418.

Rinceanu Johanna, 'The principle of legality (Nullum crimen sine lege) in Romania' in U. Sieber, S. Forster, & K. Jarvers (Eds.), *National Criminal Law in a Comparative Legal Context*, vol. 2 (1): Max-Planck-Institute für Ausländisches und Internationals Strafrecht, (2011), pp. 89-101.

Robertson Geoffrey, *Crimes Against Humanity – The Struggle for Global Justice* (Penguin Books, 3rd ed., 2006).

Robinson Mary, "Genocide, War Crimes, Crimes Against Humanity," *25 Fordham International Law Journal* (1999), p. 275.

Roméo Dallaire's, *Shake Hands with the Devil: The Failure of Humanity in Rwanda* (Carroll & Graf, New York, 2003).

Rorty Richard, *Philosophy and the Mirror of Nature* (1990).

Rosen Allen D. Kant's Theory of Justice (Ithaca, London: Cornel University Press, 1996).

Rosenstock, R. 'An International Criminal Responsibility of States?,' in United Nations/International Law Commission (ed.), *International Law on the Eve of the Twenty-First Century: Views from the International Law Commission* (United Nations New York, 1997), pp. 265–85.

Ross J. I., *Controlling State Crime* (2nd Edition, New Brunswick, NJ: Transaction Press, 2000).

Ross J. I., *Varieties of State Crime and its Control* (Monsey, NY: Criminal Justice Press, 2000).

Schabas William A. Justice, 'Democracy and Impunity in Post Genocide Rwanda: Searching for Solutions to Impossible Problems,' 7 *Criminal Law Forum* (1996).

Schabas William A., 'The Banality of International Justice,' 11 *Journal of International Criminal Justice* (2013), pp. 545–551.

Schabas William A., *An Introduction to the International Criminal Court* (Cambridge University Press, 2011).

Schabas William A., *Genocide in International Law: The Crimes of Crimes* (Cambridge University Press, 2000 and 2009).

Schabas William A., Justice, Democracy and Impunity in Post Genocide Rwanda: Searching for Solutions to Impossible Problems, 7 *Criminal Law Forum* (1996).

Schabas William A., Sentencing by International Tribunals: For a Human Rights Approach, 7:2. *Duke Journal of Comparative & International Law* (1997), pp. 461-518.

Schabas William A., *The Abolition of the Death Penalty in International Law*, (2002 and 2005).

Schachter Oscar, *International Law in Theory and Practice* (1991).

Schwarzenberger G., International *Jus Cogens? 43 Tax. L. Rev* (1965), p. 476.

Schwarzenberger Georg. '*The Problem of an International Criminal Law*,' 5 Current Legal Problems (1950).

Schwelb Egon, Crimes against Humanity, *British Yearbook of International Law* (1946) 178.

Seltzer Garry, 'The Rule of the South Africa Criminal Code in Implementing Apartheid,' 8 *Georgia Journal of International and Comparative Law* (1978), pp. 176-194.

Sevrine Knuche, 'State Immunity and the Promise of *Jus Cogens*,' *Northwestern Journal of International Human Rights* (2011), Vol. 9, No. 2, pp. 149-183.

Shaffer Thomas L., 'The Legal Ethics of Radical Individualism,' 65 *Texas Law Review* (1997).

Shelton D., 'Normative Hierarchy of International Law,' 80 *American Journal of International Law* (1986), 1.

Simmonds Nigel, *Law as a Moral Idea* (2008).

Sliedregt Elies van., *Pluralism in International Criminal Law*, 25 Leiden Journal of International Law (2012), 847.

Smith Norman Kemp, '*Commentary to Kant's 'Critique of Pure Reason'* (Humanities Press, 1962).

Smith, TS., *Lecture Delivered over the Remains of Jeremy Bentham*, Esq., in the Webb-Street School of Anatomy & Medicine, on the 9th June, 1832 (London: Effingham Wilson, 1832).

Sowilet, A., *The Problem of the Creation of a Permanent International Criminal Court* (1951).

Spiermann, 'Humanitarian Intervention as a Necessity and the Threat or Use of *Jus Cogens*' 71 *Nordic Journal of International Law*, (2002), 523.

Spooner Lysander, *Natural Law; or the Science of Justice: A Treatise on Natural Law, Natural Justice, Natural Rights, Natural Liberty, and Natural Society; showing that all Legislation whatsoever is an Absurdity, a Usurpation, and a Crime.* Part First. [1882], available at http://oll.libertyfund.org/titles/spooner-natural-law-or-the-science-of-justice-1882 (Accessed: on 18 December 2017).

Stanton Gregory H., The Ten Stages of Genocide, Genocide Watch (1996).

Stern Robert, *Understanding Moral Obligation: Kant, Hegel, Kierkegaard* (Cambridge, Cambridge University Press, 2012).

Stone Julius and Robert Woetzel, *Toward a Feasible International Criminal Court* (1970).

Sugarman David. ed., *Legality, Ideology and the State* (1985).

Svaček Ondřej, 'The Human Rights Dimension of the ICC's Complementarity Regime,' *Czech Yearbook of Public and Private International Law,* 2015, Vol. 6, pp. 273-288.

Tunnell K., *Political Crime in Contemporary America* (New York: Garland, 1993).

Unger R., The Critical Legal Studies Movement, *96 Harvard Law Review 561* (1983).

Veracini Lorenzo, "Settler Collective, Founding Violence and Disavowal: The Settler Colonial Situation," Journal of Intercultural Studies, vol. 29, no. 4 (2008).

Van Schaack Beth, Ronald C. Slye, *International Criminal Law: Intersections and Contradictions* (2020).

Van Schaack Beth, Ronald C. Slye, *International Criminal Law: The Essentials* (2008).

Van Schaack Beth, Ronald Sly. (ed.), *International Criminal Law and Its Enforcement* (University Casebook Series, 2nd).

Vanhullebusch Matthias., 'The Arab League and Military Operations: Prospects and Challenges in Syria,' 22 (2) *International Peacekeeping* (2015), pp. 151–168.

Vasilijevic Vladan A., Crimes against Peace: Between the Past and the Future, 43 *Jugoslovenska Revija Za Medunarodno Pravo* 425 (1996).

Verdross, A., 'Forbidden Treaties in International Law: Comments on Professor Garner's Report on 'The Law of Treaties,'' 31 *American Journal of International Law*, (1937), 571.

Verdross, A., 'Jus Dispositivum and *Jus Cogens* in International Law' 60 *American Journal of International Law* (1966), 55.

Virally, M., 'Réflexions sur le *Jus cogens*' 12 *Annuaire Français de Droit International* (1966), 5.

Vischer K. Robert, *Martin Luther King Jr. and the Morality of Legal Practice: Lessons in Love and Justice* (2014).

Vyver John D. van der, 'Prosecution and Punishment of the Crime of Genocide,' 25 *Fordham International Law Journal* (1999).

Wakeham Pauline, "The Slow Violence of Settler Colonialism," Journal of Genocide Research, vol. 24, no. 3 (2022), pp. 340-346;

Waldock, H., 'General Course on Public International Law,' 106 *Recueil Des Course* (1962), pp. 39-103.

Ward Ian, *An Introduction to Critical Legal Theory* (1998).

Weatherhall Thomas, *Jus cogens International Law and Social Contract* (2015).

Weil P., 'Towards Relative Normativity in International Law,' 77 *American Journal of International Law* (1983).

Weisburd, M., 'The Emptiness of the Concept of *Jus Cogens*, As Illustrated by the War in Bosnia-Herzegovina,' 17 *Michigan Journal of International Law* (1995-1996), pp. 1-51.

Weiss, T., *Military-Civilian Interactions: Humanitarian Crises and the Responsibility to Protect* (2nd ed., Rowman & Littlefield Publishers Inc., Lanham (MD), 2005).

Wet D., 'The Prohibition of Torture as an International Norm of *Jus Cogens* and Its Implications for National and Customary Law,' 15 *European Journal of International Law* (2004).

Whiteman M. M., '*Jus Cogens* in International Law: With a Projected List,' 7 *Georgia Journal of International and Comparative Law* (1977), p. 609.

Wilkes Fannie Klein & Daniel, United Nations Draft Statute for an International Criminal Court: An American Evaluation, in *International Criminal Law 526* (Gerhard O. W. Mueller & Edward M. Wise eds., 1965).

William A. Schabas, *Genocide in International Law, the Crime of Crimes* (2000).

Wippman David, Atrocities, Deterrence, and the Limits of International Justice, 23 *Forham International Law Journal* 473 (1999).

Wladyslaw Czaplinski, 'Concepts of *Jus Cogens* and Obligations Erga Omnes in International Law in the Light of Recent Developments,' 23 *Polish Yearbook of International Law* (1997–1998).

Wolfe Patrick, “Settler colonialism and the elimination of the native,” Journal of Genocide Research, vol. 8, no. 4 (2006).

Wood Allen, *Kant’s Ethical Thought* (Cambridge University Press, 1999).

Wright Quincy, Proposal for an International Criminal Court, 46 *American Journal of International Law* 60 (1952).

Wright Quincy, ‘The Scope of International Criminal Law: A Conceptual Framework,’ 15 *Virginia Journal of International Law*, (1975).

Zaman R., ‘Playing the Ace? *Jus Cogens* Crimes and Functional Immunity in National Courts,’ 17 *Australian International Law Journal*, (2010), 53.

Zarembka Paul, *The Hidden History of 9-11-2001* (New York: Seven Stories Press, 2008).

Index

#

A

B

C

D

E

F

G

H

I

T

U

V

W

Y

Z